THE INTERNATIONAL
WINE AND FOOD SOCIETY'S GUIDE TO

MEAT

by
AMBROSE HEATH

with a foreword and appendix by
ANDRÉ L. SIMON
*COLOUR PHOTOGRAPHS BY KENNETH SWAIN
AND ILLUSTRATIONS BY STEWART BLACK*

THE COOKERY BOOK CLUB

This edition published in 1971 by
The Cookery Book Club,
St Giles House, 49/50 Poland Street, London, W1A 2LG
by arrangement with
The International Wine and Food Publishing Company,
Marble Arch House, 44 Edgware Road, London, W2

© The Wine and Food Society Publishing Company, 1968

This book was designed and produced by
Rainbird Reference Books Limited,
Marble Arch House, 44 Edgware Road, London, W2

House Editors: J. E. M. Hoare, Rosemary Joekes
and Anne Crane
Designer: Anthony Truscott
Indexer: Ivan Butler

Printed and bound in Yugoslavia

Contents

Foreword	7
Introduction	9
Beef	23
Veal	73
Mutton and Lamb	107
Pork	131
Ham and Bacon	159
Offal (Variety Meats)	178
Basic Sauces and Variations	206
The Matchmaking of Meat and Wine	215
Acknowledgments	217
Comparative Cookery Terms and Measures	218
Vintage Chart	220
Fresh Food in its Best Season	221
General Index	225
Index of Recipes	230

Throughout this book, English measures are given first: the American equivalents follow (where necessary) in brackets.

Colour Plates

Rolled Sirloin of Beef	33
Roast Rolled Sirloin of Beef	34
Silverside of Beef	51
Boiled Silverside of Beef	52
Knuckle of Veal	85
Veal Fricassee	86
Leg of Lamb	103
Roast Leg of Lamb	104
Saddle of Mutton or Lamb	137
Roast Saddle of Mutton or Lamb	138
Dressed Best End of Neck of Lamb	155
Crown Roast of Lamb	156
Loin of Pork	189
Roast Loin of Pork	190
Uncooked Ham	207
Glazed Ham	208

FOREWORD

by André L. Simon

To live, all must eat, but all do not eat the same food! In the fresh waters of our rivers and lakes, and in the briny depths of the oceans, there are fishes which are strict vegetarians, others eat each other, and there are some which are scavengers, always on the lookout for dead bodies. It is the same in the air: the gentle grouse is the most pernickety feeder: it pecks the scented buds of the heather that grows on Scottish and Derbyshire moors; but the long-necked, long-fasting vultures, whenever they get the chance, will devour the putrefying flesh of dead elephants. In our fields and in the jungle, there are vegetarians eating grass, grain, roots, fruits, and when they get fit and fat they are eaten, in the jungle, by their carnivorous cousins, but in our fields, they are killed in a less brutal fashion and eaten in a more civilized manner.

Man is omnivorous, and nobody knows this better than our dentists, who will tell you that we are given a set of teeth capable of tearing meat, grinding grain, and dealing with all kinds of food in an efficient manner.

It is indeed very sad, in fact tragic, that many millions of the world's population have the teeth but nothing to bite: their anxious and daily problem is how to cheat hunger and keep alive on a handful of rice or anything that they may get hold of.

There are also quite a number of people who are vegetarians by choice: ox heart, saddle of lamb, even cheese mites or any food whatsoever of animal origin is loathsome to them. It is a question not of sense but of sensibility, that is to say of nerves.

Most of the more fortunate and sensible millions in civilized lands, who have the chance and the means to get what they want, are meat eaters. The quality and quantity of the meat which they eat is not so much a matter of taste as of opportunities. Two world wars have so thoroughly reshuffled the human packs that the population can no longer be divided into the over-fed upper classes and the under-fed lower ones. The poor are still with us, of course, and always will be, but they are fewer than before, and not so poor as they were. There are now many members of the working class in the same income group as most members of the middle class: whether they wear a tie or none, a white collar or none, they can all afford to eat meat two or three times a week, although not so long ago their mothers and grandmothers had no greater ambition than to be able to give to husbands and children the traditional Sunday hot joint, hoping that there might be some left to appear on Monday as cold meat or in shepherd's pie.

The meat problem today is twofold: first, how best to increase the cattle, sheep and pig population at home and how best to get from overseas fresh supplies of meat at the right price, to meet the rapidly increasing demand for meat; second, how to make more of the people, who are asking for more meat, appreciate the fact that it could be so much better for them to be more adventurous in their choice.

In spite of the higher cost of joints, chops, steaks and what are called 'best cuts', these are in much greater demand than the rest, not only by the rich who can well afford the price of what they fancy, but also by the not-so-rich who should be anxious, one would imagine, to get the 'best value' rather than 'the best'.

Of course, in hotels and restaurants, there are chefs who know how to prepare all kinds of meat soups, sauces, stews, entrées, casseroles, pies and puddings, made up of meat that the average housewife would hesitate or refuse to buy, afraid (as she well might be) that she would not know how to deal with it. There is also the great sausage industry, with sausage-making machines asking no questions and ready to be fed with meat that is quite wholesome but rarely if ever seen 'in the raw' in retail butchers' shops. These are, however, mere exceptions to the rule of meals cooked and eaten in the home, at the family dinner table. This is why it is so important that the housewife be given every possible assistance to get better value for the money that she spends on meat, and yet give to her family dishes which they will thoroughly enjoy: it is the food which we enjoy that brings forth gastric juices to digest it; it is more important than calories and vitamins put together.

This is the purpose of the present book. It gives recipes for the joints, chops and steaks, and all the traditional ways of roasting, boiling, baking, grilling and otherwise cooking and preparing meat for the table. The author, however, has stressed the desirability of paying greater attention than is commonly done to the many ways in which good meat dishes are easily prepared from cuts of meat which may not look as attractive as others on the butcher's table, and yet are so much better value than the rest.

How trifling is the cost of a book like this, compared with the chance it offers its owner to prepare a much greater variety of meat dishes, at lower cost than 'best cuts', food that will look good, be good and do good!

André L. Simon

INTRODUCTION

This is a book about the preparation and cooking of meat – or, to be more precise, of butcher's meat or *viande de boucherie*, since poultry and game will be dealt with in a separate volume of this series. Nor are the many meat soups described; these too are to be found in a companion volume. It is a cookery book and nothing more, even if from the extent of the ground to be covered little more than a large anthology of recipes can be assembled. These are, however, as representative as possible of the great field of meat cookery which development over the ages has placed at our command.

The basic processes of cooking meat having been first outlined, their application to the five main sources of our butcher's meat dishes – beef, veal, mutton and lamb and pork (and their offals, or variety meats as they are called in the United States) are described, a selection being made from the best-known recipes from all over the world, in particular from Great Britain, France and America.

It is not intended to discuss the relative merits of each type of meat nor to enter into arguments whether, for example, Aberdeen Angus steaks are better than those from any other breed of beef or the English South Down mutton and lamb superior to the French *pré salé*. But what will be stated, and in no uncertain terms, are the comparative gastronomical values of the cuts from the various animals, and diagrammatic drawings are introduced into the text for pictorial guidance in showing what the cuts look like in the butcher's shop and from what part of the carcass they come. The drawings show the best uses that can be made of these parts so as to obtain the best gastronomical and nutrititive value from them. Finally, drawings of the right way to carve the joints are also shown.

Meat, the finest food which we have at our command, appears in a wide diversity of ways. In countries where the animal is raised principally for eating, its quality differs only in accordance with breed and feeding, but in other lands where the animals are bred for other purposes (e.g. wool or farm work) its quality as food is subservient to the main functions for which the animal is intended, and the meat on the whole is coarse and tough. This does not mean that it will not contribute to our enjoyment of it as meat-eaters, for in countries where this state of affairs obtains the people have found many ways of dealing with their meat by a different form of cooking, and have contributed to international cuisine dishes which would never have been made from finer and more expensive meat. In the same way many countries have given a national 'stamp' to their native dishes, e.g. paprika in Hungarian dishes, olive oil and tomato in Italy, pimiento in Spain, sour cream in Russia, curry and spices in India and the East. Dishes of meat cooked to all intents and purposes in the same way become something quite different when they have passed through this transformation of national flavouring. Great Britain is an exception to this in so far as the secret of her meat cookery lies in its absolute simplicity, which stresses the fine quality and flavour of her meat. France, in spite of the elaborations of *haute cuisine*, is distinguished too by the use of butter and cream and by the innate good taste of so much of her bourgeois, provincial and peasant cookery. In the highly individual cosmopolitan cookery of the United States can be found an amalgam of most of these practices.

Meat cookery, then, can be divided into two sections, for the home and for the more formal entertainment in the hotel or restaurant. For the first the simpler dishes are mostly required (although it is astonishing how rapidly the modern home cook discovers that by no means all the subtler dishes are beyond her reach), and for the second the more elaborate dishes of the *haute cuisine*. The latter developed over the years a massive repertory of the second type of dishes, naming them after the sources of their ingredients or inspiration. They were named after countries, towns or districts famous for certain types of foodstuffs; after gastronomes and chefs who invented them and who in turn dedicated them to famous people of all kinds – actors and actresses, writers, singers, dancers and composers, statesmen, soldiers, battles and, last but by no means least, to kings and their wives and mistresses. These dishes, which were all of them a set of variations dictated by the inventor's fancy on the simple themes of the finest meat cookery, became the so-called classical repertory of the *haute cuisine* and indeed a sort of culinary short-hand by means of which such dishes could be prepared in the same way all over the world. Furthermore, André Simon, in his notes on the marriage of meat and wine, selected a number of combinations perfectly suited to the great occasion. These notes are to be found as an appendix on page 215. This makes it a compendium of the best-known examples of meat cookery, aimed at whetting and satisfying the appetite of all meat-eaters in whatever part of the world they may be living.

The dishes are taken from the traditional cookery of the nations of Europe, America and the Indian subcontinent.

INTRODUCTION

CHOOSING AND BUYING MEAT

More than with any other foodstuff, in buying meat you have to trust your tradesman, the butcher. Few shoppers are familiar with the various cuts of different meats, and still fewer able to recognize the precise state of the meat, for instance, whether it is young and freshly killed or has been sufficiently hung. Understanding meat, if only as a cook, comes with hard-won experience, and to be able to choose what cuts are most suitable for the dish in mind needs the guidance of an expert. The usual diagrams of carcasses of animals do not actually help very much, since the shopper never sees them whole and the cut is indistinguishable when detached from its meaty context. In this book, however, will be found diagrams of a more helpful kind and these, with the tables of treatments suitable for the various cuts in the kitchen, should be of considerable assistance, and will help to explain why the more muscular cuts are better suited to long slow cooking whereas the meat with less muscle in it will supply the tender portions which need a good deal less treatment by heat.

Meanwhile the butcher has to be trusted not to sell cuts unsuitable for the purpose stated by the shopper, and to resist the temptation (which in his own interests he should refuse to consider), in these days of small joints, of selling nice-looking 'roasting joints' taken from a part of the animal which only deserves, and probably responds handsomely to, stewing. The best way in which he can help is either to label the pieces on his counter by the name of the cut itself, or to simplify the whole issue by labelling pieces that might be mistaken by the young wife for roasting joints with a notice such as 'potroasting' or 'braising'. Many a shopper, too, will be influenced by the cost of meat nowadays and here (also in his own interest) the butcher should try to tell her something of the various ways in which the cheaper cuts can be used to make the most delicious dishes, instead of encouraging her to spend too great a proportion of her housekeeping money on more expensive meat that she cannot afford. But there is a native British prejudice against these cuts, from which even wartime shortages could not wean us, although in the following pages there will be found many excellent ways of cooking them in the European fashion.

The manner in which the butcher prepares his meat is also of importance. Joints should be neatly finished off and, if boned, tied compactly. Chops and cutlets should be trimmed after being chopped at the chine end, and not left full of splinters, and where the meat has a bone in it this should be sawn and not chopped. An escalope of veal is another example. This is not what our grandmothers used to call veal cutlet, but a fairly thin round cut sliced on the slant from the calf's leg or loin. Cutting up meat, however, varies from country to country, and indeed often in various parts of the same country, and while the London and Home Counties system is the one that has been adopted here, illustrations are shown of French and American cuts as well as English.

Of recent years, due probably to the enormous increase and interest in foreign travel, it has been possible to buy French cuts of meat from continental butchers in the major cities of Europe and North America, and this service is spreading. It has therefore been thought fit to include, under each section, a list of the French names with their nearest English and American equivalents.

When buying meat allow 6–8 oz. of boned meat and 8–12 oz. of meat on the bone for each person.

HANGING AND KEEPING MEAT

One of the difficulties when buying meat is that of hanging it. In the days before the last war, when butchers killed their own animals and each large village had its own abattoir or slaughterhouse, the meat used to be well hung and consequently more tender than it would otherwise have been. But since the war the tendency has been to distribute the meat to the butchers' shops from a centre, with the result that it too often reaches the home kitchen too soon after it has been killed and is thus insufficiently hung, making it tough and tasteless, whereas if the hanging were in the hands of the butcher himself, the same joint properly hung would have acquired tenderness and a finer flavour. This is another angle from which the skill of the butcher has to be acknowledged, for hanging cannot be carried out successfully in a domestic refrigerator owing to the necessity for ventilation. The length of time for which the meat should be hung depends upon various conditions; there is no hard and fast rule, but I have eaten a fillet steak which was a very dark brown on the outside. This outside was cut off before cooking and no roasted fillet could ever have been better. Offal must on the other hand be eaten as fresh as possible, and for that reason will not stand more than twenty-four hours in the home refrigerator where it should be laid on a plate or kitchen foil, heaped up a little so that the air can circulate.

Other meat should be unwrapped directly one gets home and put in the tray under the freezing compartment or in the coldest part of the cabinet. The surfaces exposed to the air will get darker, but this will not affect the flavour. If a refrigerator is not there to receive it, keep it in the larder in the cool where flies and sunlight cannot reach it, wrapped loosely in kitchen foil or plastic.

The length of time which raw meat can be kept in the home refrigerator is as follows:

INTRODUCTION

Joints of beef, mutton, lamb or pork: up to 6 days.
Beef steaks, chops, escalopes, etc: up to 4 days.
Stewing meat (cut up): beef and mutton up to 4 days;
veal and lamb 2 or 3 days.
Pork sausages up to 3 days.
Pickled pork up to 8 days.
Sliced cooked ham up to 5 days.

In general, the more cut surfaces the meat has, the shorter time it should be kept in the refrigerator. Raw mince is best cooked as soon as possible.

When the time comes for cooking, the meat should be taken from the refrigerator well before it is wanted, so that it can be well thawed out. If it is too cold the juices will be lost more quickly in the cooking. A joint should be removed the night before.

Unsalted meats can be kept perfectly satisfactorily in a deep freezer for at least six months, if properly wrapped.

COOKING MEAT

There are seven main methods of cooking meat: roasting and baking; potroasting; grilling (called broiling in the U.S.A.) and frying, both in deep and in shallow fat; sautéing, braising, stewing and boiling. In French cookery there is also a method known as *poëling*, which is really a roast cooked in a covered pan with vegetables and butter, the lid being removed towards the end of the cooking so that the meat turns brown. It differs from braising in that it is not moistened. Examples of this form of cookery are dishes *en cocotte* or *en casserole*, and a fuller explanation will be found below, as well as recipes under the section concerned. Pressure cookery will also be considered.

It must be remembered that meat cookery allows a good deal of latitude to the home cook and that allowances must be made for such things as the type of cooker, its age and idiosyncrasies and for such acts of economic pressure as the fluctuation and strength of the electricity or gas. Heat storage cookers need a quite different approach, and the cook must be prepared to treat her meat (and indeed all other) cookery not as an exact science but as an exercise with an old friend whose foibles are genially tolerated.

Roasting and Baking

To roast a joint of meat means to cook it by direct radiant heat in front of an open fire, i.e. on a spit, and to bake it means in an enclosed oven in the heat reflected from the bottom, top and sides. Only recently has it been possible to practise the former method in domestic use, as a result of the provision of electric roasters containing a revolving spit which plays the part of the old-fashioned roasting jack. The rules for the use of both are to all intents and purposes the same.

Wipe the meat, but if it can be avoided do not wash it, for this may harden the outside. Weigh it and place it either on the spit or on a grid in the baking-tin. Some cooks place this tin in another containing water, in order to prevent the drippings from burning and spluttering over the oven. In the case of roasting the dripping tin is placed under the spit.

Until comparatively recently the general practice was first to sear the meat at a high temperature (about 425°F. or 220°C.) and after 15 minutes to lower the heat to about 355°F. (180°C.) and then to cook on at this temperature for the length of time prescribed for the meat in question, but the more modern method is to cook the joint throughout at the latter temperature, and experiments are being made into cooking at an even lower heat.

In America much use is made of a meat thermometer, which is stuck into the thickest part of the joint by means of a slit in the meat before it enters the oven. This will then enable the cook to read the thermometer as the meat cooks, and to know, when it reaches a certain point, that the joint is ready. The right readings for the various joints will be found in each section under the recipes for roasting.

To return to the conventional method of 'roasting' (in fact, baking), the purpose of submitting the meat to a high temperature at the outset is to seal the outside albumen and thus prevent the escape of the juices within. To prevent the outside from becoming too dry the meat should be basted with the drippings (or if so directed in the recipe with stock, water or wine) every 20 minutes while it is cooking. Naturally, different kinds of meat require different lengths of time for their cooking, as also will different cuts of meat, and details of these will be found in their sections under the specific recipes. In general, meat on the bone will not need quite so much cooking as boned meat, stuffed joints should be weighed after stuffing and more time allowed for their cooking. There may also be the family's or guests' preferences for how much the meat should be 'done'.

The leaner cuts of beef will demand some extra fat for satisfactory cooking, and this may be supplied either by the use of a wrapping or caul (which is particularly desirable in the case of lamb and veal) or by larding or barding the piece of meat. This means the insertion of thin strips of fat bacon into the surface of the meat by means of a larding needle, or covering the tops of the piece with a thin strip of the same fat. A somewhat similar role is carried out by the process of *poêling* which is dealt with overleaf.

It is a good thing to leave a roasted or baked joint for a few minutes after the heat has been turned off, before beginning to carve it.

Potroasting

Potroasting in its simplest form is cooking a solid piece of meat in a closed utensil on a very low heat, with or without vegetables or water, wine or other suitable moistening liquid. It is in fact what might be termed a poor man's braise, as it is eminently suitable for the cheaper and coarser cuts of meat.

Poêling

In restaurant kitchens *poêling* is regularly used and, though it may not be used extensively in the home, it deserves a few words of description here, even if only as a survival of the cooking of the past. In the bottom of a deep and thick receptacle, which should be only just large enough to hold the chosen piece of meat, a layer of raw *matignon* is placed. This preparation consists of 2 onions, 2 carrots (red part only) and 2 sticks of celery, a tablespoonful of raw diced lean ham, a sprig of thyme and half a bay leaf. This is stewed in butter in the saucepan and upon it is placed the piece of meat (in much the same way as for a braise) after it has been generously sprinkled with melted butter. The pan is then covered with its lid and set to cook gently until done, nothing more in the way of moistening being added. When the meat is cooked, the lid is removed so that the surface can colour nicely and it is then ready to serve. Stock is added to the vegetables which are then boiled for 10 minutes to make the sauce or gravy. When the fat has been strained, the gravy is sent to the table in a sauceboat.

It is important to remember that at no time during the process should any liquid whatever be added, otherwise the dish would be indistinguishable from a braise. The flavour of the butter is essential for the success of this type of dish.

Grilling

Grilling is also cooking by radiant heat, this time over it, or under, if a gas or electric grill is being used. If a charcoal grill is being used (and nowadays the popularity of the barbecue has familiarised us with this method), it must be lighted so that by the time the meat is ready to be cooked the fire is bright and smokeless. One of the advantages of this form is that charcoals from different woods can be used so that different flavours are achieved.

In America, where this form of cookery first became widespread, the meat is often marinated in a sauce of some kind beforehand. For the open fire method the charcoal should be put on top of the blazing wood and left until the flames have died down and the charcoal is glowing. The meat must then be held on the grill at a height sufficient for it to escape searing by flames caused by dripping fat. It should then be turned once, with tongs or in a double grid to make sure none of the inside juices escape from any pricks.

In using a gas or electric grill, the surface of the meat should be a couple of inches or so from the heat, which should be on maximum heat when the grilling is started. The meat is seared on each side and then cooked at a lower heat for the times specified in the various recipes. When the meat is cooked, it should look plumped up, which will show that the outsides have been properly sealed at the outset. Many experienced cooks will be able to tell in a moment when grilled and fried meat is done by pressing the surface with the fingers to test the meat's elasticity. There are a very large number of ways in which grilled meat can be sauced or garnished, and a selection of these is given in the respective sections.

Broiling

To all intents and purposes broiling may be taken to mean the same as grilling. This term is in common use in the U.S.A. A grill is consequently a broiler.

Deep Frying

This form of frying is only suitable in the case of meat for egg-and-breadcrumbed cutlets, croquettes or rissoles and such dishes as brains or sweetbreads in breadcrumbs or batter. At one time, when only animal cooking fats were in use, the temperature of the frying medium could be judged by the appearance of a faint haze, but nowadays this rough-and-ready method is not as accurate as it was, owing to the varieties of frying fats in general use, and it is much more satisfactory to use a frying thermometer. 380°F. (195°C.) is the temperature for rissoles or other food that has been cooked beforehand. For egg-and-breadcrumbed raw cutlets it should register a little less, as the meat has to cook inside the coating. The experienced cook will be able to judge the temperature of the fat by the behaviour of a small crust of bread when dropped into it, and its more or less active bubbling on the fat. If the bread colours in about 70 seconds, the fat is hot enough for most purposes. Too many articles should not be put into the pan at once, so as not to lower the temperature, and if the oil shows discoloration it should be replaced by fresh at once.

Shallow Frying

In this process a small quantity of the chosen fat is melted in the frying pan and allowed to get hot, so that a faint smoke rises. This is the moment at which to put in the piece of meat, such as a steak or chop. When one side is browned sufficiently, it is turned over (care being taken not to prick it) and cooked on the other side. The first side will be found to be done as soon as the moisture from the inside begins to show on the top in small beads. This is the favourite and simplest way, after grilling, for cooking small pieces of meat (*see also* sauté, below).

Sautéing

The sauté is the fine method of shallow-frying meat which the French have passed on to us, and the large representative list of its different forms, which are given under the meats themselves, show how highly delicious it can be, simple or elaborate according to choice.

The process itself, however, is simple in the extreme. Small beef steaks, such as tournedos, entrecôte and *filet mignon*, and lamb cutlets and *noisettes* all spring to mind when this mode of cooking is mentioned. This is the way in which they are cooked. Fry them quickly in a little clarified butter so that they are browned on each side, put aside and to the gravy and congealed blood left in the pan (from which you must first have removed the grease) pour in the liquid specified by the recipe and stir and scrape the pan so that it mixes with the gravy and congealed juice from the meat. When this is done, add the liquid to the prepared sauce or garnish and pour it over the meat, the cooking of which is then completed by gentle simmering.

Care should be taken that the utensil is just large enough to contain the pieces of the sauté, which should all rest on the bottom, or the solidified meat juice may dry up and burn.

Note that the thinner and smaller the pieces of meat, the more quickly they should be fried, and that while sautés of red meat are treated as above, white meats like lamb or veal should first be fried very quickly but have their cooking completed on a very low heat, sometimes even covered.

Braising

This is really a combination of baking and steaming, and in the old days special utensils were used which had a sunken lid for holding charcoals to reinforce the cooking on top of the heat. Today there is no need for this, and braises are effectively carried out on top of the stove or in the oven at low temperatures. Vegetables are used to give the meat its special flavour and stock or wine for the moistening agent. The vegetables, consisting of carrot, turnip, onion and celery, are cut in dice with lean bacon or ham, and these, called the *mirepoix*, are first slightly browned in dripping or butter. Enough moistening liquid (stock, water, wine or both) is added barely to cover the vegetables, and salt and pepper and herbs in a muslin bag added as well. The piece of meat, which is sometimes browned first, is placed on this bed and covered with greased paper pressed down on it. The lid is then put tightly on and the contents simmered gently for two-thirds of the cooking time required. The pan or casserole is then transferred to the oven and cooked there for the rest of the time, still with the lid on. For the last 10 minutes the lid and paper are removed and the surface of the meat allowed to brown. A little of the braising stock is reduced to a glaze for painting over the piece, the rest is thickened and strained round the meat with its garnish of vegetables, extra ones being cooked separately for preference.

Braised beef will normally take at least 3–4 hours, according to the type and quality of the meat, and veal or lamb about half as long.

Stewing

This is one of the simplest and most economical ways of cooking meat and very often the most flavoursome as well. For brown stew the meat, cut in suitable small pieces, is first floured and then fried a golden brown all over. The pieces are taken out of the pan, and the vegetables fried in their turn in the same fat. The meat is returned to the pan, half-covered with a good stock or gravy, or with beer, wine or a mixture of wine and water, then seasoned with salt and pepper and possibly herbs, and simmered very gently for a good 2 hours or more until tender. A good example of a white stew is the famous Irish Stew. In this the pieces of lamb or mutton are not first browned, but are put uncooked in a pan in layers with onion and potato, the vegetables having been sliced and seasoned and covered with warm water. This is brought slowly to simmering point, adequately skimmed and cooked gently for about the same time as above. The length of the cooking time will depend upon the quality of the meat, but the less tender cuts are admirable for this form of treatment and indeed usually respond better to it than the more expensive ones.

Boiling

In boiling meat the same principles must be observed as in roasting it, in so far as the preliminary stage is the sealing of the surfaces. It must therefore be plunged,

INTRODUCTION 19

after weighing, in sufficient *boiling* water to cover it completely, boiled rapidly for 10–15 minutes and then simmered for the rest of the time at 180°F. (80°C.). Boiled meat of any suitable kind should always be very tender and well cooked, and a general guide is 20 minutes to the pound and, say, 20 minutes over, to allow for the preliminary quick boiling. This is the procedure for fresh meat, but for salt meat, the piece after being taken from the pickle and soaked for several hours according to the degree of its saltiness is plunged into warm water, brought to the boil and then simmered as above, this time for 30 minutes to the pound and 20 minutes over.

In both cases vegetables, herbs and spices can be added, and this should be done after the first skimming has taken place.

Ham and bacon come under a slightly different category and are dealt with under Pork.

Pressure Cooking

Pressure cooking serves several purposes and can achieve results very different from those arrived at by using any other piece of equipment. It is a method most useful to the cook who is short of time, as the cooking time for most meats is roughly one-third of that necessary by other means. It is possible to potroast, braise, stew, or boil meat with it. It is especially valuable for the cheaper cuts as they are made tender without loss of liquid – so difficult to control in an ordinary casserole, roasting tin or saucepan. For making stocks, glazes and meat jellies there is no equal to a pressure cooker. Bones, carcasses, or tough cuts of meat can all be reduced to a soft pulp and a rich stock or jelly obtained containing the maximum nutrition possible. It is wisest to follow the precise instructions given with different models, as these may vary and it is possible to damage the pressure cooker if this is not done.

Carving Meat

Drawings illustrating the cuts will be found throughout the text and the page reference is given in brackets. Always remember that a sharp knife is absolutely essential for carving. Some notes to help in carving follow.

Cuts of Meat

Roast sirloin of beef: when cooked on the bone, as it should be if possible, this joint is carved by first cutting slices from the undercut (or fillet), which should always be eaten hot when it is at its best. The joint is then turned over, the point of the knife is inserted between the meat and the bone to make cutting the slices easier, and long thin slices are taken along the length of the joint this side of the bone (*see* p. 26).

Rolled sirloin of beef: a thick slice is first cut horizontally off the round so as to provide a smooth surface of meat. This is then carved downwards in thin and even slices. Round of beef and rolled ribs are carved in the same way (*see* p. 56).

Roast fillet of beef: the whole fillet is used for this dish, and it should be carved downwards in thick slices across and along the length of the joint (*see* p. 56).

Roast rib of beef: first slip the knife between the meat and the bone so as to separate it and make the carving easier. Then cut thin slices off the sides (*see* p. 29).

Brisket of beef: cut in thin slices across the whole width of the joint (*see* p. 29).

Boiled silverside of beef: this cut is carved by cutting long thin slices across the face of the meat (*see* p. 202).

Stuffed breast of veal: cut downwards in thickish slices across the end and so through the rolled meat (*see* p. 92).

Roast leg of lamb or mutton: this joint is carved perpendicularly to the bone. First cut a triangular-shaped piece out of the middle of the side on which the shank-end lies. Thickish slices should then be carved alternately from each side of the cut. This joint should be carved as quickly as possible as the fat of mutton and lamb congeals rapidly and unpleasantly (*see* p. 111).

Stuffed loin of lamb or mutton: cut in thickish slices downwards from the end, as in all boned and stuffed joints (*see* p. 111).

Roast shoulder of mutton: raise the joint with a fork and cut slices along parallel to the bone and surface of the meat. When this is finished put the joint back on the dish, turn it over and start at the knuckle end, cutting slices from each side of the blade bone (*see* p. 112).

Roast saddle of mutton: saddle of mutton is carved contrary to the usual method of cutting meat. It is cut either into long 'fids' (wedge-shaped slices) running parallel

INTRODUCTION 21

to the backbone on each side which are then cut into two or three pieces across according to the size of the joint; or into ¼ in. slices cut at an angle to the backbone, as in method 2 on p. 115. The usual accompaniment is a small piece of the crisp fat taken from the bottom of the ribs where they rest on the dish (*see* p. 115).

Best end of neck: carve downwards into cutlets, making sure beforehand that the joint has been properly chined by the butcher (*see* p. 115).

Crown roast of lamb: carve down between the bones and serve in the form of cutlets, accompanying each with a little of the centre filling (*see* p. 115).

Roast rib of pork: carve downwards between the bones in thick slices, and serve in the form of cutlets (*see* p. 140).

Sucking pig: this picturesque joint usually comes to the table cut in half down the back. The head is then separated from the body and the leg is taken off next by sticking the carving fork firmly into it and slipping the knife round the outline of the joint and cutting it off the body. The triangular piece of the neck, perhaps the most succulent joint of the whole sucking pig, is removed next and then the shoulder which is tackled in the same way as the leg. The rest of the animal is then carved in thick slices (*see* p. 142).

Corner of gammon: carve in thin slices towards the corner. This joint is usually boned before cooking which makes the carving easier (*see* p. 163).

Ham: there are two ways to carve ham. The most economical is to carve it from the knuckle end, slanting the knife towards the other end. To obtain the best meat, start carving in the middle where the best cuts lie. Ham should be carved with a very thin, exceptionally sharp knife and the slices should be as paper-thin as possible (*see* p. 163).

Ox tongue: if *unpressed*, cut in fairly thick slices across the tongue starting at the thickest part and continuing towards the tip. A little of the fat near the roots of the tongue should be served with each helping (*see* p. 202). *Pressed* ox tongue is carved in thin slices across the top, parallel to the dish.

Calf's head: calf's head is very rarely served whole these days but if you should wish to serve one it should be carved in long strips from the ear to nose and a slice of the throat sweetbread should accompany each serving (*see* p. 92).

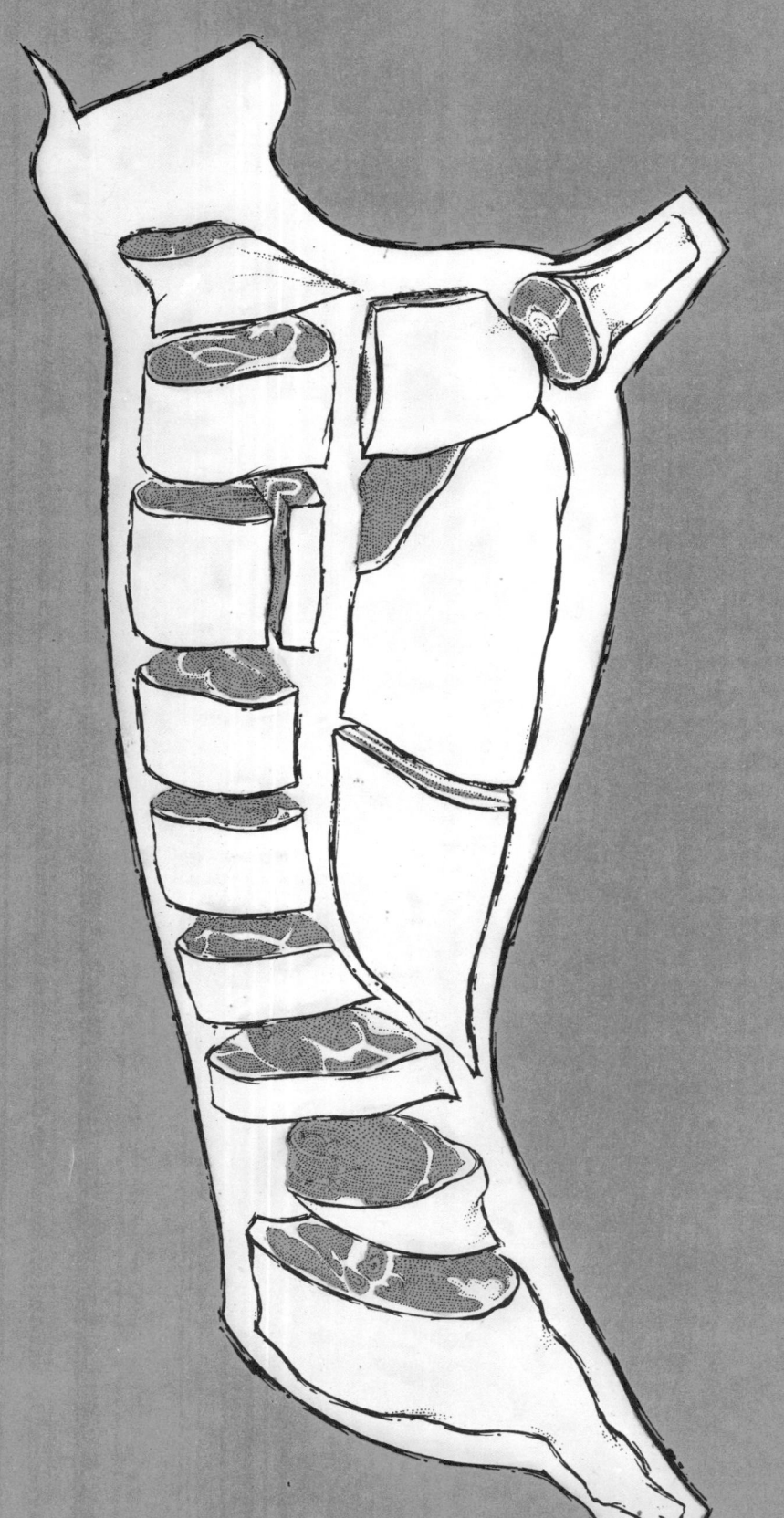

BEEF

1 HEAD
2 & 3 CLOD & STICKING
4 SHIN
5 SHOULDER
6 BRISKET
7 MIDDLE RIBS
8 FLANK
9 RIBS
10 SIRLOIN
11 RUMP
12 BUTTOCK
13 LEG

BEEF

Beef is the primest meat that the butcher has to offer. It is full of flavour, and food value and offers the greatest nutriment of all the *viandes de boucherie*. At its best it comes from oxen, steers or bullocks which have been castrated when young, or from uncalved heifers, and the finest flavour is found in animals between five and six years old. It must be hung by the butcher to ensure tenderness. Beef from cows, which is used mostly for making potroasts and stews, is lean and somewhat tough.

Beef can be classified in three categories according to its market value, which in turn depends on its qualities and uses for various forms of cooking, the best cuts obviously being the most expensive. These categories are (1) fillet, sirloin, top rump, rump steak, silverside and the inner parts of the flank and round; (2) top of sirloin, top ribs, fore ribs, shoulder, chuck end of the clod and clod itself; (3) flank, brisket, leg, neck, cheek, shin and knuckle.

Prime beef, when freshly cut, should be of a brilliant red colour, firm and elastic to the touch. The tender cuts should be surrounded and flecked or lightly marbled with fat, which should be white or slightly yellowish according to the breed of the particular animal and the manner in which it has been fed. The flesh should have a fresh, light smell, but this will become darker with hanging and the meaty odour will be more pronounced.

A diagram of the various cuts and their uses will be found opposite.

CUTS OF BEEF AND THEIR USES

Leg: stew or braise.

Thick skirt: use for puddings and stews, but the best part may be grilled or fried.

Thin skirt: stew.

Topside (round or buttock steak): potroast or braise.

Silverside: potroast or stew but usually salt or pickle and boil.

Aitchbone: roast or sometimes salt or pickle and boil.

Top rump (thick flank): salt or pickle and boil; braise, stew or use in pies.

Thin flank: roast the best quality, but mainly braise or stew.

Rump steak: grill or fry; sometimes roast.

Fillet (undercut of sirloin): roast whole; grill or fry as steaks.

Sirloin and wing rib: roast whole; grill or fry as steaks.

Fore ribs: roast whole slowly or potroast boned and rolled.

Back ribs: as above.

Flat ribs: potroast, braise or stew.

Top ribs: potroast or roast slowly.

Leg of mutton cut: roll and potroast; salt or pickle and boil.

Chuck and bladebone: braise, stew or potroast rolled.

Brisket: braise, stew or boil fresh; salted or pickled for pressed or corned beef.

Forequarter flank: as above.

Neck piece: stew or casserole; use minced.

Clod: as above.

Shin: stew or braise.

Approximate equivalent cuts of Beef

ENGLISH	FRENCH	AMERICAN
Shin (back leg)	*Gîte de derrière*	Soup bone
Shin (fore leg)	*Gîte de devant*	Shank (stew meat)
Round	*Gîte à la noix*	Round steak
Top rump	*Culotte or aiguillette*	Rump
Sirloin	*Aloyau*	Loin
Rib	*Côte de boeuf*	Rib
Shoulder	*Poitrine*	Plate, Short ribs
Brisket, best rib	*Poitrine*	Shoulder cut, brisket
Chuck	*Palernon*	Chuck
Neck	*Jumeaux or macreuse*	Chuck
Skirt	*Bavette*	Short ribs

ROAST BEEF

Beef for roasting is chosen from the best and tenderest cuts (*see* the table on pp. 23–4), sirloin, fillet and wing rib being the most often used. But these are also the most expensive and other joints such as the fore ribs can be more suitable for the ordinary cook, and so can back and top ribs which need a little moisture in the oven to make them tender. The times for the prime beef are the same. If you are using the searing method of roasting (p. 14) you should allow about 15 minutes to the pound and 15 over; if entirely at a moderate temperature, 25 minutes to the pound on the bone and 30 minutes rolled; and if you prefer slow-roasting at 355°F. (180°C.) throughout, you should allow from 40–45 minutes to the pound. Allow 5 minutes more per pound for medium-done meat and 10 minutes for well done.

If you are using a meat thermometer (and be sure that the bulb on the end when inserted does not actually touch the bone), when the beef is done it should register 140°F. (60°C.) for under-done (rare) beef, 160°F. (71°C.) for medium done and 170°F. (76°C.) for well done.

A joint of beef should be seasoned after it is cooked, and it always pays to let it stay for a few minutes with the heat of the oven turned off after cooking, before the business of carving is begun. For this a sharp knife is essential. Beef should always be carved in thin slices, except the undercut (fillet) which is carved thickly. Detailed instructions for carving roast sirloin, rolled sirloin, roast fillet and roast rib of beef will be found on pp. 19–20 and drawings on pp. 26, 56 and 29 respectively.

SIRLOIN OF BEEF 1

SIRLOIN OF BEEF 2

Accompaniments

For general purposes the best accompaniments to roast beef are of the simplest kind, and plainly cooked vegetables such as carrots, turnips, tomatoes and braised celery, onions and chicory (endive) are usually the favourites, with roast potatoes to keep them company. In France various sauces are often to hand, but in England horse-radish is the most popular adjunct, either in a sauce or, far better, I think, simply scraped thinly from the root.

One of the traditional extras in England is the famous Yorkshire pudding made of batter which was originally roasted under the meat in the drippings and in days when meat was scarce served as a separate course before the meat in order to make the latter go further. Today it is usually baked separately, either in a large baking pan or in small individual tins, and it seems to me that no better place than here could be found for the recipe.

YORKSHIRE PUDDING

¼ **lb. (1 cup) plain flour**
½ **pint (1¼ cups) milk**
1 egg
pinch of salt

Make a batter with the ingredients. Put 2 or 3 tablespoonfuls of dripping from the hot roasting meat into a baking tin and pour the batter on top. Bake in a hot oven for about 20 minutes. This will serve 4–6 people.

FILLET OF BEEF

The fillet of beef, which is rightly considered to be the finest part of the animal, is often cooked whole and not divided into steaks. This makes, in my opinion, one of the world's most delicious joints, and is usually either roasted or *poêled*. Sometimes it is larded with fat bacon strips or with tongue or truffles. A good working example is the following.

FILET DE BOEUF POÊLÉ À L'ANGLAISE (France)

The prepared fillet, is placed in the baking tin on a bed of sliced onion, carrot and celery (the carrots being cut more thinly than the other vegetables) and a bouquet garni is placed in the middle. Dot the joint with bits of butter, put on the lid and place the tin in a moderate oven (350°F., 177°C.). Baste it as it cooks and add a little salt before the end of the time. Allow 15 minutes to the pound and 15 minutes over and be careful not to overcook it, as the meat should be somewhat underdone. When it is done, take it out and keep it warm, while you scoop out the vegetables with a perforated spoon, and then add to the gravy in the pan a glass of Madeira or dry white wine or even good stock. Boil this up for a minute or two, skim off the grease and strain the sauce into a sauceboat. If you want it thick, then add a little demi-glace sauce (*see* p. 209).

POTROASTED BEEF

The potroasting which the British housewife became generally accustomed to during the last war was borrowed, like the Hamburger habit, from America, and there was nothing epicurean about it. It was welcomed as being a flavoursome way of using the cheaper cuts of beef, topside, round, chuck and clod, etc. (*see* table on p. 24) and also because this method was economical in fuel consumption since it could be cooked on top of the cooker instead of inside. The best-shaped joint for this purpose is compact and solid or tightly rolled, and it must first be dredged with flour. Potroasting is a good method of roasting small joints as there is less shrinkage. For this reason too, it lends itself admirably to pressure cooking.

POTROAST

4 lb. boned beef in 1 piece
salt, pepper
3 tablespoonfuls ($3\frac{3}{4}$ tablespoonfuls) beef dripping
Brown gravy:
fat
2 tablespoonfuls ($2\frac{1}{2}$ tablespoonfuls) beef gravy
2 tablespoonfuls ($2\frac{1}{2}$ tablespoonfuls) flour
1 cupful stock or mixture of stock, cooking liquor and milk
browning (optional)
salt, pepper

Method 1 (without water). Brown the meat all over in the dripping in a frying-pan, then transfer it to a stewpan or casserole, season, cover closely and cook over a low heat for about 3 hours, turning it over now and then for even cooking. Serve brown gravy with it made as follows: skim the fat off the strained gravy from the pan and in a small saucepan make a brown roux with equal quantities each of beef dripping and flour, and gradually stir in 1 cupful stock or a mixture of stock, the cooking liquor and, for the taste of some, a little milk, which they say gives a delicious café-au-lait coloured sauce. Five minutes' cooking will serve to thicken it, but a few drops of browning may be added if absolutely necessary. Season to taste with pepper and salt and strain into the sauceboat.

An alternative method is to brown the meat as before, and then add $\frac{1}{2}$ cup of hot water when it is in the casserole or stewpan. Cook in the same way as for Method 1. Many people place the browned joint on a shallow wire grid in the pan, so that the meat cooks in the steam made by the water as it reduces.

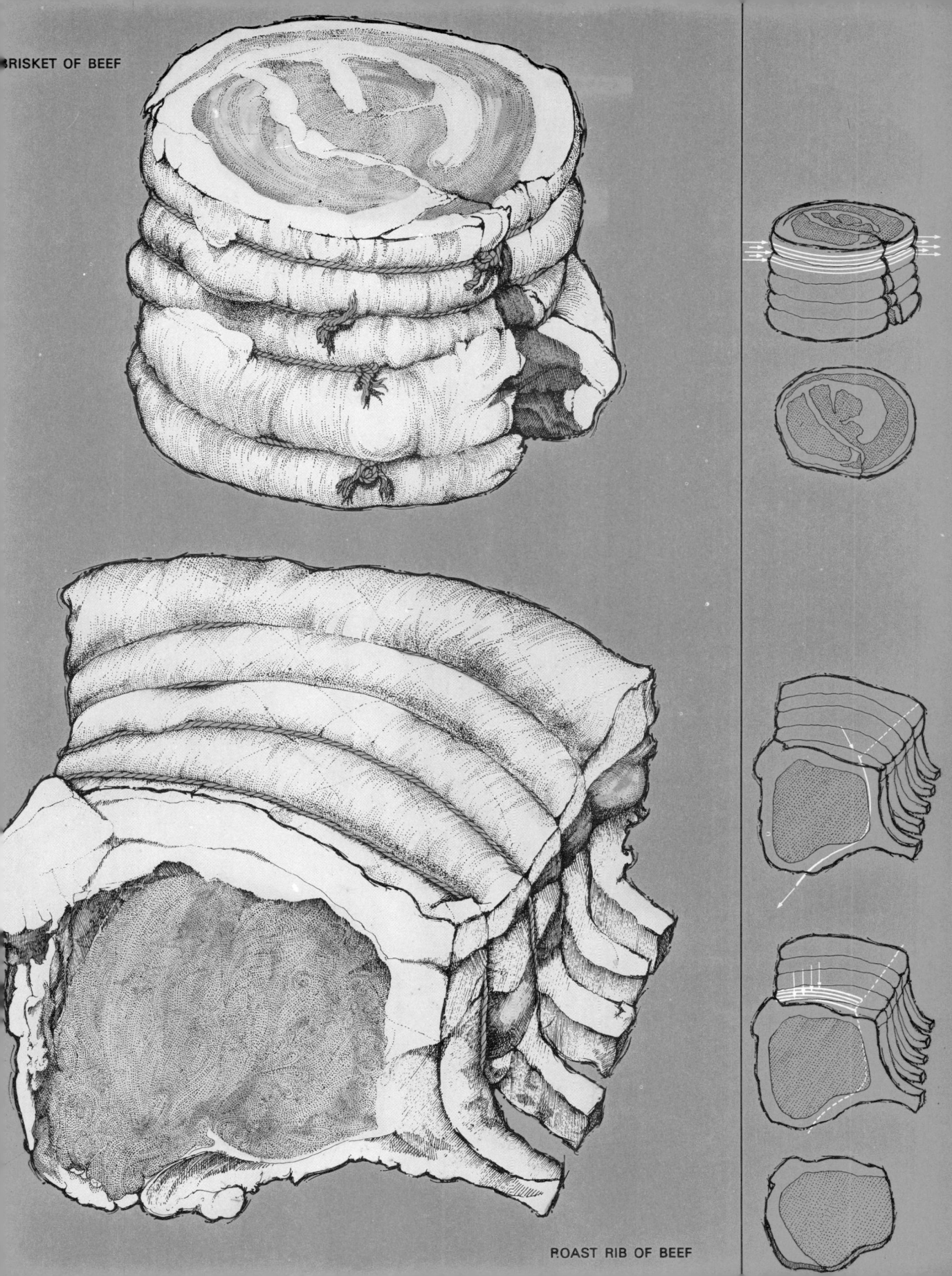

BRISKET OF BEEF

ROAST RIB OF BEEF

POTROAST WITH VEGETABLES

carrots
onions
celery
potatoes
turnips
tomatoes
leeks

Any of these vegetables may be added to the potroast when it is nearly cooked; they may be quartered, sliced or diced, and the length of their cooking dictated by the size of the pieces. If they are put in whole, they should be turned now and again to make sure that they are covered by the cooking liquor. When done, drain them well and arrange round the meat on the serving dish with a little of the gravy poured over them.

This type of potroast really becomes a braise, and my instructions for braising can apply, and wine, beer or cider can be used.

Any liquid added to a potroast should be hot when it is poured in: a cold addition tends to toughen the meat.

GRILLED OR FRIED BEEF
Cuts of steak

Entrecôte steak: taken from between the ribs, but sometimes from the sirloin; it should be about 1 in. thick and about 8 oz. for two should be allowed.

Double entrecôte: between $\frac{3}{4}$ lb. and 1 lb.

Minute steak: very thin, about 4 oz. in weight. Grill or sauté entrecôte with the exception of minute steak, which is invariably grilled. All meat to be grilled should only be beaten very lightly or when it is cooked it will bleed too much and lose its flavour.

Fillet steak: cut from the best part of the fillet and weighing 6–7 oz. at the most; cooked like entrecôtes and tournedos (*q.v.*).

Filet mignon: cut from the centre of the fillet and then in half lengthways and then cut again into flat triangles. They are seasoned lightly, dipped first in melted butter and then in breadcrumbs, brushed over with more butter and grilled. Served with various vegetables garnishes and with a *piquante*, *Béarnaise* or *Choron* sauce.

Tournedos: small round fatless slices of fillet of beef, weighing about $3\frac{1}{2}$–4 oz. and about 1–$1\frac{1}{2}$ in. thick; grilled or sautéed in butter and sometimes served on croûtons

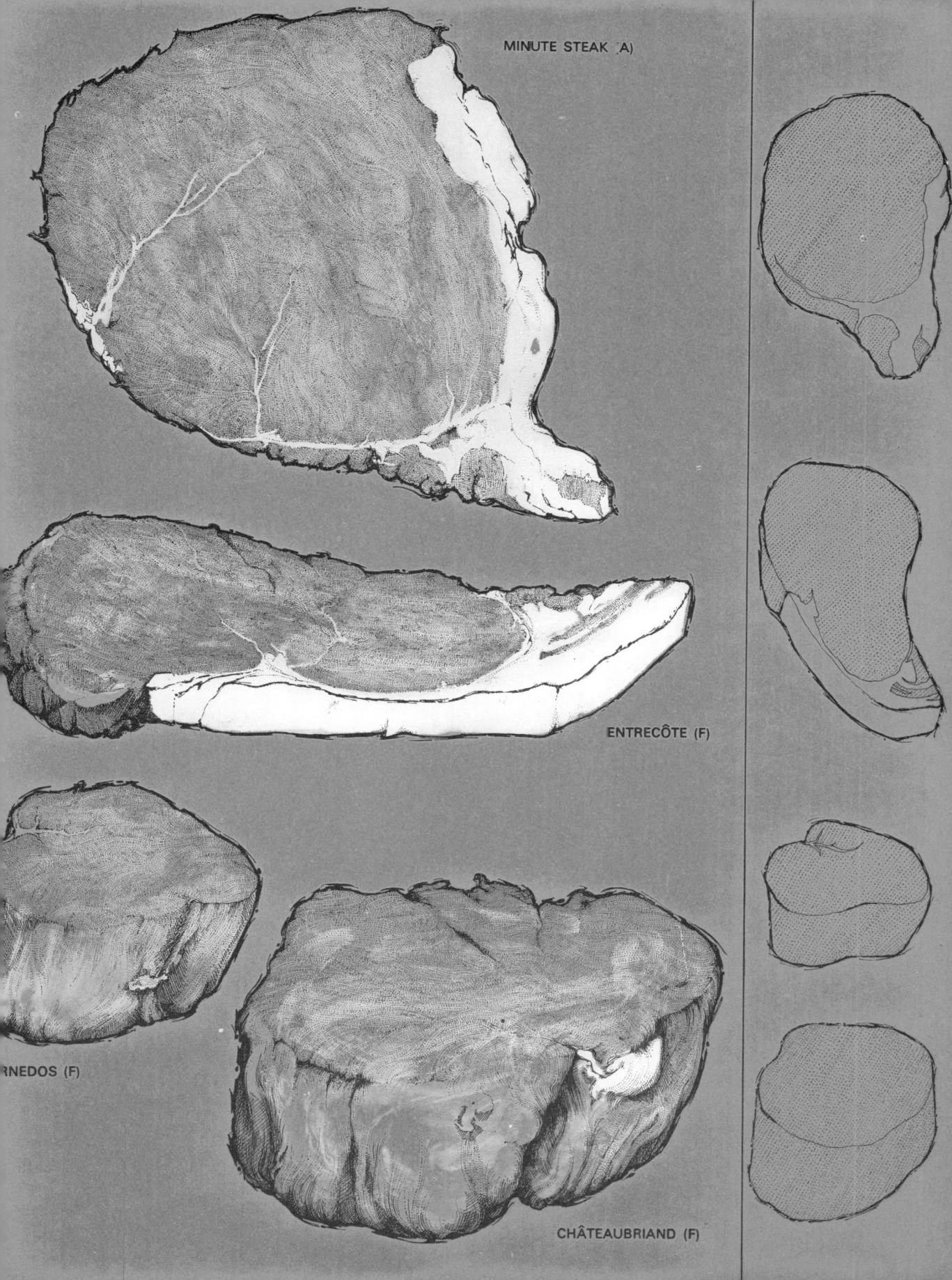

of bread fried in butter. In this case they are covered at the last moment with meat jelly as an insulation from the meat juices. The sautéed tournedos are generally accompanied by a *Chateaubriand* sauce made from this jelly, thickened with butter and finished with a drop or two of lemon juice. A selection of garnishes for tournedos will be found on p. 32.

Rump steak: cut from the end of the rump and is never less than $\frac{3}{4}$ in. thick. The English custom is to serve it, whether grilled or fried, with a thick piece of grilled kidney fat on top and some grated horseradish.

Chateaubriand: from the centre of the fillet, a good thickness weighing from 12 oz. to 1 lb. It is sometimes accompanied by a meat jelly sauce (*see* Tournedos) to which twice its weight of maître d'hotel butter has been added, and by sautéed potatoes; other garnishes suitable for grilled fillets and tournedos are good. This is an excellent steak to use for *Filet de boeuf en croûte* (p. 64).

T-bone steak: a 1 in. thick, strip cut through the sirloin, including the bone and fillet, for two or more people. It is carved by cutting alternate slices from each side of the bone towards the skin side.

Porterhouse steak: about $1\frac{1}{2}$ in. thick cut from the wing ribs (*cf.* entrecôtes which are cut from between the ribs and are half as thick).

Portmanteau steak: a thickish steak in which a deep pocket has been cut in the side. Oysters are inserted in this and the steak is sewn up again and grilled in the usual way.

Club steak: a steak cut from the fore rib; similar to a Porterhouse but cheaper.

Point steak: cut from the separate muscle to one side of the rump. This cut is held by many to have much more flavour than any other steak, though both the fillet and sirloin are more tender.

Simple Garnishes for Grilled and Fried Steaks

English: fried or mashed potatoes; fried or grilled mushrooms; fried onions. Watercress; grated or scraped horseradish; horseradish sauce; maître d'hotel butter; oyster sauce.

Rolled Sirloin of Beef and ingredients for Roast Sirloin of Beef

BEEF

French: Bercy butter; *sauce Bordelaise*; fried potatoes; onions fried in deep oil; grilled tomatoes with *fines herbes*; *sauce Béarnaise*; *sauce Chateaubriand*; *sauce piquante*; *sauce Choron*.

United States: maître d'hotel butter; mustard sauce; brown mushroom sauce; *sauce Bordelaise*; Trianon sauce.

Butter for steak: cream together 1 oz. (1¼ teaspoonfuls) butter; pinch made mustard; 1 teaspoonful Worcester sauce; ½ clove minced garlic and a little *fines herbes*. Spread on both sides of the steak and leave at room temperature for at least 30 minutes. Grill.

Platter sauce: put a little butter on a hot plate; add a teaspoonful of dry mustard, a few drops of Worcester or A.1 sauce (or both), salt, pepper, and paprika to taste. Put the grilled steak on the dish and score it with a sharp knife. Mix the juices coming from it with the butter and pour over steak to serve.

Grilled steaks

Brush the steaks on both sides with melted butter or oil, and place them on a *hot* grill. pan. Let them brown on one side under a good heat before turning them over to brown the other side. Thickness rather than weight determines the length of their cooking, and when the juice pearls on the surface of the meat, they are done. At the very last minute season them with salt and pepper.

With gas or electric grill put the grill pan 3 in. below gas flame or glowing red electric unit at 500°F. (260°C.). When seared on top, turn carefully and sear the other side of the steak. Now reduce heat to 350°F. (176°C.) and go on grilling, turning once till the steak is cooked as desired.

Alternatively, you can put the grill pan in pre-heated griller with temperature at 350°F. instead of 500°F. and turn the steak when half done as required.

For a steak with a well-browned crisp outside and a juicy inside, use the first method. For a juicier inside with a less crisp outside use the second method.

Take steaks from the refrigerator at least 30 minutes before cooking, so that the meat is at room temperature when the operation begins. Unless otherwise directed, spread with softened butter before seasoning and serving.

N.B. *Always be very careful not to pierce the lean meat with a fork, and for turning use either special tongs, two wooden spoons or the backs of two forks.*

Roast Rolled Sirloin of Beef

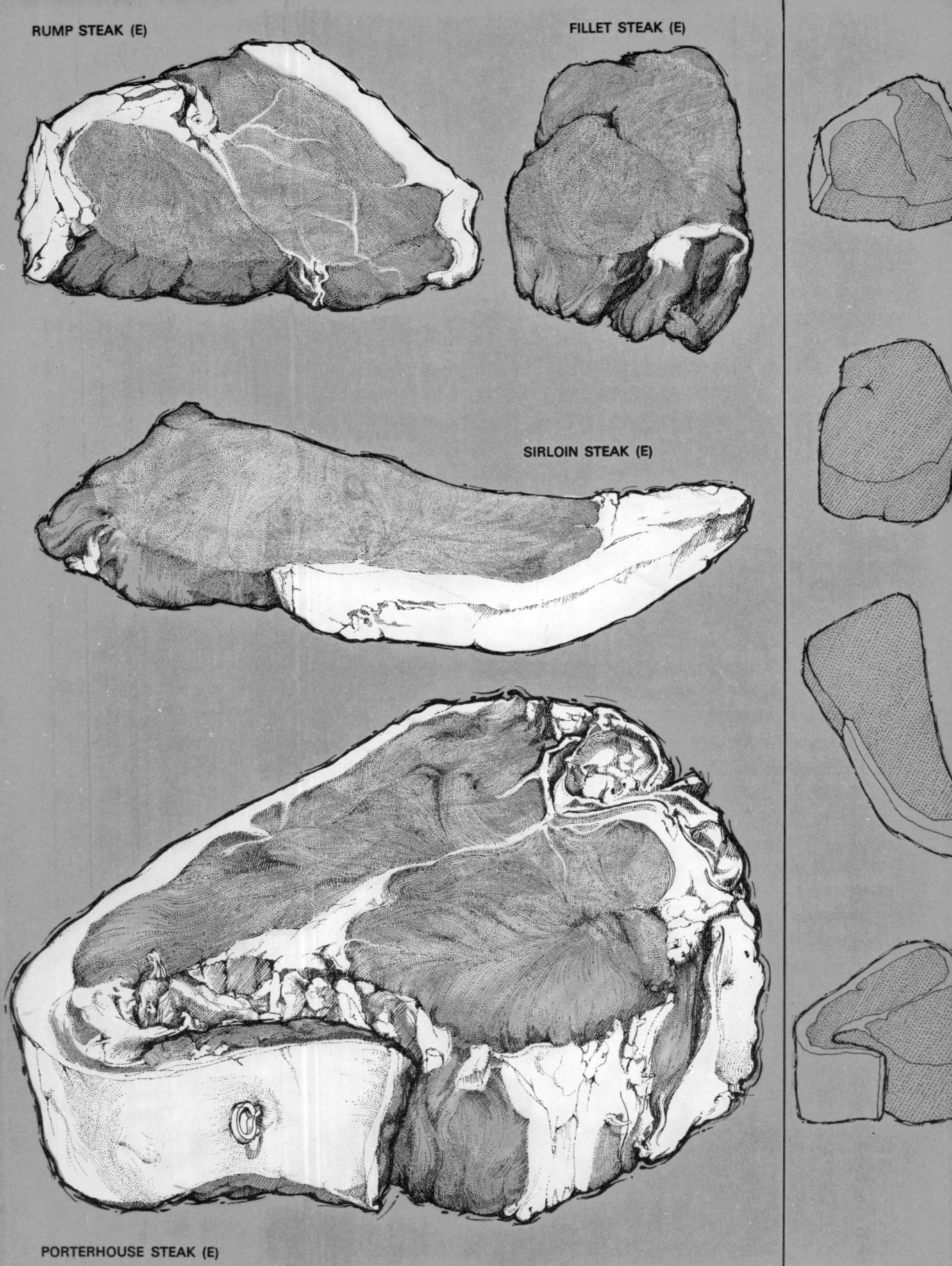

PAN-GRILLED STEAK

Heat a heavy iron frying pan till it is sizzling hot and rub it with a piece of suet or beef fat. Sear the steak quickly on each side and then cook more slowly till it is cooked as required, turning it once. If fat accumulates as it cooks, pour this away or the meat will be fried and not grilled. Brush with melted butter when done, and sprinkle with salt and pepper. This method is more satisfactory with the thicker sort of steak.

Timetable for steaks
Tender steaks 1 in. thick grill (Method 1)
    Rare   8–15 minutes
    Medium   15–20 minutes
    Well-done 15–30 minutes
1½ in. thick (Method 1 or pan-grill)
2 in. (Method 2 or pan-grill)
    Rare   15–25 minutes
    Medium   20–30 minutes
    Well-done 25–40 minutes

PLANKED STEAK

An unusual form of steak comes from the United States as the planked steak. This is a grilled (broiled) or pan-grilled steak finished with a garnish on a wooden plank in the oven. The steak should be about 2 in. thick and first seared in the usual way for 10, 15 or 25 minutes according to taste. It is then transferred to a heated plank brushed with butter or oil, the edges of which are bordered with potato or some other accompaniment. The plank is then put into a hot oven (450°F., 234°C.) and baked for about 10 minutes or till the potatoes are browned. Softened butter is then spread on the steak which is seasoned with salt, pepper and minced parsley, and hot vegetables are arranged between the meat and the border. Potatoes for the border should be mashed or *Duchesse* potatoes brushed with melted butter, milk or diluted egg yolk. Alternative cooking times are 5 minutes on each side of the steak for the preliminary grilling and a stay in a moderate oven at 375°F. (192°C.) till cooking and browning is complete.

The following observations by an authority on this form of cooking appear in *Fanny Farmer's Boston Cook Book*: 'Board for planked steak (or fish) should be made of untreated oak, 1 in. thick. It should be a little longer and wider than the meat to be arranged on it. Brush a new plank thoroughly with oil or suet and warm in a slow oven (250°F., 122°C.) for 1 hour before using. Potato border should come

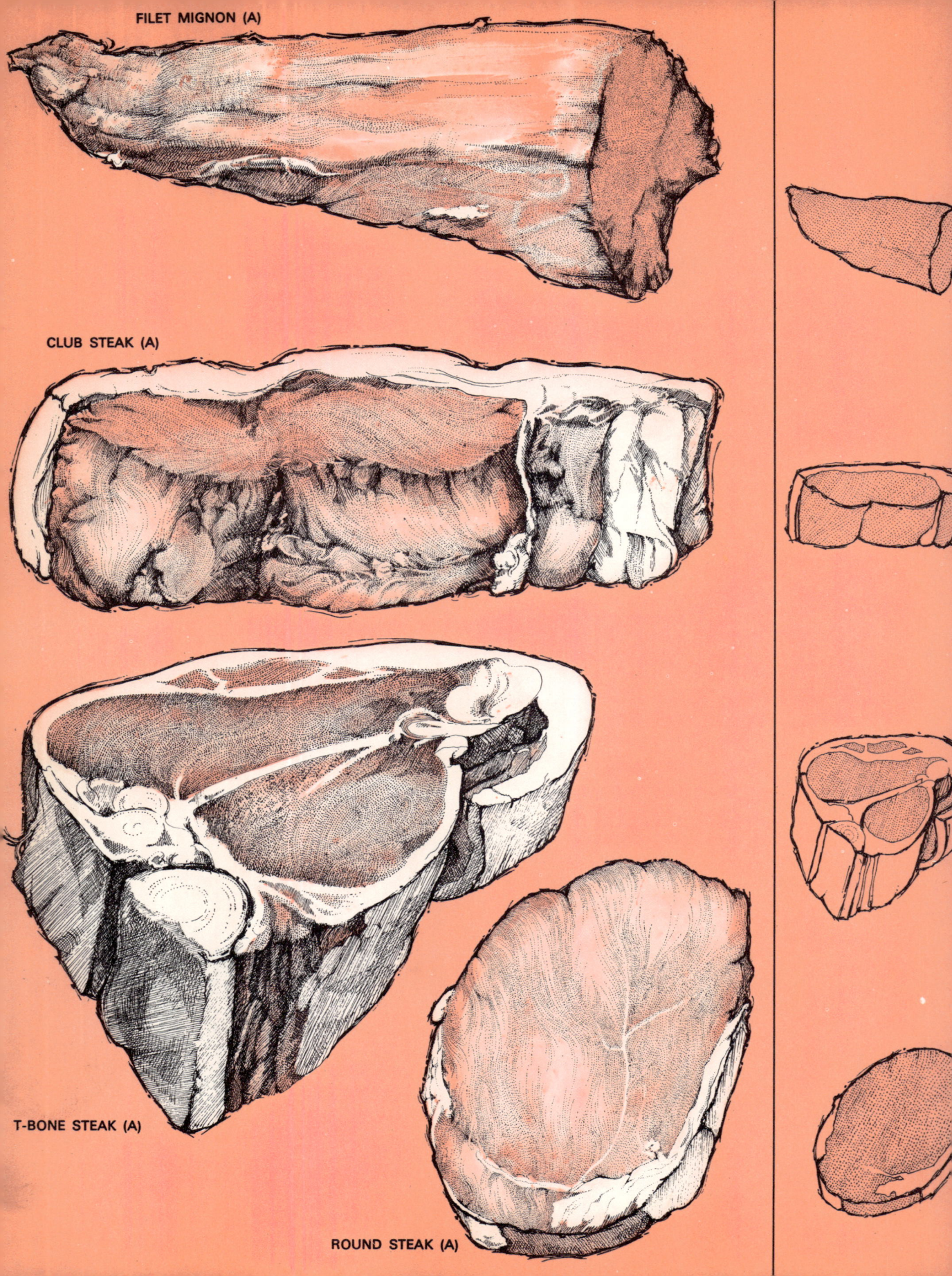

BEEF

well to edge during cooking so that wood will not scorch, and if any part of the plank is exposed, it should be well oiled'. Wipe and scrape thoroughly after use but do not wash. Wrap in waxed paper and store in dry, cool place. Planks can be purchased at a number of large stores specializing in American cookery.

SAVOURY GRILLED STEAK
Rub 3 medium-sized spoonfuls of dry mustard into a thick porterhouse steak and grill by Method 1 (p. 37). When done, spread with butter, season with salt and pepper, and surround with fried onions (English style, not French-fried).

Fried steaks

½ oz. (1 tablespoonful) butter is normally enough in which to fry an ordinary steak which, after seasoning, may be accompanied by any suitable simple sauce or garnish. In French cookery the process is carried on by using the pan in which the steak was cooked to make the sauce or garnish as in the next two recipes.

ENTRECÔTE SAUTÉ MAÎTRE D'HÔTEL
Season the entrecôte steaks lightly and fry them on both sides in a little butter till sufficiently done. Take them out and put them on a hot dish and into the frying pan (or *sauteure* if you have one) pour 3 tablespoonfuls of dry white wine (which you reduce by quick boiling to about 1 tablespoonful), scraping the bottom of the pan all the time with a wooden spoon to release the juices of the meat. When these are all dissolved, add this to some maître d'hôtel butter to make the sauce.

TOURNEDOS SAUTÉ CHASSEUR
First cut 3 oz. cleaned but unpeeled mushrooms in thin slices and fry these lightly in 2 tablespoonfuls olive oil and ½ oz. butter with the stalks upwards. Do this on a quick heat and then add 3 oz. chopped shallots and fry together for an instant. Pour off the fat and powder the vegetables with a level tablespoonful of flour. Cook gently for 5 minutes and then add 4 fl. oz. stock (1½ cups) and a tablespoonful of concentrated tomato purée. Season with pepper and simmer gently while cooking the rest of the dish. Now in a frying pan or *sauteuse* fry the steaks till properly done, and keep them hot. Drain the fat from the pan and pour in 4 fl. oz. (½ cup) dry white wine, boiling it violently and scraping the bottom of the pan with a wooden spoon. As soon as the juices from the meat are released and dissolved, and the wine reduced to about 4–5 tablespoonfuls, add the mushrooms and their sauce. After only a second or two add a coffeespoonful of chopped chervil and tarragon, stir in a small nut of butter

and pour it all over the tournedos which have been set on rounds of bread fried in butter.

Depending on how they are cut, it is sometimes necessary to tie the tournedos round with cotton which, of course, is removed before serving.

STEAK DIANE

tender steak (fillet or entrecôte)
1 shallot
butter
salt, pepper
Worcester sauce
Armagnac
parsley

Beat the meat till flat and fry the chopped shallot in butter. Meanwhile salt and pepper the steak and when the shallot is golden, put in the steak and fry it gently on both sides till it is done to taste. Add a few drops of Worcester sauce and then fire it with Armagnac or brandy serving with chopped parsley sprinkled on top.

PEPPER STEAK (France)

1 lb. chateaubriand steak
2 oz. (4 tablespoonfuls) butter
1 tablespoonful ($1\frac{1}{4}$ tablespoonfuls) olive oil
1 teaspoonful ($1\frac{1}{4}$ teaspoonfuls) black peppercorns
beef gravy
4 tablespoonfuls ($\frac{1}{4}$ cup) Armagnac or brandy
1 teaspoonful ($1\frac{1}{4}$ teaspoonfuls) cream
salt, pepper

Crush the peppercorns (black for pepperiness and flavour) on a slab or board, using a flat-iron or rolling-pin, so that you have small fragments the size of mignonette pepper, which incidentally may sometimes be purchased already ground. Salt and pepper the steak on both sides, and coat it all over with the crushed pepper, beating it well in so that it adheres firmly. Now heat the oil and half the butter in a heavy frying pan, and when hot seal the meat on each side.

When the meat is cooked to your liking, put the steak on a plate and pour off all the fat from the pan. Put the steak back into the hot pan and pour over it about 4 tablespoonfuls of brandy. Set it alight. When the flames have died down, put the steak on a serving-dish and pour into the pan a little of the gravy which you have heated and mixed with a small teaspoonful of cream. Let this reduce over the heat for a few minutes. Add a pinch of salt and a little softened butter, shaking or stirring the pan all the time, and pour this over the steak to serve. Fried potatoes of some kind are ideal for this dish, which does not really need any other vegetables.

ENTRECÔTE MIRABEAU

entrecôte steak weighing a little more than 1 lb.
2 oz. (4 tablespoonfuls) butter
anchovy fillets or paste
lemon juice
salt, pepper
green olives

Make an anchovy butter by kneading the butter with the paste or pounded fillets, and season with pepper. Brush the steak over with plain melted butter and either grill or fry it. When done to taste, season with salt and pepper and spread the anchovy butter over it. Criss-cross it with anchovy fillets and in each diamond place half a stoned green olive.

Old English cookery books often advocate the use of anchovies to supply the salt in stewed meat, but it was not till the middle of the eighteenth century that this flavour featured with beef in the French *haute cuisine*.

BEEF STROGANOFF (Russia)

1½ lb. tender steak, preferably fillet
4 onions
8 mushrooms
2 tablespoonfuls (2½ tablespoonfuls) butter
½ glass dry white wine or meat stock
salt, pepper
flour
1 tablespoonful (1¼ tablespoonfuls) tomato purée
English mustard
½ glass sour or cultured cream
parsley
olive oil

Cut the meat into thin strips 1 in. long and ¼ in. thick and leave them sprinkled with salt, pepper and a little olive oil for 30 minutes. Fry the sliced onion in the butter and then add the mushrooms, also peeled and sliced, and fry together for 5 minutes or so. Now add the meat and fry together for 5 or 6 minutes, stirring with a fork; sprinkle in a good pinch of flour and cook a little longer. Now add the tomato purée, the mustard and the wine or stock and bring to the boil. Put on the lid and just barely simmer for another 10 minutes. Finally add the cream and heat all through without letting it boil.

Note. If sour cream is unobtainable, fresh cream can be used acidulated with a little lemon juice.

BRAISED BEEF WITH ANCHOVIES

This is a more commonplace version of the same blend of flavours as in entrecôte Mirabeau, the meat being browned first with a little chopped bacon, the chopped anchovies added and the steak braised in the usual way in a moistening of good meat stock.

BRAISED AND STEWED BEEF

Braising is a simple method of steaming combined with baking, suitable mostly for tougher and cheaper joints which depend for their tenderness and flavour on a long slow cooking. It is true that many highly delicious dishes can be cooked in this way with the superior cuts of beef, but it would be more economical to use the cuts designated in the chart on p. 19, e.g. chuck, back ribs, flank and brisket. The leaner cuts like silverside and topside need a little fat to help in their cooking and this may be supplied in the form of larding or tying some fat or the outside rind of pork (*couennes*) under the meat in the bottom of the pan. The addition of a calf's foot is always an improvement to a braise especially when the meat is to be eaten cold for, like the pork rinds, it will set the gravy into a succulent jelly. Thick steaks are often braised but this form of cooking is usually reserved for a large joint which may be left for 4–5 hours while it cooks on gently without attention.

BRAISED BEEF

4 lb. fresh brisket of beef
2 large carrots
1 turnip
3 celery sticks
1 or 2 leeks
½ lb. button onions
bouquet garni
stock of diluted beef cubes
12 peppercorns
fat bacon rashers
2 oz. (4 tablespoonfuls) butter
2 oz. (½ cup) flour

Put the peeled onion aside and about ¼ pint (⅓ pint) each of the carrots and turnip cut into pieces the size of a pea; then cut into small pieces the rest of the carrots and turnip, the white part of the leeks and the celery. Put these into a stewpan or casserole just large enough to hold the meat, lay the beef on top of them and arrange the bacon rashers over the top of the meat so as to cover it completely. (If you think the rinds of smoked bacon may be too strong, use green bacon instead, but be sure to leave the rinds on it.) Now season with a little salt and add the peppercorns (in a muslin bag if preferred) and cover the vegetables only with stock. Cover very tightly and cook as gently as possible, preferably in the oven for 4–5 hours. When the meat is done, make a sauce with 2 oz. each of butter and flour and the cooking liquor in the pan; boiling this for 5 minutes and then strain it.

Meanwhile cook the carrots, turnip and onions separately and either add them to the sauce before

BEEF 43

pouring it over the meat or arrange them in neat groups round the meat, pouring a little of the sauce over them.

One of the virtues of braised meat is that it tastes almost better when warmed up again next day, a virtue which it shares with curry (*see* p. 54). As mentioned already, the presence of a calf's foot in this dish will enhance its gelatination and do wonders to the flavour as well. Brisket may be bought up to 15 lb. in weight, for a party dish.

BRAISED BEEF (France)
A favourite cut for this dish is a boned and rolled rib of beef (*côte de boeuf*), and its preparation differs from the English manner in that wine is used for the moistening liquid.

3-4 lb. rolled rib of beef
onions
carrots
pieces of green bacon rind
3-4 tablespoonfuls (3¾-5 tablespoonfuls) dripping
1 pint (1¼ pints) dry white wine
1 calf's foot
1 pint (1¼ pints) good beef stock
bouquet garni
stock
arrowroot or tomato-flavoured sauce
salt, pepper

In a casserole or braising pan put a bed of sliced onions and carrots and some fresh or salt rinds of bacon, preferably green. Season the piece of beef lightly, lay it on this bed and put in some tablespoonfuls of good dripping. Pour in 1 pint of dry white wine. Place the pan over a low heat and cook slowly till the wine is reduced almost to nothing. Add the skinned and boned calf's foot and bouquet garni. Now add the hot stock and cook the meat, covered, in a moderate oven for about 4 hours, basting it often as it cooks. The meat is served with the calf's foot which is cut into small pieces, and a little of the cooking liquor, seasoned to taste, thickened with arrowroot or a little tomato-flavoured sauce (p. 211) poured over.

The dish may be garnished with small heaps of carrots, turnips, celery, braised lettuce, glazed onions and mashed potato, or in the Italian fashion with macaroni or spaghetti or other pasta.

The wine may be diluted with a little stock if preferred, or, to make a richer dish, the meat may first be soaked in a marinade of olive oil, brandy and white wine for 5-6 hours.

Stewed Beef

STEWED STEAK (1)
1 lb. steak
1 carrot
1 onion
½ turnip
1 oz. (2 tablespoonfuls) butter
1 oz. (¼ cup) flour
¾ pint (1 pint) stock or water
salt, pepper

Trim the fat off the steak, and cut the lean into 5 or 6 pieces. Keep the vegetables, cut in dice or thin strips, in cold water till wanted. Fry the steak quickly in the butter till brown on both sides, then take the pieces out and fry the trimmings of the vegetables in the same fat with the flour till all is nicely browned. It is essential to do this properly to avoid having to add browning later on (a practice always to be deprecated). Moisten with the stock or water, stir till it boils, then put in the pieces of steak, add salt and pepper to taste and cook gently on top of the cooker with the lid firmly on for about 2 hours.

Meanwhile boil the vegetables till tender in salted water and at the last fry the fat from the meat, cut in strips, till it is nicely browned all over. Serve the steak on a dish, pouring the sauce over, and for garnish put the strips of fat on top of the meat and the vegetables in small heaps round it.

STEWED STEAK (2)
2 lb. steak
salt, pepper
onion
chopped parsley or sage
dripping
gravy

The steak should be about 1½ in. thick and scored across in squares not too deeply, with a sharp knife. Into these gashes rub a mixture of salt, pepper, finely minced onion and chopped parsley or sage, and then fry the steak in a little dripping on both sides, about 10 minutes in all. Now put it into a stewpan or casserole, just cover with hot good clear beef gravy and stew gently in the oven with the lid on for 2 hours. Serve with boiled potatoes.

BEEF WITH PEAS
2 lb. steak
fresh peas
salt, pepper
butter

A smallish, solid piece of beef is what you want, tender steak being the best. Have it cut and tied into a compact piece, season it with salt and pepper and brown it all over in butter. Butter is essential for the flavour of this dish. After about 10 minutes, turning it so that all sides are sealed, put it into a casserole which should not be much larger than the piece of meat itself, and add as many shelled small peas as the pan will hold, adding a little more salt and pepper as you go.

Now put on the lid, closed very tightly, and let the meat simmer very gently indeed for 2–3 hours. No liquid whatever should be added for the meat cooks in its own juice and this produces an admirable mixture of flavours which is really worth eating. But the dish should be disposed of at one sitting: it is nothing like as good when cold.

SPICY STEWED BEEF

1½ lb. stewing steak
fattish bacon or bacon bones
onions
4 fl. oz. (½ cup) vinegar
1 dessertspoonful (½ tablespoonful) black treacle
light ale and water
salt, pepper
cloves
bay leaf

Flatten the steak well, roll it up and tie it. Put a few bits of fattish bacon or a few bacon bones into a stew-pan with some sliced onions and just cover with a mixture of vinegar, treacle and equal parts of light ale and water. Season with salt and pepper, add 2 cloves and half a bay leaf, put the lid on closely and cook gently, preferably in the oven, for about 3 hours. Thicken the sauce before pouring it over the steak.

BEEF À LA MODE (France)

beef steak
butter
pork rind
2 onions
bouquet garni
1 clove garlic
carrots
¼ pint (⅓ pint) dry white wine
⅛ pint (⅙ pint) water

Buy a nice thick piece of beef steak (not the very best) and fry it quickly on each side in a little butter till nicely browned. Take it out and put a few fresh pork rinds into the pan. Put back the meat. Slice 2 onions on top, add a small clove of garlic and a bouquet garni and cover the whole with carrots cut in rounds. Now add ⅛ pint of water and the dry white wine, cover tightly and cook over a low heat for 2½–3 hours according to the thickness of the meat. If the sauce turns out to be too thin, reduce it till thick by rapid boiling.

The meat may be fired with brandy after being fried, and a richer and perhaps more satisfactory dish can be obtained through the addition to the vegetables of a calf's foot blanched with the pork rinds and split in two.

This dish may also be eaten cold, when the liquor will set in a jelly.

BOEUF BOURGUIGNON (France)

1 lb. stewing steak
mild or green lean bacon (or pickled pork)
butter
olive oil
button onions
1 dessertspoonful (½ tablespoonful) flour
bouquet garni
stock
red Burgundy

In a half-and-half mixture of butter and olive oil brown lightly a handful of button onions (or failing these, larger ones sliced thickly) with a thickish rasher of the bacon or pickled pork, first blanched. Then add 1 lb. stewing steak (in France the pieces of beef known as *bourguignon* approximate to our stewing steak) cut in suitably sized pieces. Toss these in the butter and oil till they are stiffened and lightly browned and then sprinkle them with a dessertspoonful of flour and brown this lightly too. Then add a bouquet garni and pour over enough Burgundy and stock till the meat is just covered. Bring to the boil, cover and simmer gently for 2½ hours, shaking the pan now and again in case the beef shows signs of sticking to the pan.

Some like to add a few mushrooms but this should not be done till ½ hour before cooking is complete and they should first be lightly fried. Garnish on serving with triangles of bread fried in oil and butter.

CARBONNADES FLAMANDES (Belgium)

2½ lb. lean beef
3 oz. (6 tablespoonfuls) butter
3 oz. lean unsmoked bacon
flour
mild ale
1 lb. onions
salt, pepper
garlic
bouquet garni
2 lumps sugar

Cut the beef into pieces about 2 in. long and 1 in. thick, season them with salt and pepper and brown them all over in the butter. Add 3 oz. lean unsmoked bacon cut into small dice and brown these too. Take out the beef and bacon and pour off all the fat except about 2 tablespoonfuls and stir into this sufficient plain flour to make a brown roux. Now by degrees add enough mild ale, stirring all the time, to make a nice sauce, and keep this and the meat hot while you brown 1 lb. finely sliced onions in the fat which you poured off. Pour the sauce into a clean casserole and fill it up with alternate layers of onion, beef and bacon, finally adding a

BEEF

chopped clove of garlic, 2 lumps of sugar, a seasoning of salt and pepper and a bouquet garni. Bring to the boil, cover closely and simmer gently in the oven for 2½–3 hours, adding a little more ale now and then if necessary, so as to keep the meat well covered. Just before serving add a dash of vinegar if desired, and simply accompany this exceptional dish by plainly-boiled or steamed potatoes, so as not to detract from its admirable flavour.

DAUBE PROVENÇALE (France)

3 lb. steak
1 lb. fresh pork (half fat, half lean)
onions
herbs
butter and olive oil
1 calf's foot
carrots
garlic
bouquet garni
salt, pepper
nutmeg
tomato purée
1 claretglassful dry white wine
water

Cut the meat into thin slices, all the same size, and beat them flat. Mince the pork very finely (uncooked pork sausage meat will do very well instead). Put the first slice of beef on a board, season it with salt, pepper, a little finely chopped onion and a good pinch of mixed herbs, preferably fresh. On this spread a layer of the pork or sausage meat to cover it, and on this another slice of beef, repeating the process till all the meat is used up, ending with a slice of beef. Now tie the whole securely with tape or string and brown it quickly in a half-and-half mixture of butter and olive oil. Put it into a stewpan not much bigger than itself and with it an onion cut in half, a couple of carrots cut in thick slices, a calf's foot blanched and cut in two, a clove of garlic, a bouquet garni, salt, pepper, a grating of nutmeg and a tablespoonful of tomato purée. Moisten with a claretglassful of dry white wine and the same of water and cover with a sheet of buttered paper. Close tightly and cook very slowly in oven for about 3 hours.

When cooked, take out the piece of beef, put it into a long shallow dish, and when it has cooled, untie it. Pour the strained hot cooking liquor into a wide basin and when it is cold, remove the surface fat from it. Warm lightly again and pour over the beef. It will be a luscious jelly when cold, and the meat will be soft enough to cut with a spoon. This *daube* is far best eaten when cold, but it is also good when served hot.

CHILI CON CARNE (Mexico)

¾ lb. round steak, cubed
8 oz. (½ cup) dried red kidney beans
1 tablespoonful (1½ tablespoonfuls) suet
1 onion
½ green pepper, chopped
½ clove garlic, minced
½ cup boiling water
4 oz. (½ cup) tinned or stewed tomatoes
salt, cayenne pepper
2 tablespoonfuls (2½ tablespoonfuls) chilli powder
Tabasco sauce

Fry the chopped onion, garlic and green pepper in the suet for 10 minutes with the lid on, stirring frequently to prevent browning, then add the beef, turn the heat up and brown the pieces well all over. Now add the boiling water and tomatoes, salt and cayenne pepper, and then the chilli powder soaked in ⅛ cup of cold water for 3–4 minutes. Finally add the drained beans which have previously been soaked overnight, put on the lid and simmer or bake in a slow oven for 1½–2 hours till the beans are soft and the meat very tender.

Now is the time to taste the sauce, and if it is not hot enough, add a drop or two of Tabasco sauce.

Peeled raw bananas sliced lengthways are recommended with this dish as a foil to its burning taste.

GAROFOLATO (Italy)

2–3 lb. topside
1 lb. tomatoes
⅛ pint (⅙ pint) red wine
garlic
parsley
mixed spice
salt, pepper
6 cloves

Brown the piece of beef all over in a stewpan in a little fat, and add the quartered tomatoes, 2 or 3 cloves of garlic, some chopped parsley, a seasoning of salt, pepper and mixed spice, ⅛ pint of red wine (Italian for authenticity) and half a dozen cloves in a muslin bag. Bring to the boil, cover and simmer gently for 2 hours or so.

GOULASH OF BEEF (Hungary)

3 lb. steak
¼ lb. (½ cup) lard
½ lb. onions
1 lb. tomatoes
salt
paprika, and possibly caraway seeds
1 lb. potatoes
water

See that you get some of the very best paprika for this delicious dish. The kind called *edelsüss* is best for the purpose, being very mild. Cut the beef into 1 in. cubes and fry these in the lard with the onions, coarsely chopped. When the onions are golden, add the salt, the peeled and quartered tomatoes and as much paprika pepper as your taste dictates, but not less than a teaspoonful. Moisten with a cupful of water, put on the lid and cook in a moderate oven for 1½ hours. Now add

BEEF

1 lb. smallish potatoes (new ones would be excellent here), whole or cut in quarters, and another cupful of water. Cook again, covered, for an hour or so longer, when the liquid should almost all disappear. Caraway seed may be added, in a muslin bag, to the tomatoes.

FRICADELLES (Holland)

1 lb. raw lean mince (ground beef)
1 grated onion
4 tablespoonfuls (5 tablespoonfuls) breadcrumbs
1 egg
4 tablespoonfuls ($\frac{1}{4}$ cup) tomato purée
$\frac{1}{2}$ pint ($1\frac{1}{4}$ cups) stock or bouillon
3-4 tablespoonfuls ($\frac{1}{4}$ cup) sour cream

Make 8 meat balls from the meat mixture, using the grated onion and working in the egg. Put them, without previously frying them, into a casserole and pour over them a mixture of the tomato purée and stock. Cover and cook very slowly for $1\frac{1}{2}$ hours. Leave the balls to soak in their sauce all night, and heat them up next day when they will be permeated with the sauce. Just before serving add the sour or cultured cream, letting it just heat through without boiling.

WÜRSTELBRATEN (Germany)

lean beef
Frankfurter sausages
onion
salt, pepper
paprika
flour
yoghurt, if desired
fat
10 fl. oz. ($1\frac{1}{4}$ cups) water

Trim the fat from a lean joint of beef and with a skewer make 5 holes right through it, along the fibres of the meat. Into each of these holes insert a Frankfurter sausage, pushing it right through and chopping off any protruding ends.

Now fry a large sliced onion in a tablespoonful of fat, dust the joint with salt, pepper and paprika and then toss it with the onion in the hot fat. Sprinkle with a tablespoonful of flour and fry for another few minutes. Then transfer it all to a fireproof dish and pour over a breakfastcupful of water into which the first pan has been scraped and swilled. Cover and cook very gently for about 3 hours till the meat is tender, adding a little more hot water if the joint shows a tendency to dry. Strain the gravy before serving and, if desired, thicken it with a little yoghurt.

Paupiettes

Paupiettes are thin slices of raw beef or other meat, rolled up with a stuffing of some kind, wrapped up in a thin piece of bacon and then braised. In England the most familiar form is known as Beef Olives, and in the United States as Veal Birds. This name appears again as *Oiseaux sans têtes* (veal) and *Loose-vinken* (beef), the latter Belgian dish being related to *Carbonnades flamandes* (p. 46), where the beef is braised in beer.

BEEF OLIVES
An English form of the paupiette. It is a simple one, popular in Victorian times.

1 lb. rump steak
6-8 oz. ($\frac{3}{4}$-1 cup) veal forcemeat
$\frac{1}{2}$ pint (1$\frac{1}{4}$ cups) brown or espagnole sauce (p. 209)

Cut the meat into rectangles as described below in *Paupiettes de boeuf*, spread on the forcemeat thinly, roll up and tie with cotton. Have the sauce ready in a stew-pan and bring it to the boil and put in the beef olives. Simmer them gently for an hour and serve on a bed of mashed potato, pouring the sauce over. Owing to a misconception about the origin of the name, the sauce was often mixed with slices of blanched green olives, and in my own opinion, this unusual addition did the dish no harm.

PAUPIETTES DE BOEUF (France)
This dish may be taken as a basic example of cooking in this way, the nature of the different stuffings and braising ingredients being varied in the other forms. The paupiettes, then, are thin slices about $\frac{1}{8}$ in. thick and weighing about 3$\frac{1}{2}$ oz. taken from the sirloin or rump, and flattened to measure 8 × 4 in. They are spread with a mixture of sausage meat, breadcrumbs, onions and herbs, and rolled up in a thin rasher of streaky bacon. They are tied with cotton (which must not be forgotten when they are served) and braised slowly, covered with meat stock or other suitable liquid, on a bed of thinly-sliced onions, carrots and blanched green bacon rind. When they are cooked, they are arranged on the serving dish and the reduced cooking liquor, from which the grease has been removed, thickened perhaps with a little *demi-glace* sauce, is poured over them.

PAUPIETTES DE BOEUF FLAMANDES (Belgium)
The paupiettes are prepared as in the basic recipe, and are browned quickly all over

Silverside of Beef and some of the ingredients for Boiled Silverside of Beef

in a little dripping. Transfer them to a casserole and add a little butter to the pan in which they were cooked and brown some chopped onions in it. Add these to the casserole in alternate layers with the beef, and place a bouquet garni in the middle. Add some beer to the sediment in the frying pan; bring it to boiling point and thicken with flour. Now add a little brown sugar and cook the paupiettes in this for 2 hours or so in a slow oven. In this case the paupiettes are served round a large piece of cooked, smoked bacon.

PAUPIETTES DE BOEUF À LA CRÈME
A curiously attractive recipe in which, like *Entrecôte Mirabeau*, beef and anchovies are combined.

tender beef **anchovy fillets** **parsley** **onion** **garlic** **butter** **bouillon** **cream** **lemon** **chives or the green part of a spring onion** **pepper**	Make a stuffing with fillets of anchovy, parsley and a small onion chopped up together, with a touch of garlic if desired. Spread this on the prepared beef slices and roll and tie them up. Brown them all over in butter, then season with pepper only and moisten with bouillon. Put on the lid and cook in a slow oven for 1 hour. Before serving thicken the sauce with cream (but do not allow it to boil), and sprinkle with a few drops of lemon juice and a good pinch of chopped parsley and chives or the green part of a young onion, very finely minced. As will be seen there is a great variety of stuffings for paupiettes as well as many different liquids in which they can be braised.

BEEF DOVES
Another form of paupiette, in which a cabbage leaf is used for the wrapping.

8 oz. minced raw beef (ground) **2 oz. (scant ⅓ cup) uncooked rice** **salt, pepper** **cabbage leaves** **tomato sauce** **cayenne pepper** **bacon fat or butter**	Mix the beef and rice together and season with salt, pepper and cayenne pepper. Remove suitable leaves from the cabbage, trim them and blanch them for 2 minutes in boiling water to make them pliable. Place a couple of tablespoonfuls of the beef mixture along each leaf, and fold over and tie compactly. Brown the little packets all over in butter or preferably bacon fat and then simmer them for 1 hour in a thinnish tomato sauce. Cooked rice or breadcrumbs can be used if pre-

Boiled Silverside of Beef

ferred, and the seasoning of the beef mixture can be varied in a number of ways.

Curry

BEEF CURRY

It is simple enough to make a good curry, provided that you do it properly and have the right ingredients. These are, apart from fresh meat, a good proprietary curry paste and powder, onions, garlic, fresh or desiccated coconut, good stock for moistening, some suitable fat, a bay leaf, saffron, ginger and some lemon juice.

In order that the coconut shall play its important part in the sauce you must make some coconut milk. The milk in the coconut is not what you want, but an infusion made in this manner. Put the freshly grated coconut, or desiccated coconut, into a small saucepan and add just enough cold water to cover it. Bring it to the boil and let it stand, off the heat, for 20 minutes. Then press through a sieve or a potato ricer. The stock is important, as it is this that will give body to the flavour and you can make it from the trimmings of whatever meat you are using. When it is ready, measure out $\frac{1}{2}$ pint ($1\frac{1}{4}$ cups) and have ready the same quantity of coconut milk. Now put 2 oz. ($\frac{1}{4}$ cup) oil or butter into a saucepan and fry 2 small onions and a small clove of garlic, finely minced, till a light gold (no darker). Stir in a heaped tablespoonful of curry powder and the same of curry paste, and cook it for 3 or 4 minutes on a low heat, stirring all the time to remove the raw taste of the powder. Then add by degrees a wineglassful of the coconut milk and the whole of the stock, simmer for about $\frac{1}{4}$ hour, and keep it hot.

Cut up the pieces of raw meat and fry them in another pan in 1 oz. (2 tablespoonfuls) of the fat with a small onion or shallot cut in pieces. Turn the pieces over with a wooden spoon till they are lightly browned all over, and then take them out and put them into the curry mixture, leaving the fat and onion in the pan. Leave the meat to soak in the curry for at least 30 minutes, then put the pan over a very low heat, adding a little more stock if the pieces are not quite covered. Add a bay leaf, garlic, saffron and lemon juice and cook, covered, in the slowest possible way till the meat is tender. Then add another wineglassful of coconut milk and cook for another 5 minutes or so. If the sauce is not thick enough by then, you must reduce it by taking the lid off the pan till it is, but on no account should flour be used (other than for flouring the meat). Salt may now be added to taste, and if you have a sweetish tooth, a little chutney liquid may be mixed in. Plainly boiled rice is served with the curry, usually as a border, but better as a separate dish.

BEEF

Meat curries are undoubtedly best when made with fresh meat, but if you want to curry cold cooked meat, you can use the same curry sauce for them. If these directions are followed carefully, an excellent curry will result. The main points are that the onions are not fried too much, that the coconut milk is added exactly as directed, that the stock is well flavoured and as rich as possible, that the meat is allowed to soak in the curry mixture and that it should be stewed as slowly as possible. Many people find this spicy impregnation so important that they insist on their curries being made the day before and then warmed up. It is, I think, an admirable idea. But always turn the curry out into a china or earthenware bowl, for if it is left standing in a metal saucepan it may be found very unpleasant indeed.

For mutton and lamb curry *see* p. 122.

BOILED BEEF

In England, boiled beef is always salted and hardly anywhere save in small continental restaurants will you find the delicious spicy dish which fresh boiled beef can be. In the United States, boiled fresh beef is featured in some cookery books, but it is much less elaborate than the French *pot-au-feu* which is internationally famous. Instructions for carving silverside and brisket will be found on p. 20 and drawings on pp. 29 and 202 respectively.

BOILED FRESH BEEF (U.S.A.)

4 lb. brisket, chuck silverside or larded round of beef
horseradish sauce
salt
horseradish sauce:
1 cupful white sauce
¼ cup grated horseradish
pinch dry mustard

Brown the piece of meat all over, and put it into a pan. Pour in enough boiling water to come half-way up and simmer, covered, till the meat is tender. This will take about 3–4 hours, the time depending on the quality of the beef. Half-way through the cooking (not before) add salt in the proportion of ½ teaspoonful for each 1 lb. of meat. Serve with horseradish sauce. To a cupful of white sauce made with butter, flour and milk, add ¼ cup grated horseradish and a pinch of dry mustard.

POT-AU-FEU (France)

In France, boiled fresh beef is a classical dish in which the soup, meat course and vegetables are all cooked in one. Any lean meat is suitable but silverside is normally used, and additional bones and chicken giblets will provide a better flavour. The preliminaries are important. If you set more store by the boiled beef itself, the meat

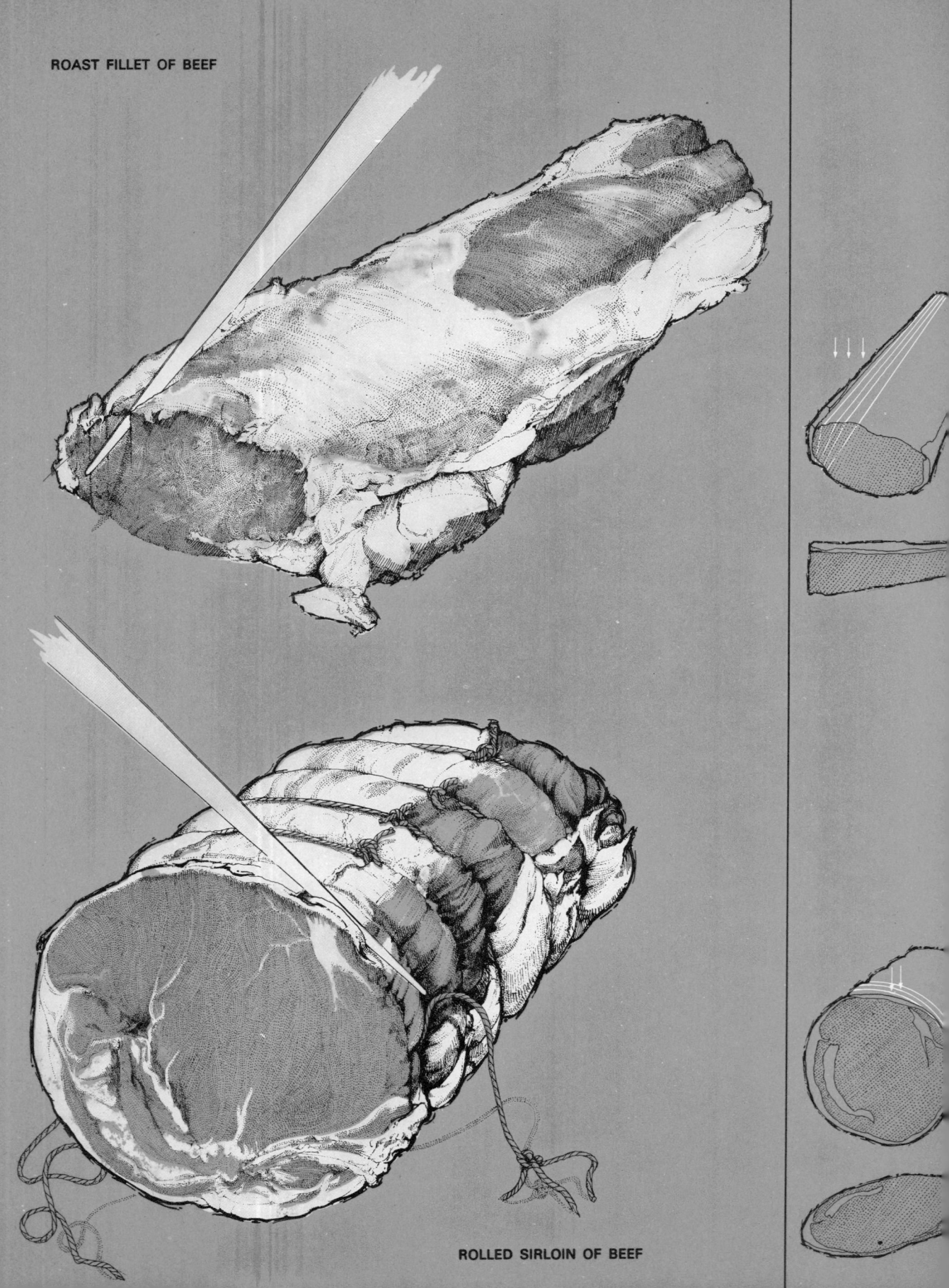

BEEF 57

should be put into boiling water and salt added after it is cooked, but if it is the soup you want then put it into cold salted water and heat it gradually. In either case you must see that the liquid just trembles slightly during the cooking and that it never actually boils. Skimming throughout is essential. This is a good orthodox *pot-au-feu*:

2 lb. lean beef
1 lb. chickens' giblets without the liver
1 lb. bones
cold water
salt
2 onions
cloves
3 carrots
1 turnip
celery or celeriac
4 leeks
bouquet garni
garlic
cloves
peppercorns
a marrowbone if possible

Get the butcher to chop the bones up small and put them with the giblets into a heavy saucepan with about 8 pints (10 pints) cold water. Add salt and bring to the boil. Skim carefully, then add a glass of cold water to produce more scum, and skim again. Stick 2 onions with cloves (it is useless to be didactic about the number of cloves, as tastes vary so much), add them to the pot with 4 leeks tied in a bundle and the carrots, turnip and some celery or celeriac cut in long slices, and the piece of beef. Skim again after bringing to the boil, put the lid on the pan, leaving it a tiny bit open and simmer for 4 hours, keeping an eye on the heat to make sure that it never reaches boiling point. The marrowbone, tied in a piece of muslin, is added 30 minutes before the *pot-au-feu* is to be eaten.

It not only adds richness to the whole, but gives marrow addicts a special treat when it is served on toast.

In Languedoc a special touch is given to the local *pot-au-feu* by the use of a piece of blanched pickled or salt belly of pork instead of the giblets, and throughout France the famous *poule-au-pot* contains, instead of the giblets, a chicken or fowl stuffed with a mixture of chopped ham, garlic, onion, its own liver and sausage meat. To give colour to the soup, the skins of the onions (well-washed, of course) are left on, or they are skinned and roasted before the cloves are stuck in.

The *pot-au-feu* is served first in soup plates for the broth and vegetables cooked in it, and then the meat appears in a separate dish with boiled or steamed potatoes and extra vegetables round it. French mustard, pickles, gherkins and horseradish sauce are among the accompaniments which help to give the meat some piquancy.

CROÛTE AU POT (France)
Remove the fat from the *pot-au-feu*. (This is best done when the fat is cold.) Heat the soup to boiling point. Add a few scraps of the boiled beef and some diced cooked

vegetables and pour into an earthenware casserole or marmite, after putting a toasted square of bread for each person at the bottom. Grated cheese is usually served with it.

BEEF AND BEANS

3 lb. brisket of beef
salt, pepper
1 pint (1¼ pints) haricot beans
2 rashers smoked bacon
1 onion
½ oz. (½ tablespoonful) bacon fat or lard
3 tablespoonfuls (3¾ tablespoonfuls) flour
1 dessertspoonful (½ tablespoonful) vinegar (optional)

An hour before you want to cook it, rub 3 lb. brisket of beef with salt and pepper. Meanwhile put 1 pint soaked haricot beans into some fresh cold water, add ½ teaspoonful of salt and 2 rashers of smoked bacon, bring to the boil and simmer for 1 hour. Now add the brisket and continue to cook gently for about 3 hours more after it has come to the boil again.

When the beef is done, put it into a dish, cut the bacon into strips and lay them over the meat. Keep the beef hot while you brown a sliced onion in ½ oz. bacon fat or lard, and make a thick sauce by adding 3 tablespoonfuls of flour and a cupful of the cooking liquor. Add the drained beans. Pour over the meat to serve. Vinegar may be added to the sauce for flavour.

PRESSED BEEF (U.S.A.)

3 lb. flank of beef
salt
peppercorns
bay leaf

Remove unnecessary fat, roll and tie up the piece of flank. Put it in a pan with any bones available and pour over enough boiling water to cover the joint. Season with salt and peppercorns, add a small piece of bay leaf. Bring slowly to the boil and simmer very gently indeed for several hours till the meat is in shreds and almost all the cooking liquor gone. Then arrange in a deep pan, pour the remains of the liquor over it and press under a heavy weight. Let it get quite cold before serving.

COLD SALT BEEF

Alexis Soyer, the famous chef to the Reform Club in London in the 1830s, had this special way with boiled salt beef. He filled two large basins with iced water just before the meat was cooked, and then plunged the joint into one of them and left it there for 1 minute, then he took it out and plunged it into the other. He continued this process for about 20 minutes, renewing the iced water the while, and then put the meat on a dish and let it get quite cold. This method leaves the fat deliciously white and preserves all the juices in the joint.

BOILED SALT BEEF (U.S. Corned beef)
Beef to be cooked in this way is invariably salted and there are various proportions of salt and saltpetre used. This brine or pickle is a good representative English one.

4-6 lb. salt beef
2-3 medium-sized onions
3 turnips
4 carrots
12 peppercorns
bouquet garni
suet dumplings
pickle for beef:
8 pints (10 pints) cold water
1 lb. (2 cups) common salt
brown sugar
¾ oz. (1¾ tablespoonfuls) saltpetre
suet dumplings:
4 oz. (1 cup) flour
1 oz. (¼ cup) shredded suet
salt, pepper
pinch of baking powder
(if desired half an onion chopped and a little chopped parsley)

Boil the ingredients for the pickle together for 10 minutes, skimming frequently, then strain into an earthenware basin. Let the pickle get cold before putting the meat into it. For English tastes it should remain there for 10 days. If it is not entirely covered, turn it every day.

The meat – aitchbone, round or brisket should be skewered or bound with tape into a compact shape, and put into a large pan just big enough to hold it and the cooking water. This should be warm, unless you know the meat is very salt, in which case it should be cold. Very gradually bring it to the boil and skim it well. Now add the onions peeled and left whole, the turnips cut into thick slices, the carrots cut in 4 lengthways, 12 black peppercorns tied in a muslin bag and the bouquet garni. Bring to the boil again and simmer for 20–30 minutes to the pound and serve garnished with the vegetables.

It is customary to serve suet dumplings with this joint when hot, and these should be put into the cooking liquor 30 minutes before serving, bringing the liquor to the boil before they are added.

For the dumplings mix all the ingredients well and then add enough cold water to make a light dough. Divide into a dozen small balls.

NEW ENGLAND BOILED DINNER (U.S.A.)
4 lb. boned cut of salt or pickled beef
water or stock to cover
carrots
turnips
new potatoes
small cabbage

Wash the meat under the cold tap and tie it up. Cover with cold water or good stock and bring slowly to the boil and cook for about 5 minutes. Skim and then simmer for 2½ hours when it will be nearly done. Let it cool a little and remove most of the fat. Bring to the boil again and add the carrots, turnips and new potatoes. Leave these whole if they are small or cut into pieces.

Cook for 15 minutes and then add a small cabbage, cut into quarters and with the centre stalk removed and continue cooking for another 20 minutes. Serve hot with the vegetables arranged in heaps round it and a little of the cooking liquor in a sauceboat.

Horseradish sauce or mustard pickles are traditionally served with this dish and small hot cooked beetroots are sometimes added to give colour to the garnish. If you require a more elaborate dinner, try cooking a small stewing chicken or a piece of pickled pork with the meat.

GLAZED CORNED BEEF (U.S.A.)

Cook the corned beef as for boiled salt beef, and when drained put it in a baking-tin. Cover the top with 2 oz. ($\frac{1}{4}$ cup) brown sugar and stick it with half-a-dozen cloves. Then put the tin into a moderate oven (350°F., 177°C.) and bake for about 30 minutes, when the melted sugar will glaze it. As with many beef dishes, horseradish sauce provides a suitable accompaniment.

SPICED BEEF

10 lb. pickled brisket
spices:
1 dessertspoonful ($\frac{1}{2}$ tablespoonful) black pepper
pinch of ground ginger
pinch of powdered cloves
pinch of grated nutmeg
pinch of ground mace
$\frac{1}{2}$ pint ($1\frac{1}{4}$ cups) claret or stock
flour and water paste (optional)

Drain and wipe a piece of pickled brisket of beef and spread it out. Mix together the spices and seasonings, and sprinkle them over the meat. Roll it up and bind or skewer it into a solid piece. Put it into an earthenware pot of a size which will just contain it comfortably and pour over it $\frac{1}{2}$ pint of claret or good beef stock. Put 2 or 3 thicknesses of greaseproof paper over the top and then press the lid firmly on. No other liquid is necessary and the closure must be as airtight as possible. If you have the right sort of receptacle, it would be better to cover the edges with a flour-and-water paste. Cook in a slow oven for a good 4 hours, and press the joint between 2 plates or boards till it is cold.

BEEF-HAM (Scotland)

For this recipe for the traditional Scots way of preparing a beef-ham, I am indebted to Miss Marian McNeill's *The Scots Kitchen*.

BEEF

20 lb. rump of beef
3 lb. (3¾ cups) salt
¼ lb. (½ cup) saltpetre
¼ lb. (½ cup) unrefined sugar
½ oz. (1 tablespoonful) cloves
allspice
black pepper

For a rump of about 20 lb. take ¼ lb. saltpetre, 2 lb. salt, ¼ lb. sugar, ½ oz. cloves, some Jamaica pepper (allspice) and black pepper, the spices all ground. Mix all these ingredients thoroughly together, rub the beef all over, and stuff as much as possible into the bones. Let it lie for 2 or 3 days. Then add another 1 lb. salt, rub in well and turn every day. It will be ready in 3 weeks.

Drain it from the brine and hang it up. If you want it smoked, hang it over a barrel in which you burn peat or turf. The smoke will soon taste it, if you turn it well on every part. Then hang it up to dry. Or it may be boiled when taken out of the pickle, and allowed to stand till cold in the water in which it was boiled, or it may be baked in a deep dish, covered with a coarse paste.

MINCED BEEF

The trimmings of steaks will serve perfectly for providing the raw minced beef which, ever since the last war, has become increasingly popular in England. Mince was popular too, as I remember from my childhood days, in Victorian times, when Viennese steaks were frequently served for lunch. For some reason or other the voyage across the Atlantic changed the name to Hamburgers.

The mince for the Hamburger steak should be made from the better cuts, but the cheaper kind from the neck and flank is often used. If you think that your butcher may be a little unreliable about the quality of the meat he uses for mince, buy the meat in a piece and ask him to mince it for you or do the mincing at home yourself. Steak for Hamburgers, by the way, is generally minced more finely than the usual sort. Mince, or ground beef, is the basis, too, of Italian meat sauces, served with many pasta dishes.

HAMBURGER STEAK

1 lb. finely minced lean raw beef
salt
pepper
butter

Form the meat into about 6 round flat cakes, but do not press it too tightly together. In fact, handle it as little as possible, but if it is too dry moisten it slightly with tomato juice. Fry in butter or grill the steaks quickly on each side, and serve sprinkled with salt and pepper, and spread with softened butter.

PLANKED HAMBURGER STEAK

These steaks lend themselves admirably to planking (*see* p. 37). Follow the basic recipe for Hamburger steak with a little salt and pepper and moisten with lemon juice to taste; shape into one large steak of a size to fit the plank and about $1\frac{1}{4}$ in. thick, and grill this on each side just enough to sear it. Place it on the ready-greased plank, spread the top of the meat with melted butter, and season it with salt and pepper. Now surround it with mashed potato and brush over with egg yolk mixed with a little milk, and bake in a hot oven (450°F., 233°C.) till the top is browned.

MEAT BALLS

1 lb. lean minced beef
4 oz. ($\frac{1}{2}$ cup) minced fresh or pickled (salt) pork
1 small onion (chopped)
butter
3 oz. (1 cup) breadcrumbs
$\frac{1}{8}$ pint ($\frac{1}{6}$ pint) milk
flour
1 oz. (2 tablespoonfuls) dripping
salt, pepper

Season the beef and pork mince with salt and pepper to taste and add the onion, first lightly-fried in the butter, the breadcrumbs and the milk. Mix well together, shape into a dozen small balls, roll in flour and brown well in the dripping. These may be served as they are, but it is more usual to continue cooking them in a casserole with various vegetables (e.g. tomatoes, potatoes, carrot, onion, celery and green sweet pepper, diced, chopped or minced) and to finish cooking them with lid on for about 45 minutes in a moderate oven.

BIFTECK À LA RUSSE (Russia)

1 lb. raw minced beef
flour
4 oz. ($\frac{1}{2}$ cup) butter
4 oz. ($1\frac{1}{4}$ cups) breadcrumbs
pepper, salt
nutmeg
2-3 tablespoonfuls ($2\frac{1}{2}$-$3\frac{3}{4}$ tablespoonfuls) demiglace sauce (p. 209)
4 fl. oz. ($\frac{1}{2}$ cup) sour or cultured cream

Shape the meat mixture into 8 small balls, roll them in flour and cook them in butter. Arrange them in the serving-dish, drain the butter from the pan and pour in the sour cream. Let this reduce for a few seconds, then mix in the half-glaze sauce. Strain the sauce over the meat balls, which are usually accompanied by a dish of sauté potatoes.

BEEF

BIFTECK À L'AMERICAINE
To eat raw steak has always been considered a sign of virility, dating from the days when the Tartars consumed their horseflesh in this way. In its simplest form nowadays this dish consists of fillet of steak from which the fat and gristle have been removed, minced and seasoned with salt and pepper and shaped into small round flat cakes for each person. A raw egg yolk is placed in a hollow in each, and the dish is accompanied by chopped raw onion, capers and parsley in separate dishes, the mixture being made at the table by the diner himself.

STEAK TARTARE
This is a more elaborate version of *Bifteck à l'Américaine* originating, I believe, in the United States, where some ceremony has developed in its making. Make a *piquante* mayonnaise sauce with 4 egg yolks, 4 tablespoonfuls ($\frac{1}{4}$ cup) olive oil, 1 tablespoonful ($1\frac{1}{4}$ tablespoonfuls) Worcester sauce, French mustard, salt, pepper and good vinegar (to taste). 1 lb. rump or fillet of steak, freshly minced, is stirred into this lightly with a fork along with a finely chopped onion, 1 dessertspoonful minced parsley and 2 dessertspoonfuls (1 tablespoonful) whole capers.

   For service at the table the steak is piled in a dish and egg yolks, each in its half-shell, arranged in hollows on it and the onion, capers and parsley piled in heaps round the edge. The steak mixture is tossed together in the bowl, the yolks, onion, etc. being added according to the tastes of the guests. It saves a good deal of trouble, however, and tastes just as well, if the operation is conducted in the kitchen.

   It is obvious that in dishes of this kind there is room for many variations. For example, a hot sauce like Tabasco may be added to the sauce; beetroot, gherkins and red or green pepper, or both, all cut in small dice may be used as additions to the little heaps round the steak. Again, the steak can be served on a large plate and the heaps arranged round the outside, so that the guests may themselves make their own mixture on their plates, choosing accompaniments from the variety before them.

MINCE
1 lb. mince
$\frac{1}{4}$ lb. ox kidney
salt, pepper, mustard
chicken or beef stock
onion

Put the mince into a heavy-bottomed pan, without any flavouring or fat. Beat with a wooden spoon to break up the meat as it browns. When it is well browned, season with salt, black pepper and mustard. Add the kidney, cut into small pieces and just cover with boiling chicken stock. Add the onion, cover and stew gently 1 hour.

   Serve with triangular pieces of toast and plain boiled rice. Tomato purée may be added for variety.

MINCED COLLOPS OF BEEF (Old English)

1 lb. minced steak
1 small chopped onion
butter
1 tablespoonful (1¼ tablespoonfuls) flour
¼ pint (⅓ pint) stock
bouquet garni
1 tablespoonful (1¼ tablespoonfuls) mushroom ketchup
salt, pepper
toast

Fry the onion in the butter till light brown, then stir in the flour and brown this a little too. Add the mince and stir over the heat for a few minutes. Add the stock, bouquet and ketchup, season with salt and pepper and cook very gently for ¼ hour. Serve garnished with small pieces of toast.

PIES AND PUDDINGS

These make splendid winter dishes. Beefsteak pies and puddings and all their variants are one of the triumphs of the English kitchen. In the nineteenth century larks were a common addition but, fortunately, this barbarous practice has died out.

All cuts suitable for stewing are equally satisfactory for pies and puddings. For a superlative dish use rump steak instead of a cheaper cut in pies or puddings.

FILET DE BOEUF EN CROUTE (France)

brioche paste:
8 oz. (2 cups) flour
⅓ oz. (⅓ cake) yeast
4 eggs
scant 4 oz. (½ cup) butter
1 fillet steak
1 egg yolk
Périgueux sauce

Roll out the pastry into a rectangle. Seal the steak, previously well larded, over a good heat so that the outsides are well browned and crisped. Then put it aside to cool. Lay the meat in the middle of its pastry bed, gather the paste over it, seal the edges together and brush over with yolk of egg to gild it. It is then baked in a moderate oven till the pastry is done. Serve with *Périgueux* sauce.

Alternatively, the meat can be coated when cold and before it is wrapped up in the pastry with, say, a thick mushroom purée.

Périgueux sauce is made from ½ pint (1¼ cups) much reduced *demi-glace* sauce to which 3 dessertspoonfuls (2½ tablespoonfuls) peeled and chopped truffles and a little Madeira are added at the end.

Raymond Oliver, whose restaurant in Paris, the Grand Véfour, is internationally famous, has suggested using the following method instead: 'Cut the fillet into small tournedos, two for each person. Fry these very quickly, being careful to keep them just seared and hardly cooked at all. Then reshape the fillet, patting a stuffing or a purée between the tournedos'. He insists that all these operations should be accomplished as quickly as possible, so as not to have to re-heat the meat too much.

STEAK PIE

2 lb. steak
1 tablespoonful (1¼ tablespoonfuls) flour
1 egg yolk
salt, pepper
water
clear beef gravy
shortcrust pastry:
1 oz. (2 tablespoonfuls) lard
1 oz. (2 tablespoonfuls) butter
4 oz. (1 cup) flour
salt
water

To make the shortcrust pastry, cut the fat into small pieces and rub into the flour and salt till the mixture looks like fine breadcrumbs; using very little water mix to a stiff dough and roll out.

The meat should be cut into pieces about 3 in. long, which are then rolled in a mixture of 1 tablespoonful flour, 1 teaspoonful (1¼ teaspoonfuls) salt and pepper. Put them into a piedish well raised up in the middle to support the pastry in cooking. Sprinkle what is left of the seasoning between the pieces of meat as you arrange them, and pour over them enough boiling water to come three-quarters of the way up the dish. Line the edges of the dish with puff pastry or shortcrust pastry and cover the dish with more pastry, making a hole in the top, and decorating with pastry leaves and brushing over with yolk of egg. Bake in a hot oven at first till the pastry has risen and set, and then at a lower temperature to cook the meat. This will take about 2 hours. Before serving, pour a little clear beef gravy through the hole in the top. If this is not available, use hot water seasoned with salt and pepper.

STEAK AND KIDNEY PIE

1½ lb. steak
2 sheeps' kidneys *or*
½ lb. ox kidney

Cook as for steak pie, cutting the kidney across in thin slices and rolling each one up tightly. Arrange the little rolls of kidney on end in the piedish.

STEAK AND OYSTER PIE

steak
oysters

Cook as for steak and kidney pie, substituting 2 dozen small oysters for the kidney. The opened oysters should be bearded and rolled up in the steak like the kidneys. The beards are blanched and their liquor strained and added to the gravy or water which is put into the pie before serving.

STEAK AND POTATO PIE

1½ lb. steak
potatoes to line the dish
1 tablespoonful (1¼ tablespoonfuls) flour
salt
1 small onion
pepper
shortcrust pastry (p. 65)
salt, pepper
water
gravy

Cut the peeled potatoes into thick slices and the meat into thin ones about 2 in. long and 1 in. wide. Dip the meat into the flour, seasoned with salt and pepper, roll the pieces up tightly and put them into the piedish which has already been lined with the potato slices. Sprinkle a little of the parboiled and finely chopped onion over them and repeat these vegetable and meat layers till the dish is full, sprinkling with more of the seasoning as you go. Then pour in enough boiling water to fill the dish three-quarters full, cover with the pastry and bake in a moderately hot oven for about 2 hours. Before serving, pour in hot beef gravy or water seasoned with salt and pepper, through the hole in the top crust.

STEAK PUDDING

suet pastry:
10 oz. (2½ cups) flour
2 teaspoonfuls (2½ teaspoonfuls) baking powder
salt

2 lb. steak
1 tablespoonful (1¼ tablespoonfuls) flour
salt
pepper
water

To make the suet pastry, sift the flour with the baking powder and salt to your taste. Then add the suet and mix well. Using a knife, mix in enough water to make a soft dough. Add the water as quickly as possible.

Cut the beef into thin slices about 3 in. long and dip these in the seasoned flour. Roll out the suet crust and set aside about three-quarters of it to make the lid of the pudding. Grease a pudding basin well, line it with the crust and put in the meat, sprinkling the rest of the seasoning between the layers. Do not pack too tightly or the water will not be able to percolate freely and the pudding will tend to be dry. Fill the basin three-quarters full with boiling water, and put on the suet crust cover, previously rolled out to fit the top, and seal the edges together. If the pudding is to be boiled, tie over the basin a scalded and floured pudding-cloth and boil for 3½ hours at least. However, if it is to be

BEEF

steamed, it must be covered with a greased paper and will take another 30 minutes to cook.

The water should be boiling when you put the pudding in, and kept on the boil all the time.

Variants on this theme are of course *Steak and kidney pudding* and *Steak, kidney, oyster and mushroom pudding*. To make either of these dishes, remember to use less beef in order to make up the correct weight. The English traditional steak, kidney, oyster and mushroom pudding is a masterpiece of which any nation might be proud.

CORNISH PASTY

Beef is the authentic meat for a Cornish pasty, but lamb or mutton are sometimes substituted. Any good pastry can be used, but it must be neither flaky nor too rich. This recipe gives a variation of the suet pastry given in the recipe for steak pudding.

pastry:
1 lb. (4 cups) flour
4 oz. ($\frac{1}{2}$ cup) lard and suet
salt
water to mix

$\frac{3}{4}$ **lb. raw steak**
2 potatoes
1 onion

Roll the pastry out $\frac{1}{4}$ in. thick and cut it into rounds with a plate. Lay these pieces on a pastry board with half of the round over the rolling pin and put in the filling on the bottom half. The proper filling for this pasty is a mixture of small pieces of raw steak and raw potato flavoured with a little minced onion, but sometimes a little of the red turnip found in Cornwall is used as well. Damp the edges lightly, and fold over into a semi-circle. Shape the pastry nicely with your finger and thumb and crimp the edges where they join. Cut a slit in the middle of the pasty, lay it on a baking sheet and bake it in a quick oven first so that it keeps its shape and then lower the heat to cook the contents.

SAUSAGES

BEEF SAUSAGES

Beef is used in making sausages for those who are, for one reason or another, intolerant of pork, and they can be used in any of the recipes given for pork sausages (*see* p. 152). It is hard to better the traditional English breakfast of bacon, egg, and sausages. The small cocktail sausage or chipolata is increasingly popular grilled and served on sticks either hot or cold. Here is a recipe in case anyone wishes to make them at home.

2 lb. lean beef
1 lb. beef suet
pinch powdered allspice
salt, pepper
sausage skins

The beef and suet should be chopped or shredded as finely as possible and well mixed with the seasonings. The mixture should be pressed lightly into the skins or, when these are not available, formed into sausage shapes or flat round cakes and fried. The following recipe is particularly suitable for this type of sausage.

BEEF SAUSAGES IN BEER

1 lb. beef sausages
butter
bay leaf
peppercorns
salt
1 pint (1¼ pints) beer or old ale or porter
1 tablespoonful (1¼ tablespoonfuls) potato flour or arrowroot

Blanch the sausages for a minute by pouring boiling water over them, then drain and dry them, and brown them in butter to which you have added a bay leaf, a few peppercorns and a little salt. Add ½ pint (1¼ cups) beer, bring quickly to the boil, and boil for a few minutes to reduce it a little. Then add the rest of the beer, just enough to cover the sausages bring to the boil again, and simmer for 15 minutes. Thicken the sauce before serving with a tablespoonful of potato flour or arrowroot, and serve in a border of mashed potatoes.

LEFT-OVERS

For most of these dishes cold fresh boiled beef is recommended, but roast beef can be used instead. For dishes which require sliced cold beef, carve very thinly.

BOILED BEEF AU GRATIN

cold minced boiled beef
onion
butter
salt, pepper
grated nutmeg
tomato sauce (p. 211)
parsley
garlic
mashed potato
breadcrumbs
grated cheese

Chop the onion and fry it lightly in a little butter till golden-brown, then add the cold minced beef and a seasoning of salt, pepper and grated nutmeg. Pour in some tomato sauce, some chopped parsley and a little garlic and simmer gently for 9–10 minutes. Turn into a fireproof dish so that the mixture fills it three-quarters full, and spread a covering of mashed potatoes over the top. Now sprinkle with a mixture of breadcrumbs and grated cheese, dot with some small flakes of butter and brown in a hot oven.

BEEF

BEEF ARLÉSIENNE (France)

cold boiled beef	Arrange the cold sliced beef on a dish. Fry some thinly-sliced onion in olive oil till browned, then add peeled and sliced aubergines and fry on for 6–7 minutes. Add peeled, de-seeded and chopped tomatoes and the red peppers, first grilled and then cut in strips. Season with salt, pepper, chopped parsley and a touch of garlic. Cover and simmer for about 20 minutes, then pour it over the beef slices and heat through for a few minutes in a moderate oven.
onion	
olive oil	
aubergines	
tomatoes	
red sweet peppers	
parsley	
garlic	
salt, pepper	

BEEF LYONNAISE (France)

cold boiled beef	Fry some onions, thinly sliced, in some butter till they begin to brown, then add the cold beef in thin slices or diced, season and sauté for 7–8 minutes on a low heat. When thoroughly hot, add a few drops of vinegar, toss again and sprinkle with chopped parsley.
onions	
butter	
salt, pepper	
vinegar	

BEEF PROVENÇALE (France)

cold boiled beef	Cook the coarsely chopped tomatoes in the oil with salt, pepper and chopped parsley and garlic with the lid on for 15 minutes. Then add the beef, cut into small walnut-sized cubes, and simmer for 15 minutes longer. If you like, at the end of this time some black or green olives may be added, and some finely chopped mushrooms previously fried lightly in oil. This dish is generally served in a border of pasta or mashed or boiled potatoes.
tomatoes	
olive oil	
salt, pepper	
chopped parsley	
garlic	
a few black or green olives or mushrooms (optional)	

CORNED BEEF HASH

potatoes	Chop up some cold potatoes and mix them with an equal amount of chopped corned beef mixed with a lightly-fried chopped onion. Heat the fat in a heavy frying pan and press in the meat mixture, cooking slowly till the underside is nicely browned. Then turn it over and brown the other side. See that it is well seasoned. If the mixture looks too dry at the beginning, a little stock, milk or cream may be added.
corned beef	
onion	
dripping or butter	

CANNELON OF BEEF

1 lb. (2 cups) cooked beef, finely chopped
8 oz. cooked lean ham or bacon, also finely chopped
mixed herbs
a little grated lemon rind
salt, pepper and nutmeg
1 egg to bind
gravy

Mix all the dry ingredients together and moisten with the beaten egg. Shape into a short thick roll, wrap in greased paper or kitchen foil and bake for 1 hour in a moderate oven. Serve with good gravy poured round it.

BEEF CECILS (U.S.A.)

1 lb. (2 cups) finely chopped cold beef
salt, pepper
onion juice
Worcester sauce
3 tablespoonfuls (scant ¼ cup) breadcrumbs and more for coating
1 oz. (2 tablespoonfuls) melted butter
1 egg
fat for frying

Season the chopped beef with salt, pepper, onion juice and Worcester sauce to taste and then mix well with the 3 tablespoonfuls breadcrumbs and melted butter and bind with a slightly beaten yolk of egg. Shape into small cigar-shaped croquettes, pointed at each end, coat with the white of egg, roll in fine breadcrumbs and fry them golden in fat or oil. Serve with tomato sauce.

MIROTON OF BEEF

cold beef
½ oz. dripping or butter
3 onions
flour
3 tablespoonfuls (scant ¼ cup) tomato purée
½ pint (1¼ cups) stock
vinegar
parsley

Slice the onions thinly and brown them in the dripping or butter. Sprinkle with a little flour and let that brown too, moistening with the stock (preferably beef) well mixed with the tomato purée and a little vinegar to taste. Cook this all together over a low heat for about 10 minutes, and then pour it over the slices of cold beef arranged in the serving dish, and heat them through. Sprinkle with chopped parsley. Serve with mashed potato.

HACHIS EN PORTEFEUILLE (France)

finely chopped cold beef **Lyonnaise potatoes** **sauce Robert** **mashed potato** **breadcrumbs** **butter**	Butter a fireproof dish and in the bottom put a layer of *Lyonnaise* potatoes. On these put a layer of finely chopped cold beef bound with *sauce Robert*, and repeat the layers till the dish is nearly full. Then spread over the top a thin layer of mashed potato, sprinkle this with breadcrumbs and melted butter and brown in the oven.

(*Lyonnaise* potatoes are sliced cooked potatoes sautéed with onion.)

BEEF SALAD

cold boiled beef **vinaigrette dressing** **chervil** **tarragon** **hard-boiled eggs** **onion** **chives**	Arrange the cold beef slices in a salad bowl and pour over them a vinaigrette dressing of mustard, salt, pepper, vinegar and olive oil. Leave for 30 minutes, then add the herbs and decorate with hard-boiled egg. Chopped chives or onions may be served separately. Dress with cold cooked French beans and potatoes, or uncooked tomatoes and cucumber, attractively arranged and dressed with a vinaigrette sauce or mayonnaise if preferred.

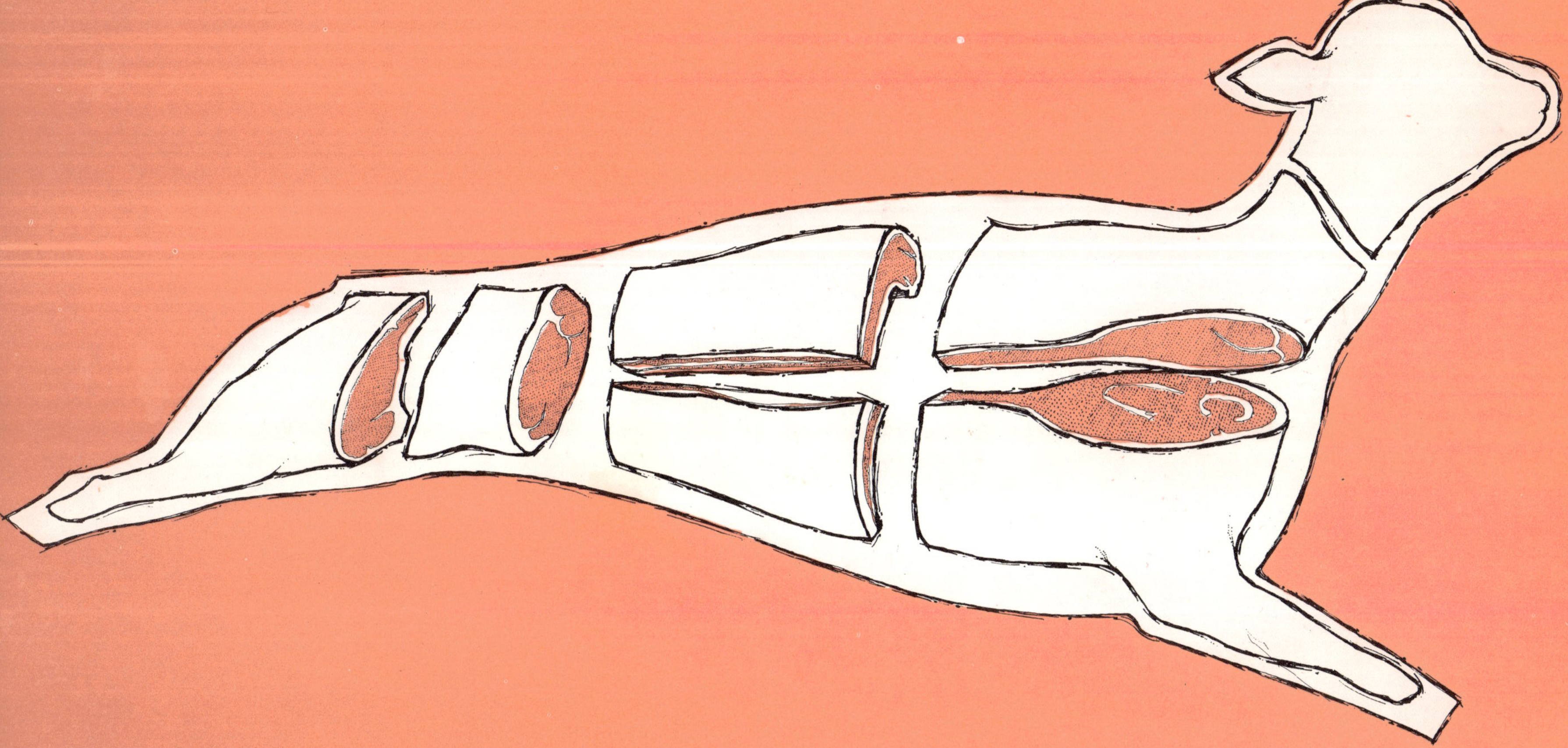

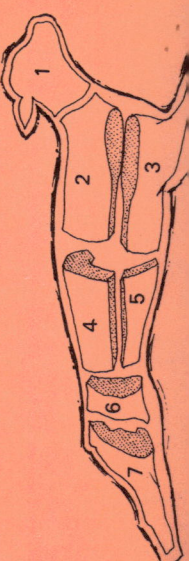

1 HEAD
2 MIDDLE NECK
3 BEST END AND SHOULDER
4 BEST LOIN
5 CHUMP END LOIN
6 LEG VEAL
7 SHIN VEAL

CALF

VEAL

The best veal should always be milk-fed. The bulk of supplies in England come from Europe. The finest veal comes from calves of from four to six months old which have been specially reared for the table. The flesh should be white or palest pink, and any hint of redness is suspicious. It should look somewhat moist with the fat abundant and pure white. Meat with a dry outer skin or any hint of flabbiness or clamminess should be avoided. The bones should be tender and translucent.

It is a dryish meat, which demands comparatively long and slow cooking. It is not greatly appreciated in England, though veal cutlets and veal and ham pie figure among the dishes for which the English kitchen has long been famous.

Mashed potatoes, noodles, chestnut purée, spaghetti, French beans, green peas, baby carrots, fried tomatoes, mushrooms, spinach, sorrel and chicory all go well with veal. Those who find the flavour of sorrel alone too much for them may find a half-and-half purée of spinach and sorrel more to their liking.

VEAL STOCK

As veal is inclined to be tasteless, it is always better to use veal stock in its cooking instead of water, for by this the flavour will be very much improved.

veal bones
calf's foot
onion
carrot
celery
salt, pepper
3½ pints (4¼ pints) water
tarragon, rosemary or thyme

The butcher will sell you some veal bones separately if necessary and you must put them into a saucepan with the cold water, carrot, onion and a stick of celery and half a blanched calf's foot. Bring to the boil and simmer for at least 2 hours, then add a bouquet of tarragon, rosemary (be careful of this as it is very pungent) or thyme and go on simmering gently for another 15 minutes. Strain into a basin and leave till cold.

If you do not have veal or chicken stock handy, you can do worse than use a diluted chicken *bouillon* cube for cooking with veal. It is better than water, and the veal will impart its own flavour to it as well.

Cuts of Veal

Fillet: for roasting (larded or stuffed) and for escalopes.

Knuckle: for stewing (pie veal) and pies, sautés, ragoûts, blanquettes and fricassées. The shin, used for *Osso buco* (*see* p. 96) contains more marrow. Use the feet and bones for enriching braises and for jellifying.

Loin: roast as a joint; also for sautés and braises. Grill or fry as chops.

Best end of neck: roast or braise. Fry or sauté as cutlets.

Middle neck and scrag: braise in a piece, or use for stewing and for pies.

Shoulder: roast whole or stuff and roll. The 'oyster' is used for braises, blanquettes and ragoûts.

Breast: stuff and slow-roast, or stew or braise.

Escalopes: cut from fillet, best end of neck or topside. Oval in shape and should weigh about 3 oz. Ideally they should be cut on the bias. Fry.

Grenadins: smaller but thicker than escalopes and cut from the meat left over when escalopes are cut on the bias. Stud with bacon fat and braise.

Medaillons: diminutive escalopes. Fry.

Noisettes and mignonettes: small round slices from the fillet. Always cooked with butter. Garnish as for escalopes.

Chops: loin chops and chump chops from the loin. Fry. Thick chops can also be braised.

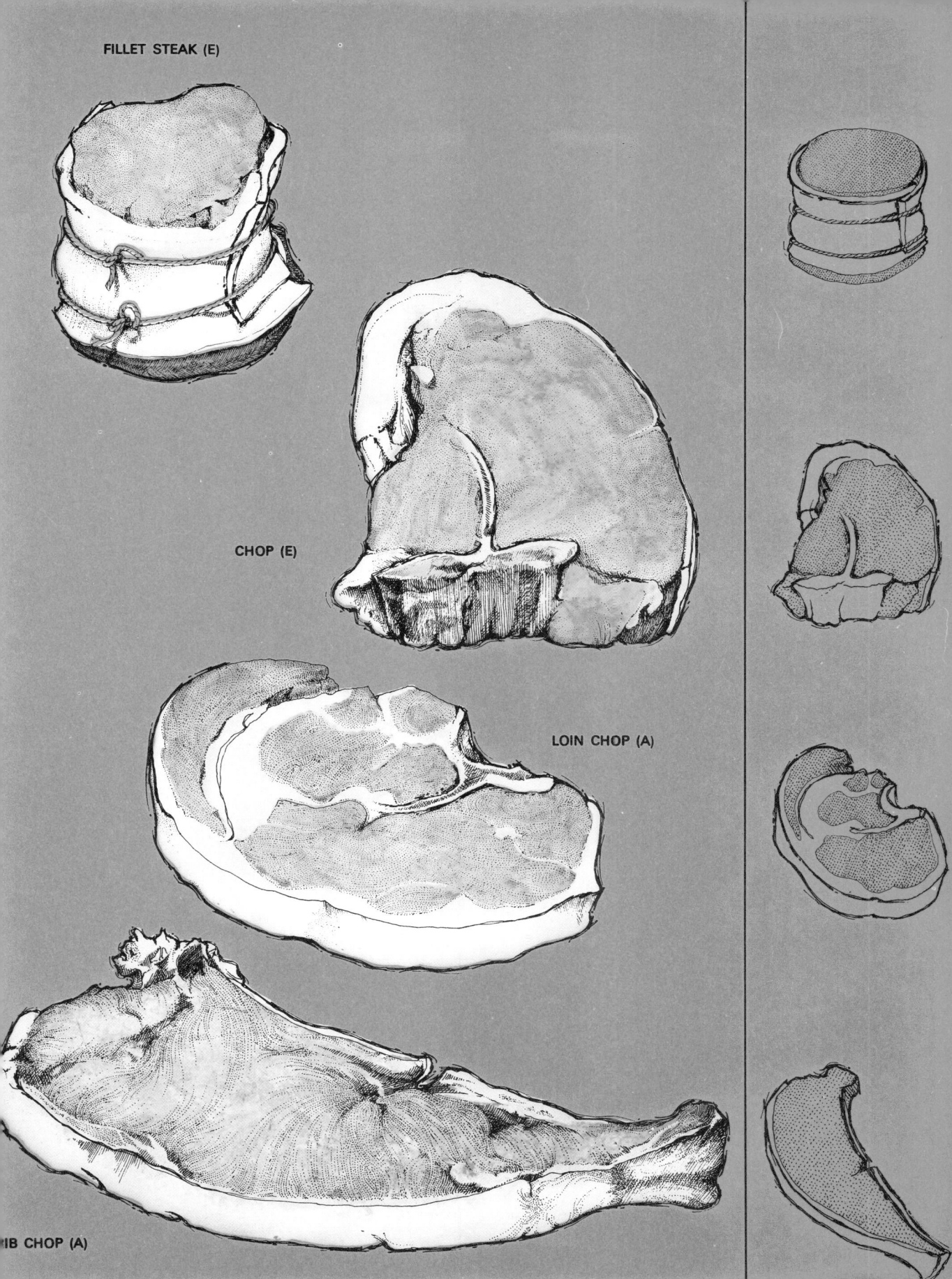

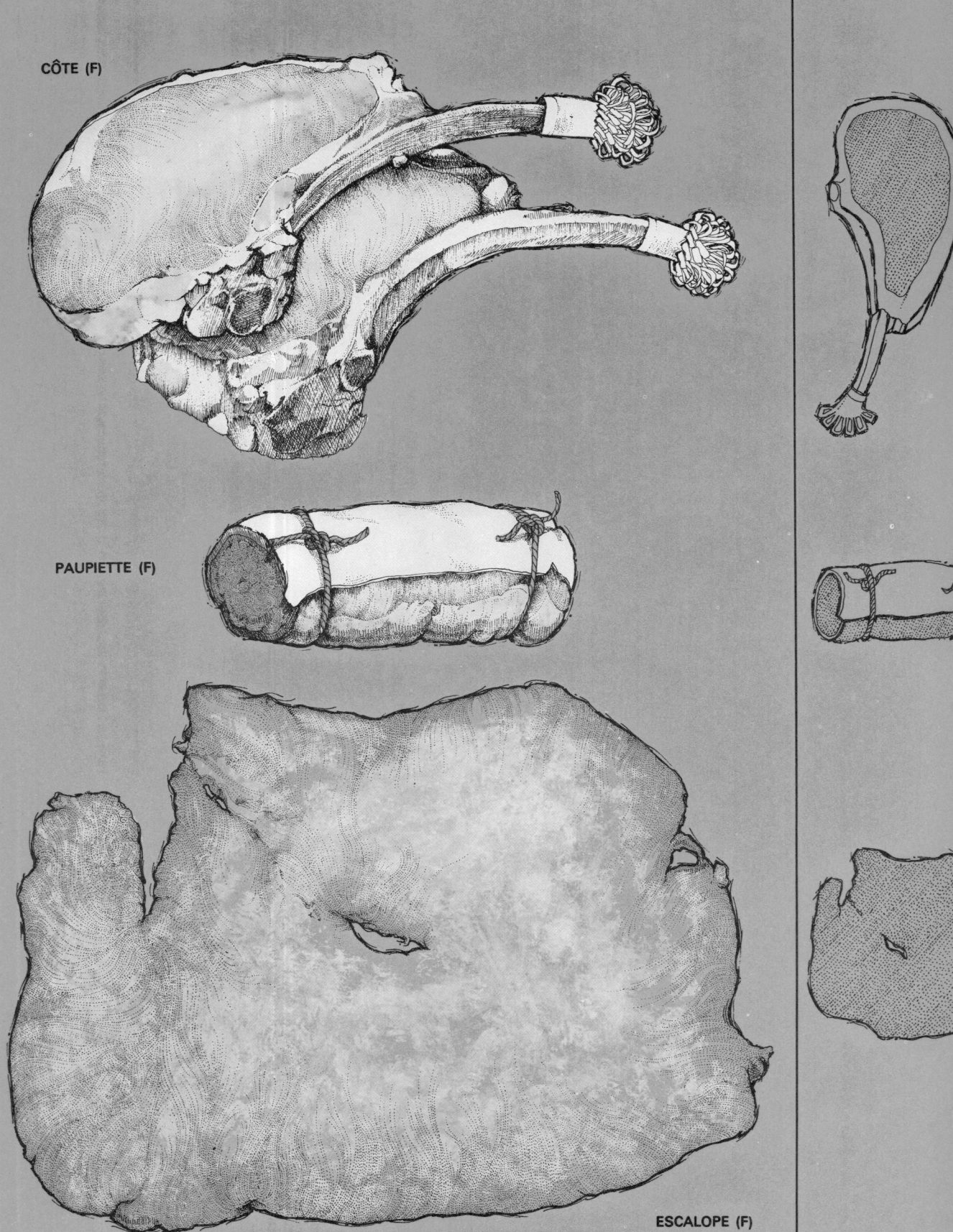

Approximate equivalent cuts of Veal

ENGLISH	FRENCH	AMERICAN
Chump end of loin	*Cul or Quasi*	Heel or Round
Topside	*Noix*	Rump
Fillet	*Rouelle*	Round toast
Loin	*Longe*	Loin
Best end of neck	*Carré*	Rib roast
Knuckle	*Rouelle Cuisseau* or *Jarret*	Knuckle
Shoulder	*Epaule*	Shoulder
End chops	*Basses Côtes*	Shoulder chops
Breast	*Poitrine*	Breast
Belly	*Ventre*	Flank
Middle-cut breast:	*Tendrons*	Riblets
Shin	*Jarret*	Leg

ROAST VEAL

ROAST LOIN OF VEAL

Veal is a dry meat and must be roasted slowly and with plenty of fat. It should never be overdone and never subjected to fierce heat at the outset, as red meat is. It is probably better as a joint when braised, but if it is roasted, you should give it a steady temperature of 380°F. (195°C.) for 40 minutes to the pound. If you are using a meat thermometer, it should register 165°F. (74°C.) when the veal is done.

Have the loin boned and fill the cavity with savoury forcemeat (p. 84). Tie the meat up well and lay some rashers of pickled pork or fat bacon on the top. Season with salt and pepper and add a little butter or dripping and about ½ pint (1¼ cups) of water to the pan. Bake in the oven in the same way as roast beef (p. 13).

The fillets, shoulder and breast of veal should be roasted in the same way.

SADDLE OF VEAL

The saddle of veal is a dish of occasion and hardly ever makes its appearance in the home, but a note about its cooking may be of use in case this noble joint is wanted. Instructions for carving stuffed breast of veal on p. 20 and a drawing on p. 92.

The kidneys are usually removed first and cooked for 30 minutes before the joint is to be served, and the flank is trimmed on each side so that it can be drawn over the filets mignons and tied round with tape. The cooking time for the whole saddle, whether roasted, braised or potroasted, will be in the neighbourhood of 3 hours, and this should be done at a regular temperature of about 380°F. (195°C.) It is most important that the cooking fat should not burn, and this can be prevented by adding a few tablespoonfuls of water to the pan now and then.

ROAST VEAL WITH VEGETABLES

4 lb. veal
12 button onions
pinch of thyme
1 sprig fresh, or a pinch of dried, basil
4 small carrots
1 teaspoonful (1¼ teaspoonfuls) chopped parsley
1 lemon
good pinch each cloves and mace
6 small potatoes
1 oz. (2 tablespoonfuls) bacon dripping
hot water
flour
salt, pepper

Rub well into the meat a mixture of ½ oz. bacon dripping, the chopped or dried herbs, salt, pepper, the juice of a lemon and the two spices. Melt the rest of the bacon dripping in a large pan, add the onions, and, when they begin to brown, put in the piece of veal. After browning this on all sides, transfer it to a baking-tin with the onions and put it into a slow oven. Dredge with flour, basting with the drippings every 15 minutes. At the end of the first hour add the quartered carrots and the potatoes, whole, and if the liquid shows signs of drying up, add a little more hot water. Serve on a dish surrounded by the vegetables, with the thickened gravy poured over.

ROAST LOIN OF VEAL WITH KIDNEY

1½ lb. loin of veal, with the kidney
salt, pepper
3 tablespoonfuls (3¾ tablespoonfuls) melted butter
3 tablespoonfuls (3¾ tablespoonfuls) fresh cream
2 tablespoonfuls (2½ tablespoonfuls) veal stock

Have the butcher bone and roll the piece of veal round the kidney, and rub it all over with salt and pepper. Put it into a fireproof dish and pour over it the cream and butter. Roast it in a moderate oven for 1 hour, adding the hot stock after 15 minutes. Turn the joint once during the whole of the cooking, and if it shows signs of drying up add a little more hot stock. The kidney should be left encased in its own fat, which gives the dish a specially delicious flavour. Breast or shoulder can also be used for this dish.

VEAL

FILLET OF VEAL EN COCOTTE

Filet mignon de veau is a joint not often found in England. The exact equivalent to the fillet of beef, it is simple but exquisite.

Cook the whole trimmed fillet in butter, adding a tablespoonful of water as it begins to brown, and repeat this from time to time till you achieve a perfect gravy. When the fillet is done, transfer it to an earthenware dish, pour the gravy back over it, and garnish it with mushrooms. A Provençal or Tyrolean sauce may be substituted for the plain gravy, and any sort of vegetable purée or pasta goes with it.

FRIED VEAL

BAVARIAN VEAL CHOPS (Germany)

6 veal loin chops
½ onion, sliced
8 slices carrot
2 sticks celery
4 cloves
peppercorns
1 oz. (2 tablespoonfuls) butter
salt, pepper
egg
flour
breadcrumbs

Put 6 nicely trimmed veal loin chops into a pan, add the vegetables and pepper, cover with boiling water and cook till tender. Drain (but keep back the liquor for making soup) and when cooled, season with salt and pepper, flour them and egg-and-breadcrumb them.

Fry in deep fat or oil, arrange on a serving dish when drained and surround with boiled macaroni mixed with onion sauce.

VEAL CHOPS BORDELAISE

2 veal chops
butter
1 glass dry white Bordeaux
a little veal stock
a little meat glaze
6 small glazed onions
2 tablespoonfuls (2½ tablespoonfuls) cubed potatoes
artichoke hearts
fried parsley

Brown the veal chops lightly on both sides in butter, and set them on the serving dish. Swill the contents of the pan with a glass of white wine, the meat glaze and the veal stock. Pour this sauce over the chops which you have garnished with the onions, some potato cubes cooked in butter and some thinly-sliced artichoke hearts tossed in butter. Finally add a garnish of fried parsley.

FRIED VEAL CHOP

1 veal chop for each serving
butter
flour
2-3 tablespoonfuls (2½-3¾ tablespoonfuls) stock
salt

Season with salt, coat lightly with flour and brown lightly on both sides in butter, then reduce the heat and go on cooking slowly till the meat is done. Make a gravy with the contents of the pan and 2 or 3 tablespoonfuls stock, and pour this over the chop on serving.

VEAL CUTLETS WITH CUCUMBER

veal cutlet
butter
cream and lemon juice or soured cream
salt, pepper
paprika
cucumber

Fry some thin veal cutlet slices in butter till browned on each side, take them out and keep hot while you add to the juices in the pan enough cream to make your sauce and a seasoning of salt and pepper. Add a pinch of paprika for colour. Pour this over the cutlets and the thin slices of cucumber, stewed in butter, with which you have surrounded them. A touch of lemon might be added to the cream, or soured cream used.

VEAL CUTLETS SUÉDOISE

veal cutlets
onion
parsley
thyme
bay leaf
lemon
olive oil
butter
breadcrumbs
apple purée made with dry white wine
grated horseradish

First let the cutlets lie for 30 minutes sprinkled with minced onion, parsley, thyme and bay leaf, the juice of a lemon and a few drops of olive oil, turning them over once or twice. Then dry and wipe them, brush with melted butter, coat with fine breadcrumbs and cook under the grill. Serve with them a purée of apple, stewed in a little white wine instead of water. Some like to mix a little grated horseradish with the apple.

VEAL ESCALOPE MODENESE

The escalope is egg-and-breadcrumbed and fried in butter in the usual way, and served coated with a tomato sauce to which has been added a little strong veal gravy, some chopped lightly-fried onion and some very small dice of cooked lean bacon.

VEAL ESCALOPES BOLOGNESE

1 veal escalope for each serving
flour
butter
Marsala
Parmesan cheese
veal stock

Each escalope should be about 3 oz. in weight and be cut about ¼ in. thick. Season and flour them lightly and brown on each side in butter on a fairly quick heat. Then add 2 large spoonfuls Marsala for each escalope and stir well into the butter. Spread each escalope thickly with grated Parmesan cheese and sprinkle over each a few drops of stock, adding 1 good spoonful also to the sauce. Reduce the heat and cook gently for 5 minutes longer with the lid on, or till the veal is tender and the cheese melted.

French beans or braised endives offer a suitable accompaniment, with potatoes to your choice.

VEAL ESCALOPES À LA CRÈME MOUTARDÉE

1 veal escalope for each serving
salt, pepper
cream
1 teaspoonful (1¼ teaspoonful) French mustard
butter or lard
flour

Season the escalopes with salt and pepper and dredge them lightly with flour. Fry them in butter or lard and, when they are nicely browned on each side, put them into the serving dish. Now pour a cupful of cream into the frying pan, adding 1 teaspoonful French mustard (*à l'estragon* is the best flavour here) and scrape and stir till you have a coffee-coloured thickish sauce. Pour over the escalopes and serve with a fine purée of potatoes and perhaps a little boiled salsify.

VEAL ESCALOPES MARÉCHALE

1 veal escalope for each serving
breadcrumbs
egg
grated cheese
spinach
orange sauce:
2 oranges
1 lemon
8 fl. oz. (1 cup) brown gravy
salt, pepper

Egg-and-breadcrumb the escalopes, mixing an equal amount of grated cheese with the crumbs. Fry them slowly in butter till golden-brown, and serve with a purée of spinach and orange sauce. To make the sauce cut the red part of the rind of an orange into thin matchsticks and pour boiling water over them. Leave for 5 minutes and drain. Add to them the juice of 2 oranges and 1 lemon and 1 cup rich brown gravy or sauce. Season to taste with salt and pepper.

VEAL ESCALOPES PERSILLÉES

1 veal escalope for each serving
egg
breadcrumbs
parsley
garlic
butter or lard

Egg-and-breadcrumb the escalopes, using a mixture of breadcrumbs, chopped parsley and the faintest suspicion of minced garlic. (If this is too much garlic for your taste, simply rub the bowl in which you mix the parsley and crumbs with a cut clove of garlic beforehand.) Fry in butter in the usual way, and serve with French beans.

VEAL ESCALOPES SAVOYARDE

for 2 escalopes:
salt, pepper
lemon juice
1 oz. (2 tablespoonfuls) butter
¼ pint (⅓ pint) double cream
4 tablespoonfuls (5 tablespoonfuls) dry white vermouth

Season the escalopes with salt, pepper and lemon juice and fry them quickly on each side in the butter. Now add the vermouth and let it boil up, but turn down the heat at once and add the cream. Shake this in the pan with the vermouth till they are completely amalgamated and then simmer on a still lower heat for a minute or two longer till the cream thickens.

If you can, use Chambéry vermouth from the Savoy.

WIENER SCHNITZEL (Austria)

1 veal escalope
salt, pepper
egg
breadcrumbs
lard
lemon
oil or butter

The Vienna escalope fancier will brook no fancy garnishes to his beloved *Schnitzel*, but having beaten and trimmed the slice, will make a few cuts round the edge (to prevent its curling up) and will then egg-and-breadcrumb it after seasoning with salt and pepper. It is then fried in plenty of deep smoking oil till golden-brown (no darker). The average weight is about 4 oz. and as it must be very thin, the ideal version should almost cover a dinner plate. Some people prefer to fry them in butter in a frying pan, but this is a matter of personal taste. Keep warm on a plate over a pan of steaming hot water.

Wiener Schnitzel are often garnished with chopped hard-boiled eggs, parsley, and an anchovy fillet curled round an olive.

VEAL

VEAL EN BROCHETTE

1 lb. lean veal cutlet
½ lb. fat fresh pork
seasoned flour
2 oz. (4 tablespoonfuls) butter or lard
salt, pepper
brown gravy

Cut the veal into ½ in. thick slices and the pork into thin ones, and then into 2 in. squares, and arrange them alternately on small skewers; about 4 of veal and 3 of pork on each.

Roll the laden skewers in seasoned flour and fry them in 2 oz. butter or lard in a heavy frying pan. When they are browned all over, put on the lid and cook slowly for about 1 hour, turning frequently, till tender. Serve with thick brown gravy or make a creamy lemon sauce with the cooking liquid.

VEAL KNOTS (U.S.A.)

1½ lb. veal cutlet, ½ in. thick
salt, pepper
flour
4 oz. (½ cup) butter
bay leaf
2⅔ fl. oz. (⅓ cup) dry white wine

Cut the veal into thin strips about 8 × 1 in., roll them in flour seasoned with salt and pepper and then tie each into a knot. Fry them in ½ cup butter till well browned, then add half a bay leaf and cook slowly with the lid on for about 20 minutes, turning now and then. When done, pour in ⅓ cup dry white wine, heat to just under boiling point and serve at once, adding a little more salt and pepper if necessary.

VEAL WITH MARSALA (*Piccate alla marsala*) (Italy)

veal escalopes
salt, pepper
lemon juice
flour
butter
Marsala
veal stock

The veal should be cut very thinly indeed in 3 in. squares each weighing not more than 1 oz. These are beaten out, and after being seasoned with salt, pepper and lemon juice, are tossed lightly in flour. Enough butter is melted in a thick frying pan to cover the bottom and the *piccate* are browned quickly in it on each side. For 8 pieces now add 2 large spoonfuls of Marsala and, after it has bubbled up, add 1 good spoonful veal stock. Stir this sauce over a good heat till the liquids are well amalgamated and let the contents of the pan simmer for another minute or so on a reduced heat till the sauce becomes syrupy. Serve with a dish of mushrooms.

Three or four of the little *piccate* are enough for each person.

BRAISED VEAL

BRAISED TOPSIDE OF VEAL

2-3 lb. topside of veal
bacon fat and rind
carrots
onions
bouquet garni
salt
veal stock

Put the piece of veal into a casserole with the sliced vegetables, the bouquet, a little salt and some bacon fat and rind. Add ½ pint (1¼ cups) veal stock, and after bringing to the boil cook till it has disappeared. Then add more stock, enough to come half-way up the meat and boil for a few minutes. Now put on the lid, transfer the pan to a moderate oven and continue to cook, basting the joint frequently. When the joint is nearly ready, take the lid off for the meat to brown, but do not stop basting it. Serve with the strained braising liquor. A little dry white wine added to the stock will enhance the flavour.

BRAISED LOIN OF VEAL

loin of veal
salt, pepper
butter
flour
stock or water
onions

Sprinkle the joint with salt, pepper and a little flour, and brown it all over in butter, turning it over all the time to prevent burning. Now add a little stock or water and 2 or 3 onions, put on a closely-fitting lid and cook slowly till the meat is quite tender, adding a little more liquid when necessary. Serve with the gravy thickened with flour and water.

STUFFED SHOULDER OF VEAL

shoulder of veal
salt, pepper
mirepoix vegetables
forcemeat:
1½ lb. sausage meat
8 oz. (2⅔ cups) fresh breadcrumbs
stock
2 eggs
nutmeg
parsley
salt, pepper

Mix all the ingredients for forcemeat together. Bone the shoulder and stuff it with the forcemeat. Roll it up and tie it and braise in the usual way (p. 17). The cooking time will be between 1½ and 2 hours. Serve the braising liquor as sauce.

Knuckle of Veal and some of the ingredients for Veal Fricassee

VEAL

VEAL BRAISED WITH BACON AND SOUR CREAM

8 rashers streaky smoked bacon
1½ lb. veal cutlet
flour
½ pint (1¼ cups) sour cream
¼ pint (⅓ pint) hot water
1 teaspoonful (1¼ teaspoonfuls) paprika

Grill the rashers of bacon till they are quite crisp, then take them out of the pan and keep them hot. Dredge the veal with seasoned flour and fry it lightly in the bacon fat. Now add the hot water, put on the lid and simmer for 30 minutes. Then add the heavy sour cream mixed with paprika and simmer for 15 minutes more. Serve with the cream gravy made from the contents of the pan. Cream gravy is made in the same way as basic white sauce, substituting 2 tablespoonfuls of the dripping in the pan for the usual butter. Some people may find smoked bacon too strong: if so, unsmoked or 'green' bacon should be used.

FRICANDEAU OF VEAL

The fricandeau is a larger piece taken from the same source as the escalope, that is, from the topside of veal, cut with the grain; it should not be more than 1½ in. thick.

1 lb. topside of veal
bacon lardons
thin slice of pork fat
carrots
bouquet garni
onions
1 pint (1¼ pints) good meat stock
salt, pepper

Beat the meat slightly, and lard it with pork lardons seasoned with salt and pepper. Then wrap the piece up completely in a slice of fresh pork fat and put it into a heavy braising pan with the vegetables and bouquet, and add more salt and pepper and the meat stock. Cover the pan and cook gently for 3 or 4 hours, then take the slice of pork fat from the meat, put the joint into a clean braising pan and pour back the liquid over it. Do not put on the lid again, but increase the heat and go on cooking for the joint to dry out, turning it frequently. Serve with its own gravy with the fat removed, and with a purée of spinach or sorrel (or a half-and-half mixture). A cold fricandeau makes an excellent dish for a summer luncheon. Put it into a serving-dish as soon as it is cooked, and pour over it the strained stock, which will set in a jelly when cold. A green salad goes well with this.

STUFFED SHOULDER OF VEAL À LA BOURGEOISE

Stuff the shoulder as above and partly braise it. Then add some more onions, carrots

Veal Fricassee

and a bouquet garni with enough good stock to come two-thirds of the way up the meat. Put on the lid of the pan and finish cooking on a moderate heat. The stock of the braise should be thickened before serving with a little flour and butter or with potato flour.

Paupiettes

Paupiettes are cut from the topside in thin slices 4–5 in. long by 2 in. side. Flatten and trim them and spread on one side with forcemeat made from fresh breadcrumbs, 6 oz. ($\frac{3}{4}$ cup) sausagemeat, 1 egg, cream or milk, salt, pepper, grated nutmeg and chopped parsley all mixed well together. Roll the paupiettes into cork shapes, wrap them in a thin slice of fat bacon and tie with cotton. Braise them on a bed of carrots and onions like sweetbreads (p. 197) or cook them gently in butter, adding a little cold water from time to time to prevent them drying and colouring too much. Serve with one or more of the vegetables appropriate to veal dishes.

SALTIMBOCCA (Italy)

thin slices of veal
thin slices of ham
sage leaves
butter
Marsala

Take 2 or 3 slices of veal for each person, and flatten them as thin as possible. Trim them and trim the slices of ham to the same size, laying them on each one. Put a leaf of fresh sage in the middle and roll them up, fixing each with a small skewer or cocktail stick. Fry them gently in butter till well browned all over, then pour a small glassful of Marsala over them and just bring it to the boil. Cover the pan and let the little rolls cook with the lid on till quite tender which will take about 15 minutes. They are served with croûtons of fried bread. If there is no Marsala to hand, any white wine can be used instead.

VEAL OLIVES (U.S.A.)

The simplest method is to cut the veal from the leg and pound it in pieces 2 × 4 in. till it is $\frac{1}{4}$ in. thick. Have ready some thin rashers of streaky bacon slightly longer than the veal pieces, lay them on the meat so that the bacon extends beyond the meat. Roll them up and tie or fasten with cocktail sticks.

Now brown them all over in a little butter, season with salt and pepper (go easy on the salt) and put in a baking dish. Pour in enough hot water to come half-way up the rolls, and bake with the lid on for 30–45 minutes. Make a brown sauce with the

VEAL 89

liquid remaining in the tin, and pour it over the olives. Tomato juice is sometimes used instead of water, in which case it should simply be thickened before serving.

VEAL PAUPIETTES À LA CREME WITH ANCHOVIES
(*See* similar dish under Beef. p. 53.)

STUFFED VEAL SANDWICH

2 veal escalopes
cooked ham or bacon
mushrooms
parsley
tomato sauce
butter
small tomatoes

Buy 2 slices of veal ½ in. thick, and on one of these lay some thin slices of cooked ham or bacon as lean as possible. On top spread a mixture of the fat of the bacon and some mushrooms and parsley, all chopped together and bound, if desired, with a little thick tomato sauce. Place the other slice of veal on top, tie the 2 together and brown the sandwich on both sides in butter. Let it simmer thus for 30 minutes, turning it once, and then pour in some more tomato sauce, a little thinner this time, put on the lid and cook for another 30 minutes or till the meat is done. Untie it, strain the sauce over and serve it garnished with small baked tomatoes and grilled mushrooms.

RAGOÛTS AND STEWS

RAGOÛT OF VEAL

The popularity of the ragoût of veal stems, I think, from the fact that it is a useful vehicle for the disposal of the various lesser cuts of veal and indeed of the trimmings of other cuts. It is a very delicious and savoury method of cooking this delicate meat. Ragoûts can be made with shoulder, breast, middle neck or scrag, the meat being boned and cut into pieces 2 in. square. Ready-cut veal for this purpose can be bought from the ordinary butcher under the name of pie veal, though on the whole it is generally more satisfactory to buy and cut up your own and so be able to rely on its absolute freshness.

Ragoûts are either light in colour, like *blanquettes* of veal (p. 93), or the meat is first browned and floured before the hot liquid is added. The principal secret of success is, however, never to let the ragoût reach boiling point but always to keep it at a gentle simmer. Veal ragoûts re-heated in a cream and egg sauce make excellent fillings for vol-au-vents. The bland flavour marries well with such garnishes as mushrooms, diced tongue, peas, asparagus and prawns.

RAGOÛT OF VEAL WITH PEAS

2 lb. breast of veal
butter
flour
salt, pepper
stock
2 or 3 onions
green peas

Cut the veal into suitable pieces and brown them in butter. Sprinkle lightly with flour seasoned with salt and pepper and colour this too. Moisten with sufficient stock and add the chopped onions. Cover and simmer for at least 1 hour, then add some freshly shelled petit pois or green peas and continue cooking together till the veal is tender.

VEAL RAGOÛT À LA CREOLE

1½ lb. brisket of veal
¼ lb. green bacon
onion
carrot
1 dessertspoonful (½ tablespoonful) lard
1 clove garlic
1 dessertspoonful (½ tablespoonful) flour
3 tomatoes
bouquet garni
cayenne pepper
1 teaspoonful (1¼ teaspoonful) vinegar
1 pint (1¼ pints) water

Cut the brisket of veal into 2 in. squares, the bacon and potatoes into cubes and a large onion and a medium carrot into slices. Fry the veal, seasoned with salt and pepper in the lard till browned, then add the bacon, potatoes, onions and carrot with a clove of garlic, minced or crushed, and brown them too. Stir in the flour, let that brown as well and add the sliced tomatoes, a bouquet garni and a tiny pinch of cayenne pepper; pour in 1 pint (1¼ pints) water mixed with 1 teaspoonful vinegar, and when it begins to boil, cover tightly and simmer for about 2 hours.

STEWED KNUCKLE OF VEAL

3 lb. knuckle of veal
small turnip
2 small carrots
onion
stick of celery
salt, pepper
bouquet garni
2 oz. (⅓ cup) Patna rice
parsley sauce

Have the knuckle sawn into 2 or 3 pieces and put these into a saucepan with just enough boiling water to cover them. Bring to the boil again and skim. When the scum has all disappeared, add the vegetables cut in pieces, salt and pepper to taste and a bouquet garni. Simmer for 2 hours, then add the rice and go on cooking for another 20–30 minutes till the rice grains are soft. Serve the meat hot with parsley sauce.

In England it is often partnered by boiled gammon of bacon; the strained stock in which it cooked is invaluable for soup.

VEAL

VEAL KNUCKLE PAYSANNE

3 lb. knuckle of veal
flour
butter
16 small onions
20 small carrots
bouquet garni
20 small new potatoes
1 lb. green peas
stock

Have the knuckle sawn into 2 in. pieces, season and flour them and brown all over in butter. Then add the onions and carrots with the bouquet, and pour in enough white stock to cover the vegetables. Put on the lid and cook over a low heat for about 30 minutes. Now add the potatoes and the peas and a little more stock to keep the vegetables just covered, put on the lid again and simmer for 45 minutes to 1 hour longer till the meat is quite tender.

VEAL FRICASSEE

This is made all too often in the English kitchen with cooked meat, but when made from fresh meat, as below, it is incomparable.

1½ lb. knuckle of veal
2 oz. (¼ cup) butter
1 large onion
salt, pepper
3 tablespoonfuls (3¾ tablespoonfuls) flour
stock
bouquet garni
3 eggs
3 tablespoonfuls (3¾ tablespoonfuls) cream
nutmeg
lemon juice

Melt the butter, add the veal cut in small pieces and a large sliced onion, and season with salt and pepper. Stew very gently with the lid on for about 15 minutes, then add the flour, mix all well together and just cover with boiling veal stock. Stir while you bring this just to the boil and then add the bouquet. Put on the lid again and simmer for 1–1½ hours. Put the meat into a deep serving dish and thicken the cooking liquor with 3 yolks of egg beaten with the cream. Add nutmeg and lemon juice to taste, correct the seasoning and pour over the meat. Garnish with small mushrooms and button onions cooked in stock. Some people like to add *fleurons* of puff pastry.

VEAL CUTLET WITH SOUR CREAM

veal cutlet 1½ in. thick
butter or lard
3 onions
salt, pepper
paprika
4 fl. oz. (½ cup) sour cream
flour

Brown the sliced onions in the chosen fat, then season the cutlet with salt and pepper and brown that too. Sprinkle with a little paprika, according to taste, and pour over the sour cream. Put on the lid and cook very gently over a low heat for about 1 hour, turning the cutlet once during that time. Serve with plain boiled noodles.

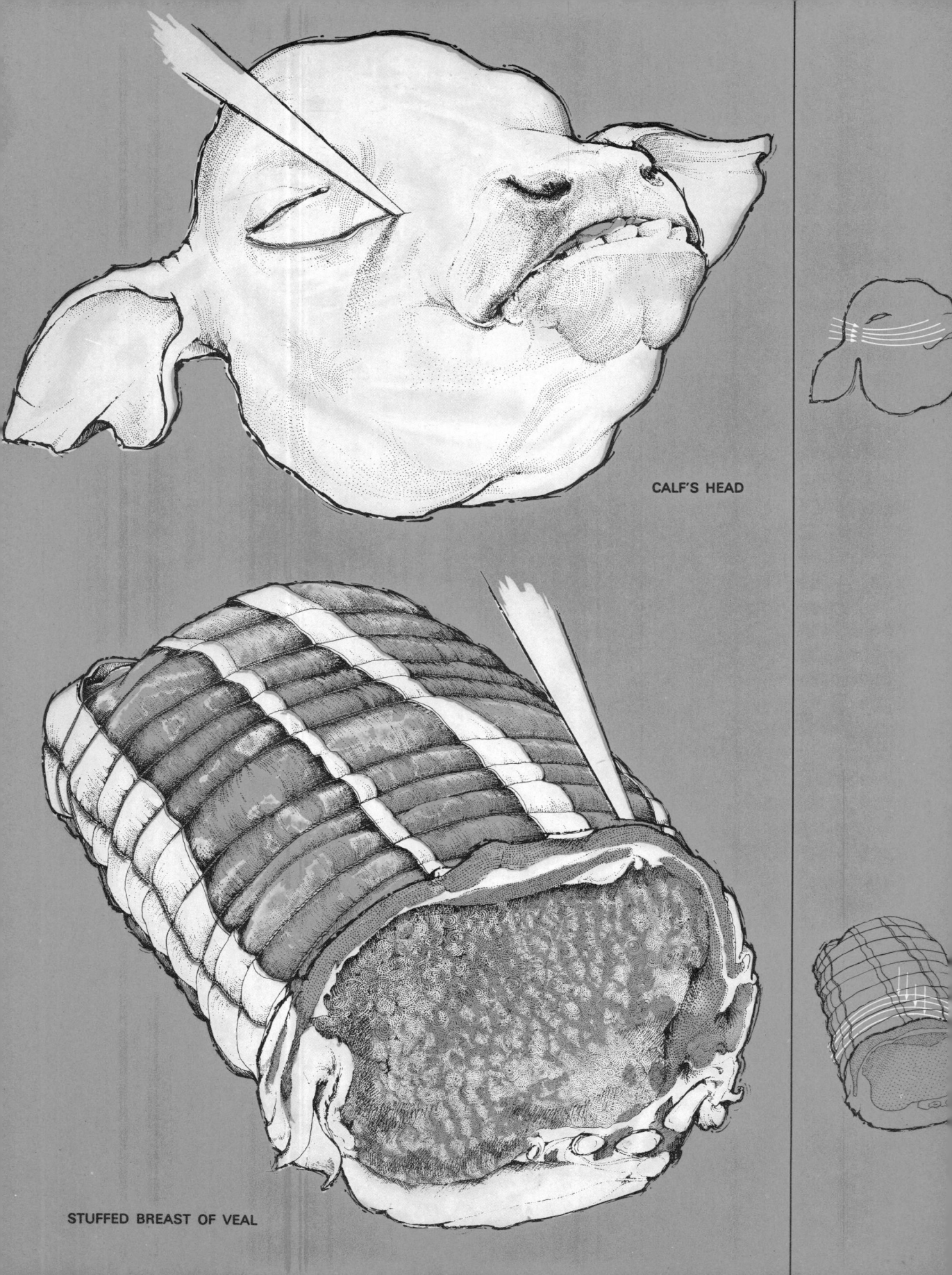

CALF'S HEAD

STUFFED BREAST OF VEAL

VEAL

BLANQUETTE OF VEAL (*Blanquette de veau à l'ancienne*) (France)

1½ lb. veal cut from breast or shoulder and divided into 1½–2 oz. pieces
2 small carrots
onion
cloves
bouquet garni
6 oz. (¾ cup) butter
3 tablespoonfuls (3¾ tablespoonfuls) flour
3 yolks of eggs
lemon juice
grated nutmeg
salt
rice
water or stock

Put the pieces of veal into a saucepan with enough cold salted water or stock to cover them, bring gently to the boil and after skimming add 2 small carrots, an onion stuck with a clove and the bouquet. Cover and cook gently for about 1½ hours. Meanwhile make a white sauce with 3 tablespoonfuls flour, 3 oz. butter and some of the cooking liquor, and simmer this for 15 minutes or so. Place the pieces of veal in a dish and keep them hot while you thicken the sauce with 3 yolks of eggs, a further 3 oz. butter and a seasoning of nutmeg and lemon juice to taste. Strain this over the meat and serve with a dish of plain rice or pilaff. Some people like to mix with the meat some button mushrooms and onion cooked in stock.

STEWED STUFFED BREAST OF VEAL

2 lb. breast veal
2 carrots
2 onions
turnip
forcemeat:
3 oz. (1 cup) fresh breadcrumbs
chopped parsley
1 teaspoonful (1¼ teaspoonfuls mixed dried herbs
little grated lemon rind
1–2 oz. (¼–½ cup) shredded suet
salt
pepper
1 egg
milk

The stuffing for this dish is often made with breadcrumbs, sausagemeat and mixed herbs bound with egg, but the more common herb stuffing is made by mixing together all the dry ingredients, and moistening it with egg beaten with a little milk.

Bone the breast, spread with the stuffing and tie it up in a roll. Wrap it in a butter muslin bag and put it in a saucepan with just enough cold water to cover it. Bring to the boil, skimming, then add the vegetables cut in pieces and a seasoning of salt and pepper. Simmer gently for about 3 hours till tender, and serve with parsley sauce.

CONFEDERATE VEAL (Missouri, U.S.A.)

slice of veal
1 lemon
nutmeg
½ small onion
1 sprig thyme
3 sprigs parsley
1 teaspoonful (1¼ tea-
 spoonfuls) celery seed
½ oz. (1 tablespoonful)
 lard
1 tablespoonful (1¼
 tablespoonfuls) flour
mushrooms
salt, pepper
cayenne pepper
2 teaspoonfuls (2½
 teaspoonfuls)
 Worcester sauce
16 fl. oz. (2 cups) water

Rub a ¾ in. thick slice of veal from the leg all over with salt, pepper, the juice of a lemon and a good pinch of grated nutmeg, spread it out and sprinkle it with the minced onion, the finely chopped herbs and the crushed celery seed. Grate the lemon rind over all, and roll the piece of meat up like a roly-poly and tie with string. Dredge it with flour and fry it in the lard till it is a rich brown all over. Add the flour, let this brown as well and add a little salt, pepper and cayenne pepper and moisten with 2 cups of water and the Worcester sauce. Close the pan tightly and simmer gently till the meat is done. Then add some fresh or canned mushrooms, first lightly fried, heat all through and serve the veal with the thickened strained sauce over it.

VEAL MATELOTE (France)

1¾ lb. stewing veal
flour
1 oz. (2 tablespoonfuls)
 dripping or butter
1 onion
2 cloves of garlic
bouquet garni
salt, pepper
1 claretglassful red
 wine
4 fl. oz. (½ cup) veal
 stock
button onions
button mushrooms
parsley
fried bread croûtons

Cut the meat into 2 in. squares and roll these in flour. Brown them in the fat in a fireproof casserole, add the sliced onion and brown that lightly too. Add the garlic, crushed, the bouquet garni and a seasoning of salt and pepper, then pour in the wine and, with the lid off, let it reduce by half. Now pour in the warmed stock, put on the lid and simmer for 1½ hours. Finally, brown some small button mushrooms and onions in butter, add them to the meat and cook all together for a further 30 minutes. Serve sprinkled with chopped parsley and garnished with fried bread croûtons.

LEG OF VEAL BOURGEOISE

slice of leg of veal
2 thick rashers of bacon
butter
salt and pepper
button onions
bouquet garni
carrots
½ calf's foot
dry white wine
stock

Get a thick slice of leg of veal and brown it in butter with the rashers of bacon cut into small dice, seasoning well with salt and pepper after browning. Now add a handful of small button onions, the bouquet garni, a number of small young carrots and the half calf's foot. Moisten with a glass of dry white wine and enough white stock to come half-way up the meat, and cook very gently with the lid on for 2 hours or so, basting and turning the meat frequently. Serve with the boned calf's foot and the vegetables (which need no more sauce than that in the pan). Some green peas and tiny new potatoes add to the appeal of this dish, which can be further enhanced by the addition of a little brandy to the wine and stock.

SAUTÉ DE VEAU PRINTANIÈRE

1¾ lb. veal
2 oz. (4 tablespoonfuls) dripping or butter
2 tablespoonfuls (2½ tablespoonfuls) seasoned flour
1 wineglassful dry white wine (optional)
4 fl. oz. (½ cup) stock
bouquet garni
10 young carrots
10 young turnips
12 spring onions
12 small new potatoes
10 oz. (1 cup) fresh green peas
parsley
chervil
chives
salt, pepper

Cut the meat into large squares and brown them all over in the fat. Sprinkle with the flour and let that brown as well. Pour in the wine and let it reduce with the lid off for 5 minutes, then add the same quantity of stock and simmer, covered, for 1 hour. Add all the vegetables with a little more salt and pepper, cover again and cook for another 30 minutes. On serving, sprinkle with a mixture of chopped parsley, chervil and chives.

This dish can be made without the wine, with stock alone, but in this case do not reduce the stock as you do the wine.

STEWED SHIN OF VEAL (*Osso buco*) (Italy)

2 lb. shin of veal
¼ pint (⅓ pint) dry white wine
stock
¾ lb. ripe tomatoes
2 oz. (4 tablespoonfuls) butter
garlic
parsley
lemon
rice or pasta
salt, pepper

Have the butcher saw the shin into 2 in. pieces and brown these in 2 oz. butter. When browned arrange them upright in your pan so as to ensure that the marrow in the bones does not come out in the cooking. Pour the wine over them and let it cook for about 10 minutes with the lid off. Now add the skinned and chopped tomatoes and a cupful of stock, season with salt and pepper, put on the lid and simmer for 1½ hours. While it is cooking, mix together a handful of chopped parsley, a clove of garlic and the grated peel of half a lemon, and when it is cooked, sprinkle this on top of the veal before serving with rice or some pasta or other.

VEAL SAUTÉ MÉNAGÈRE

1½ lb. veal breast
salt, pepper
flour
3 tablespoonfuls (3¾ tablespoonfuls) oil
2 tablespoonfuls (2½ tablespoonfuls) butter
onion
dry white wine
¼ pint (⅓ pint) tomato purée
1 pint (1¼ pints)
bouquet garni
garlic

Cut the veal in pieces for serving and toss them in seasoned flour. Fry them lightly till browned with a chopped onion in a mixture of oil and butter. Now add a glass of dry white wine, the tomato purée, 1 pint stock or water and a bouquet garni and a clove of garlic.

Put on the lid and simmer for 1½ hours and serve. Serve noodles, sprinkled with cheese or buttered, as an accompaniment.

MADEIRA VEAL STEAK

2 lb. veal cutlet
2 oz. (4 tablespoonfuls) butter or lard
salt
pepper
Madeira scallion sauce (p. 213)

Brown the meat, which should be cut in a piece about about 1 in. thick, in half the butter or lard and then cover and cook slowly for 20 minutes until it is tender. Put it on the serving dish, sprinkle with seasoning and spread on the rest of the butter or lard. Finally pour Madeira scallion sauce over and round it before serving.

VEAL

VEAL SAUTÉ MARENGO

1 lb. breast of veal
1 tablespoonful (1¼ tablespoonfuls) **flour**
olive oil
2 onions
8 oz. tomatoes
4 oz. mushrooms
8 fl. oz. (1 cup) veal stock
8 fl. oz. (1 cup) dry white wine

Cut the veal in suitable pieces for serving and brown them in the olive oil. Add the chopped onions, colouring a little, and then sprinkle in the flour, and brown that too. Moisten with the stock and wine mixed together and, if desired, a very little finely minced garlic. Now add the sliced mushrooms and the chopped and peeled tomatoes and close the pan tightly. Let the sauté simmer gently for a good 1½ hours, when it should be ready to serve.

VEAL HOLSTEIN (U.S.A.)

2 slices of veal, ½ in. thick, from the leg
breadcrumbs
salt, pepper
egg
pork fat
butter
12 fl. oz. (1½ cups) brown sauce (p. 209)
poached eggs

Cut and trim the meat into 6 slices, and beat them flat. Sprinkle with salt and pepper, then dredge in crumbs, beaten egg and then in crumbs again. Fry in shallow pork fat and butter (twice as much pork fat as butter) till well browned on both sides. Pour the brown sauce over them and simmer with the lid on till the veal is tender, which will take 1–1½ hours. To serve, strain the sauce round, not over, the cutlets and garnish each with a poached egg on top

VEAL CUTLET À LA CREOLE

1½ lb. veal cutlet
1 oz. bacon dripping
2 tablespoonfuls (2½ tablespoonfuls) **flour**
1 onion
½ green sweet pepper
½ red pepper
2 teaspoonfuls (2½ teaspoonfuls) **parsley**
thyme
1 ripe tomato

Brown the veal cutlet on both sides in the bacon dripping, then take it out and keep it hot. Now in the same fat fry a chopped onion and the chopped red and green peppers, and when the onions are nicely coloured, sprinkle with flour and brown this too.

Chop up the skinned tomato and add this with the parsley and thyme chopped and a moistening of water. Mix well together and put back the cutlet. Cover the pan and simmer the meat gently for 45 minutes. Serve with plain boiled rice in a separate dish.

POACHED VEAL

VEAL QUENELLES
½ lb. boned fillet of veal without any gristle
small pinch white pepper
fraction of grated nutmeg
4 oz. butter
1 whole egg
2 yolks of eggs
white stock
panada:
½ pint (1¼ cups) water
2 oz. (4 tablespoonfuls) butter
salt
5 oz. (1¼ cups) flour

Prepare the panada as usual. Put onto a buttered dish and put aside until cool.

Cut the meat up finely and pound it with the seasonings. Now remove it from the mortar, put in the panada which you pound in its turn and then add the butter. Return the meat and pound all well so as to amalgamate well together. Then add the egg and the yolks, one by one, and when well mixed rub all through a sieve, and keep on ice or in the refrigerator till wanted. Have ready some boiling white stock and test a small bit of the veal mixture for solidifying before making the quenelles. If too soft, add a little more flour. Butter a fireproof casserole. Shape the quenelles between two spoons, as you do with meringues, put them into the casserole and cover them carefully with the stock, or even boiling salted water. Cover the casserole and poach them on the lowest possible heat for 10-12 minutes, seeing that the liquid does not boil.

Escoffier gives another way of poaching them, which he says is the most practical. The quenelles are put into small buttered dariole moulds which are then placed in a deep pan and covered with the boiling liquid. They are poached slowly without letting the water boil, and when they are done they leave the moulds and rise to the surface of the liquid.

PIES AND PUDDINGS

VEAL POT PIE
1 lb. veal
¼ lb. pickled (salt) pork
salt, pepper
stock
½ lb. potatoes
shortcrust pastry

Cut the veal into neat pieces and cut ¼ lb. pickled pork (or blanched bacon) into thin slices. Put the meats in layers into a piedish, season with plenty of salt and pepper and three-quarters fill the dish with well-flavoured stock made from the veal trimmings or bones. Cover with another piedish upside down and bake in a moderate oven for 1½ hours. Now add more stock to replace what has boiled away, cover the top with ½ lb. parboiled thickly sliced potatoes, put on a shortcrust pastry lid and bake in a moderately hot oven for about 45 minutes. Chopped parsley is sometimes added to the contents.

VEAL, HAM AND CALVES' LIVER PIE

8 oz. each cold roast veal, cold boiled liver and cooked ham, all finely chopped
8 oz. sausage meat
little finely chopped parsley
½ pint (1¼ cups) gravy
salt, pepper
puff or rough puff pastry

Reduce each meat separately to a purée in a blender if possible and put in layers into a piedish, sprinkling each layer with salt, pepper and the parsley. Add a little gravy and cover with pastry. Bake in a moderate oven for 35–40 minutes, and pour more gravy through the hole in the top. The pie can be eaten hot or cold.

VEAL AND HAM PIE

3 lb. neck or breast of veal
puff or rough puff pastry
¼ lb. ham (or bacon)
hard-boiled eggs
herb forcemeat balls (p. 93)
salt, pepper
mace
butter
cold water

Cut the meat into 1½ in. pieces, put them into a fireproof dish, season with salt and pepper, just cover with cold water, and cook gently on top of the cooker or in the oven for about 2 hours.

Line the piedish with the chosen pastry, while the meat is cooling, then cover the bottom of the dish with it, adding a few strips of ham or bacon and thin slices of eggs sprinkled with salt, pepper, ground mace and grated lemon rind, interspersing these with herb forcemeat balls first lightly fried in butter. Repeat these layers till the dish is full enough, piling the contents up in the middle, half-fill the dish with gravy made from the meat trimmings, and cover with the paste. Decorate this, making a hole in the top, brush over with egg to gild it and bake for 45 minutes to 1 hour in a moderately hot oven. As soon as baked, pour a little more well-seasoned gravy through the hole in the top and serve more gravy separately.

If the pie is served cold, leave small spaces between the meats to allow a jelly to form.

VEAL PUDDING

1 lb. lean veal
4 oz. bacon (green or smoked) or pickled pork
suet pastry (see p. 66)
mushrooms
veal kidney

Cut up the veal into smallish pieces, keeping the bones and trimmings aside to make a well-flavoured stock. Next cut the bacon or pickled pork into thin strips and put the meat into a pastry lined pudding basin in the same way as for steak pudding (*see* p. 66) adding bits of the veal kidney and mushrooms here and there. Cover with more pastry and steam for 3 hours. Serve with gravy made with the stock from the bones, etc.

VEAL AND SAUSAGE LOAF

8 oz. cold minced veal
4 oz. ($\frac{1}{2}$ cup) sausage-meat
1 tablespoonful ($1\frac{1}{4}$ tablespoonfuls) fresh breadcrumbs
salt, pepper
egg
veal stock
mixed herbs
flour

Mix together the veal, sausagemeat, salt and pepper and breadcrumbs, adding some mixed herbs if desired and moistening with the beaten egg and sufficient stock to moisten thoroughly.

Shape into a loaf and either coat lightly with flour or egg-and-breadcrumb the top and sides. Bake in a moderate oven for 1 hour, basting now and then with fat. Serve hot or cold.

FLADGEON OF VEAL

8 oz. finely chopped lean raw veal
4 oz. (1 cup) suet
2 tablespoonfuls ($2\frac{1}{2}$ tablespoonfuls) fresh breadcrumbs
lemon rind
grated nutmeg
salt, pepper
2 eggs
milk or stock

Mix together the veal, suet and breadcrumbs and the seasonings of salt, pepper, nutmeg and a pinch of grated lemon rind, stir in a beaten egg and as much milk or stock as will moisten the whole thoroughly. Turn into a greased piedish so that it is half-full, then beat another egg with $\frac{1}{4}$ pint ($\frac{1}{3}$ pint) cold stock, season to taste and pour this into the piedish. Bake till set in a slow oven for about $1\frac{1}{2}$ hours.

VEAL 101

SAUSAGES

VEAL SAUSAGES
1 lb. lean raw veal
1 lb. fat bacon
little chopped fresh sage
salt
black pepper
flour
egg
breadcrumbs

Chop the meats together finely and mix well with the sage and plenty of salt and pepper. With floured hands, shape into small round cakes, egg-and-breadcrumb them and fry in shallow fat.

VEAL AND OYSTER SAUSAGES
1 lb. lean raw veal
1 or 2 dozen small oysters
4 oz. (1⅓ cups) fresh bread
4 oz. (1 cup) shredded suet
egg
butter for frying

Open the oysters, and strain their liquor over the crumbs. When it is absorbed, mash up the bread with a fork. Now add the veal, minced as finely as possible and mix it and the soaked bread with the suet, seasoning with salt and pepper to taste. Mix well and add the oysters cut in small pieces and beaten with an egg. Pound all well together again, shape into small sausages, flour them and fry in butter.

They can be eaten hot or cold, and if served on cocktail sticks make an unusual and admirable snack.

LEFT-OVERS

MARBLED VEAL
equal amounts of cold veal and cold tongue
hard-boiled eggs
salt, pepper
some cold jelly stock

Chop the veal and tongue separately and very finely, or better still, blend to a stiff purée, seasoning well with salt and pepper. Cut the egg up into suitable pieces and use these to make a pattern in the bottom of the mould or pudding basin. On this place irregularly-shaped pieces of the veal and tongue in layers, warming the jelly stock slightly and pouring it between the lumps of meat, so as to give a marbled effect when set. When the mould is filled, put it aside until set and cold.

SALPICON OF VEAL

1 lb. diced cooked veal
1½ cups (12 fl. oz.) thick veal gravy
sherry
onion juice
cayenne pepper
Worcester sauce
mushrooms
butter
green olives and button onions if desired

Heat up the cold veal in the thickened gravy, flavouring it with a little sherry if you wish, and seasoning with a few drops of Worcester sauce, a little onion juice and a touch of cayenne pepper. Add a few mushroom slices (first fried lightly in butter) and, if desired, some sliced green olives and whole button onions first cooked in butter. The best kind of little onion for this garnish is the white pickling one.

VEAL EN COQUILLES

cold veal
white sauce
veal stock
duchesse potatoes
grated cheese
scallop shells
milk

Make a good white sauce with milk and veal stock and heat up in it some cold veal cut into very small dice. Now make a surround of *duchesse* potatoes in scallop shells and fill up the centres with the veal mixture. Sprinkle with a little cheese (a mixture of Parmesan and Gruyère is best) and brown in the oven.

On no account mince veal with a machine as this seems to deprive it of all its flavour. If you want a less plain dish, add to the veal some equally small dice of ham, bacon or tongue, a little lightly fried minced onion and a few chopped mushrooms.

VEAL KROMESKIS

cooked veal
ham or bacon
onion
mushrooms
béchamel sauce (p. 206)
egg
fritter batter
tomato sauce
fat or oil

Cut the cold veal into tiny dice and mix them with diced cooked ham, bacon or tongue, a little lightly fried chopped onion and mushrooms. Bind with a little thick béchamel sauce, incorporating the yolk of an egg. Let the mixture cool on a plate, then form into small rolls shaped like corks. Wrap each of these in a thin piece of cooked ham or bacon or a very thin rasher of streaky raw smoked bacon. Dip them into fine fritter batter made with white of egg only and fry in deep fat or oil till crisp and golden. Tomato sauce is usually served with them.

Leg of Lamb and some of the ingredients for Roast Leg of Lamb

VEAL

There is a Polish way of encasing the little rolls in the thinnest of thin cooked pancakes and egg-and-breadcrumbing them and frying them in deep fat or oil, but in my opinion this makes them too heavy. Their fascination lies in their lightness when simply fried in batter.

VEAL SALAD

cooked veal
celery
hard-boiled eggs
stuffed olives
chives
mayonnaise or cream or sour cream dressing

Mix together 12 oz. (1½ cups) diced cooked veal, half that quantity of diced celery, 2 chopped hard-boiled eggs and 8 sliced stuffed olives. Dress with mayonnaise, cream dressing or sour cream dressing, and finish by sprinkling with chopped chives.

For sour cream dressing add 2 tablespoonfuls (2½ tablespoonfuls) soured cream to 4 fl. oz. (½ cup) French oil-and-vinegar dressing.

VEAL TETRAZZINI (Italy)

cooked veal
veal gravy
anchovy paste
Parmesan cheese
noodles

Put a layer of cooked noodles into a shallow fireproof dish, and cover with minced cooked veal. Cover this with a good layer of gravy blended with flour and milk, flavoured very lightly indeed with anchovy paste. Sprinkle thickly with grated Parmesan cheese (or a mixture of Parmesan and Gruyère) and put in the oven or under the grill till the cheese melts and browns very slightly.

In my own experience an additional refinement to this delicious dish can be obtained by using, instead of plain anchovy paste, the more attractive *Patum Peperium* or Gentleman's Relish.

Roast Leg of Lamb

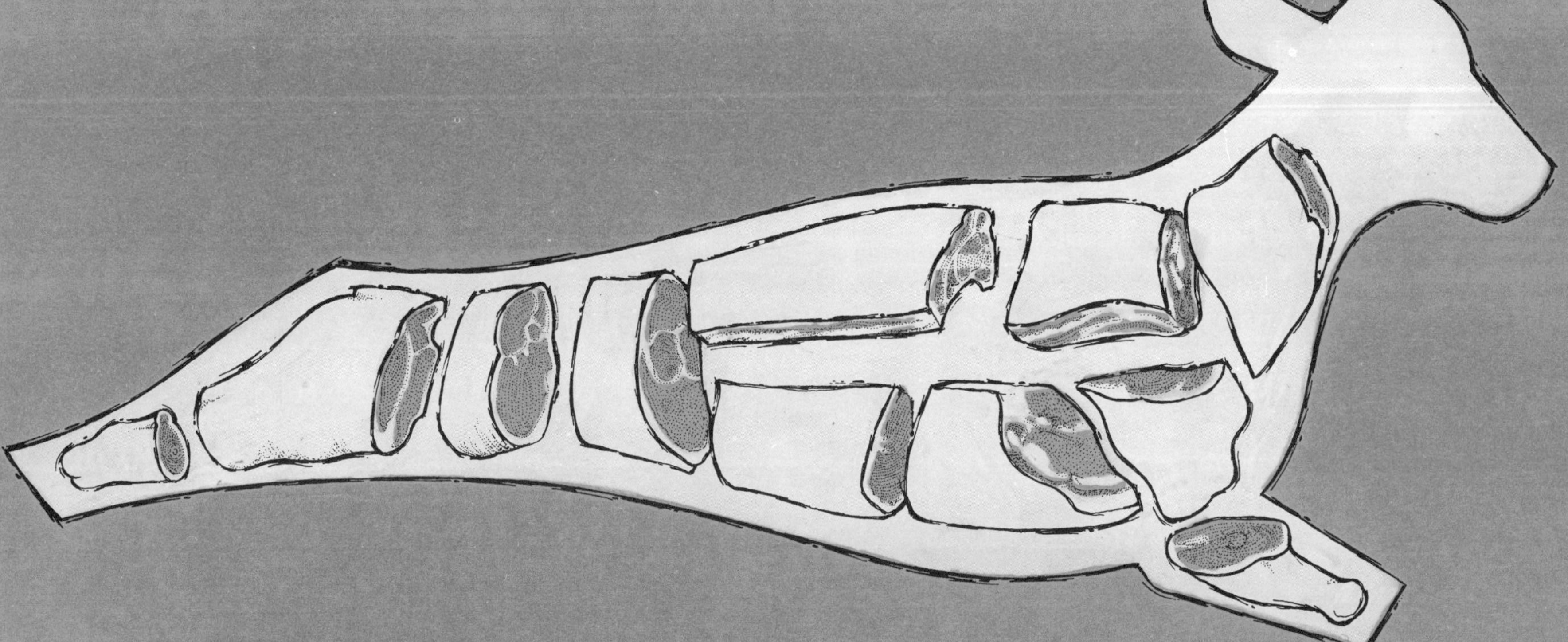

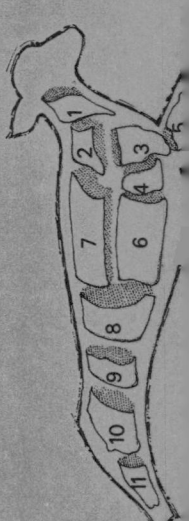

LAMB OR MUTTON

1 HEAD
2 SHOULDER PIECE
3 SCRAG
4 MIDDLE NECK
5 SHOULDER
6 BREASTS
7 BEST END
8 LOIN
9 CHUMP
10 LEG
11 KNUCKLE LEG

MUTTON AND LAMB

The meat of the sheep is known in the kitchen as mutton and lamb. The best joints of lamb and mutton are the saddle and the shoulder, neither of which can be surpassed when roasted, and after these the leg and the loin. The prime age for mutton is three to four years, and to be at its best it must be well fed and hung in a cool, airy place for two or three weeks after it has been killed. Joints of mutton should be plump, with small bones, the lean having a slightly brown tinge, firm and close in texture. The fat should be hard and shiny white. After hanging, it may get a dark and slightly unappetizing look, but normally this will be a sign that it has been properly treated by the butcher. Good lamb should be bright red when cut, with not too much fat.

The best of English mutton and lamb comes from Southdown and Hampshire sheep and from the Welsh and Scottish mountain breeds, the last two having a richer and gamier flavour due to the pasture which the animals have enjoyed. The grazing has a notable effect on the meat and a famous example of this is the French *pré-salé* lamb from animals grazed on salt marshes, where a proportion of aromatic herbs in the grass play their part in flavouring the meat.

For many years before the war, chilled New Zealand (or Canterbury) lamb, as it was then called was increasing in popularity, and is now almost a staple diet of the English. The New Zealand Information Bureau have recommended that this should be put into a cold oven set at 350°F. (180°C.) and roasted for 30–35 minutes per pound, allowing 40–45 minutes if the joint is boned and stuffed.

Cuts of Mutton and Lamb

Leg: roast, braise or boil. It can be boned and stuffed. Transverse slices from the fillet end (opposite to the knuckle) are fried, grilled or casseroled. This part is the best to use for *brochettes*.

Loin: middle of back (saddle) is the best roasted dish from this animal, but is usually divided down the backbone into two joints and roasted on the bone or boned and stuffed.

Best end of neck: roast or braise whole, or divide into cutlets.

Middle neck: stew and for casseroles and broth.

Scrag (neck): as middle neck.

Shoulder: roast whole or bone, stuff and braise, or cut in pieces for fricassées, stews or *brochettes*.

Breast: bone, stuff and roll, roast or braise, or stew, then egg-and-breadcrumb and bake or fry. It can also be boiled.

Chops: loin chops come from the rib end, chump chops from the leg end of the loin; they are generally fried or grilled.

Cutlets: cutlets are chops from the best end of neck and have a curved bone. Again, they should be fried or grilled.

Noisettes: one of the most delicate cuts of mutton and lamb, *noisettes* are really cutlets trimmed without the bone. They weigh 2–3 oz. each and frying suits them better than grilling. All recipes for tournedos of beef suit them.

Approximate equivalent cuts of Mutton and Lamb

ENGLISH	FRENCH	AMERICAN
Leg	*Gigot*	Leg steaks, loin end of leg
Loin	*Longe*	Loin
Best end of neck	*Carré*	Cutlet
Middle of neck	*Côtelettes découvertes*	Rib chop, crown roast
Breast	*Poitrine*	Breast
Shoulder	*Epaule*	Saratoga chop, shoulder
Scrag end of neck	*Collet*	Neck
Saddle	*Selle*	Saddle
Chop, cutlet	*Côte, côtelette*	Chop, cutlet

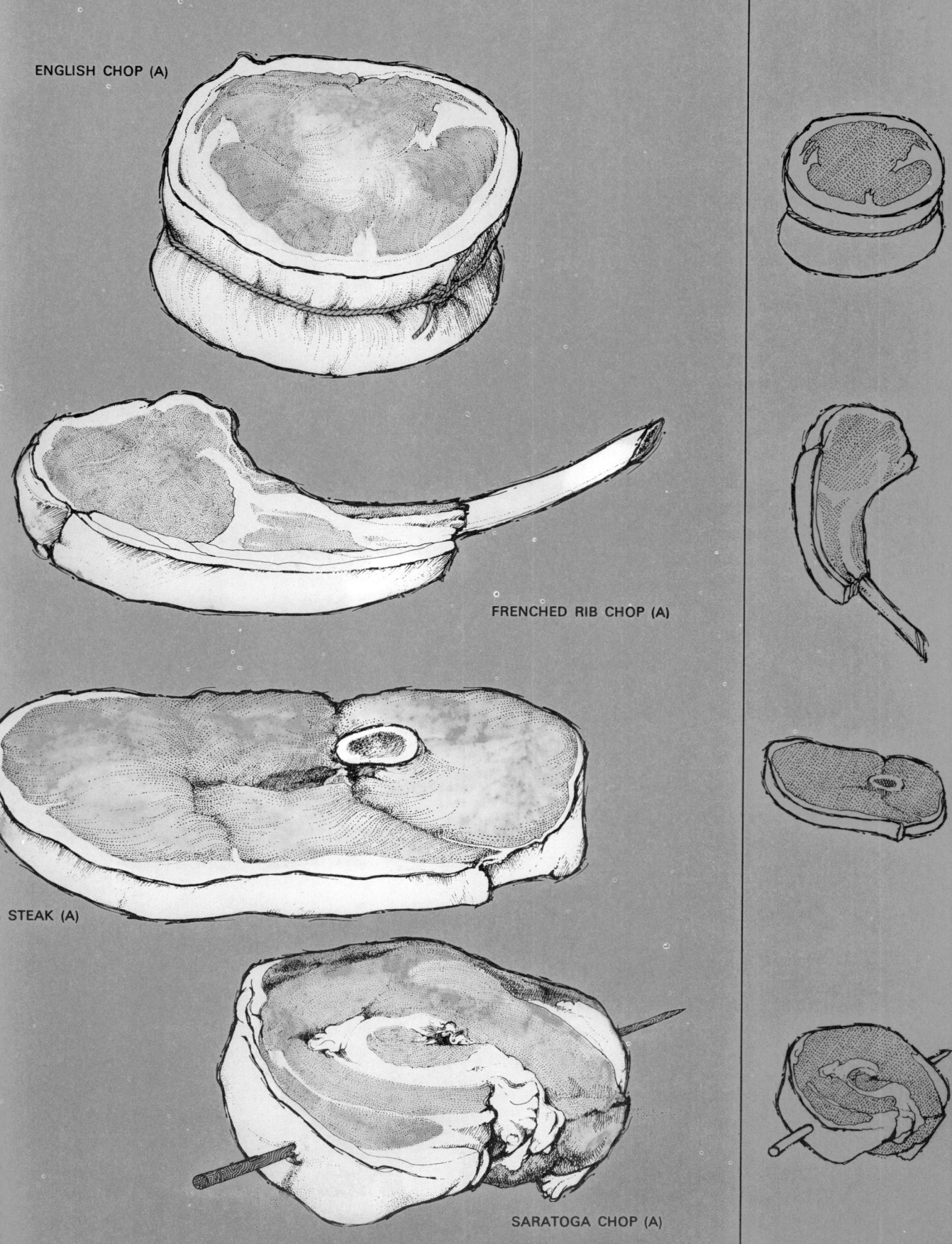

ROAST MUTTON AND LAMB

CROWN ROAST OF LAMB

Although many people attribute this dramatic dish to the old English kitchen, its origins are American and comparatively modern.

1 whole best end of neck of lamb
fresh pork fat
2 shallots
½ oz. (1 tablespoonful) butter
6 oz. (¾ cup) minced raw lean veal
1 tablespoonful (1¼ tablespoonful) chopped parsley
salt, pepper

You will have to get the butcher to prepare this joint for you by chining it and then bending the cutlets round in the shape of a crown (with the *noisettes* outwards) and stitching the two ends together. Then wrap the whole thing with a large piece of fresh pork fat.

For the filling cook 2 chopped shallots in ½ oz. of butter till soft then add the minced raw veal and the meat cut off the bones between the cutlets; and also 1 tablespoonful of chopped parsley and a seasoning of salt and pepper. Cook together for a few minutes, and put the mixture in the middle of the crown, covering the ends of the cutlet bones to prevent their burning.

Roast for 30 minutes in a fairly hot oven (400°F. or 200°C.). Instructions for carving this joint will be found on p. 21 and a drawing on p. 140.

ROAST LEG OF LAMB OR MUTTON

A roast leg of lamb or mutton needs a moderate oven (380°F. or 195°C.) and will take 30 minutes to the pound. If slow roasting is preferred, the temperature should be 335°F. (170°C.) and 5 minutes longer given per pound. If you are using a meat thermometer it should register 170°F. (76°C.) for a medium done joint and 180°F. (82°C.) if it is to be well done.

Many people nowadays like to insert a clove of garlic into the flesh of the shank, and also prefer the French fashion of marinating the joint for a day or two before cooking in a mixture of sliced vegetables, herbs, spices, vinegar and white wine.

Another variation, particularly suitable for older meat, is to add a large spoonful of juniper berries and a bay leaf or two to such a marinade.

ROAST LEG OF MUTTON MARINATED WITH PORT

leg of mutton
bottle of dry port wine

Take a fine leg of mutton and make a few deep holes in the shank end with a thick skewer, working the flesh away from the bone but without tearing it. Hang the leg

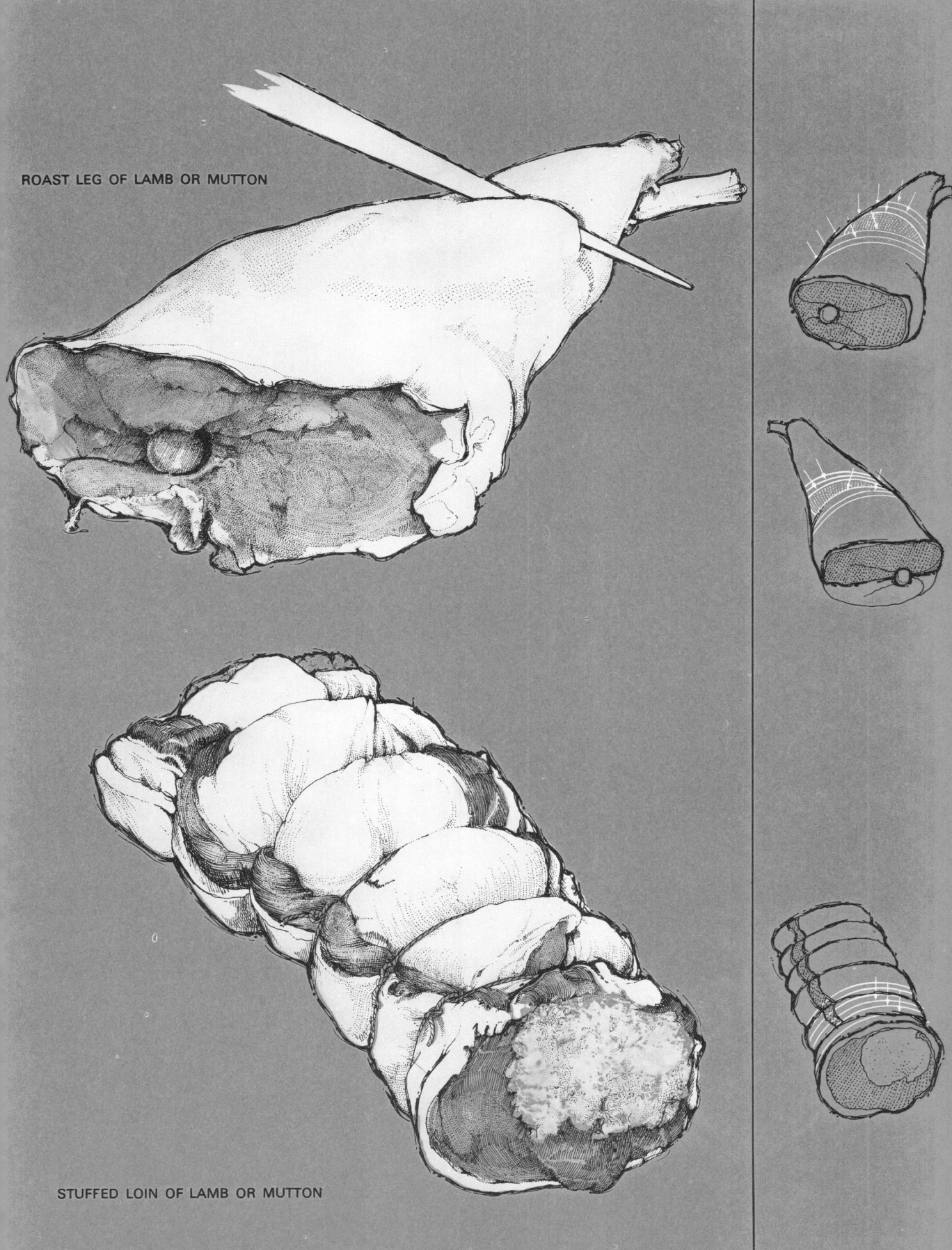
ROAST LEG OF LAMB OR MUTTON

STUFFED LOIN OF LAMB OR MUTTON

ROAST SHOULDER OF MUTTON 1

ROAST SHOULDER OF MUTTON 2

MUTTON AND LAMB

up in a cool larder (not a refrigerator) and commence to pour very slowly a bottle of dry port into the leg through these holes, massaging it in towards the shoulder end till it is all absorbed. Go on doing this daily pouring in the port little by little and massaging it down, till the bottle is empty. This should take a week or so, perhaps longer.

When the process is complete, roast the leg in the usual way. You will want to serve nothing more with it than its own gravy, which is magnificent.

To carve this joint follow the instructions for roast leg of lamb on p. 20 and see the drawing opposite.

ROAST LOIN OF BABY LAMB

loin of baby lamb
garlic
onions
potatoes
butter
stock

Some people like to spread the joint with French mustard, but this is a matter of personal taste. The garlic, however, is essential, and pieces of it should be inserted in the loin here and there. Having done this, butter the joint well.

Peel and slice some potatoes and onions thinly and cook them in butter in the baking dish without browning them. Season them well and place the loin on these, and put the dish into the oven heated to 425°F. (220°C.) and cook for 45 minutes and then lower the heat to 355°F. (180°C.) and cook for another 30 minutes. Just before serving pour in a few tablespoonfuls of reduced stock.

If another joint of baby lamb has been used instead of loin, it should be turned over and left unbasted when the heat is decreased for the finishing.

Accompaniments

With roast lamb, spring vegetables and new potatoes are served, and clear gravy and mint sauce (*see* p. 213) accompany them. With roast mutton serve roast potatoes, haricot beans, turnips and onions with onion sauce (*see* p. 213), and red or blackcurrant jelly and thick gravy. In America cranberry jelly takes the place of the other jellies.

ROAST STUFFED SHOULDER OF MUTTON OR LAMB

The shoulder of leg of mutton or lamb is very often boned and stuffed, and a stuffing for this purpose is recommended here. To make this mix together 2 oz. finely chopped bacon, 4 tablespoonfuls breadcrumbs, 2 finely chopped shallots, 2 tablespoonfuls shredded suet, 1 teaspoonful chopped parsley, ½ teaspoonful grated lemon rind and the same of dried mixed herbs, a saltspoonful of grated nutmeg and salt and pepper to taste. Moisten with egg beaten in milk and press the mixture into the cavity where the bone was. Skewer or tape it in position, and roast as for leg of mutton or lamb accompanying it on serving with brown sauce or thick brown gravy.

Instructions for carving this joint will be found on p. 20 and a drawing on p. 112.

ROAST LAMB CHOPS

lamb chops
streaky bacon
salt, pepper
flour
fat

Have the chops cut 2½ in. thick and boned; wrap each round with a rasher of streaky bacon. Sprinkle them with salt, pepper and flour and brown them well on both sides in fat. Then put them on a rack in a baking tin. Roast in a moderate oven for 40 minutes or so.

SADDLE OF MUTTON

The saddle of mutton consists of the two loins attached to the backbone, and represents this admirable meat at its very best. Unfortunately family meals are much smaller than they once were, and so even the lamb's saddle is too much for the average family and that of the adult sheep unthinkable save for a large dinner party. In England it is usually served with redcurrant jelly or even rowan jelly, the sharpness of which acts as a foil to the richness of the meat. I tasted at a Vintners' banquet many years ago an accompaniment of seakale and pickled walnuts which had much the same effect and the benefit of the unusual as well.

The skin from the saddle of mutton should be removed and the surface of the joint smeared thickly with softened butter or good dripping. It is then sprinkled with salt and a little pepper. A breakfastcupful of water should then be poured into the baking dish, and the joint is put into a hot oven to seal it for 10 minutes or so. Then continue to cook at a reduced heat with frequent basting, allowing 15 minutes for each pound weight. The kidneys, which some butchers use for decorating the neck end of the joint, should be cooked with it for the last 15 minutes. Serve with plain gravy.

STUFFED LAMB CHOPS

Leave the bone on some loin chops, allowing 2 per serving, trim off most of the fat and cut through the meat horizontally, so that a deep pocket is made through to the

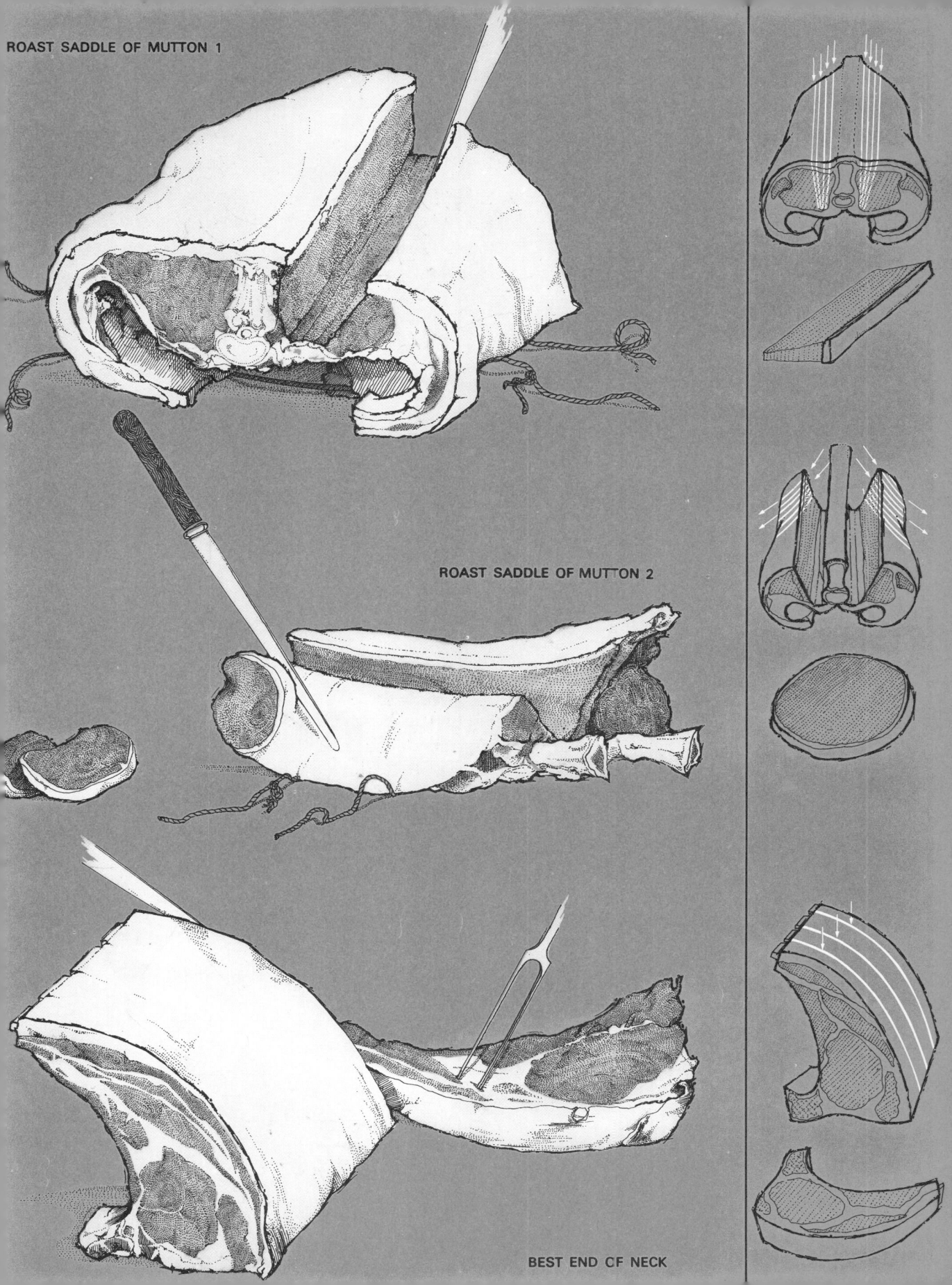
ROAST SADDLE OF MUTTON 1

ROAST SADDLE OF MUTTON 2

BEST END OF NECK

bone. Stuff this with a suitable filling, e.g. mint stuffing, sage and onion or herb forcemeat or sausagemeat, and press the cut sides of the chops lightly together again. Now dip the chops in crumbs, then in beaten egg and then in crumbs again, and bake them in a hot oven, basting with butter or other suitable fat and turning them over once during the cooking. Sprigs of watercress would be a suitable garnish.

MINT STUFFING

3 cups dry breadcrumbs
½ cup fresh mint leaves finely chopped
3 oz. (6 tablespoonfuls) butter
3 tablespoonfuls (3¾ tablespoonfuls) chopped celery
chopped onion

Cook the celery and onion in half the butter for 2 minutes, then add the mint or watercress as a substitute and a seasoning of salt and pepper. Cook till all liquid evaporates and then add to the crumbs which have been mixed with the remaining 1½ oz. melted butter. This stuffing, incidentally, is excellent with roast chicken.

GRILLED AND FRIED MUTTON AND LAMB

GRILLED BREAST OF MUTTON

breast of mutton
salt, pepper

Divide the breast into suitable pieces for serving, having first trimmed the unnecessary fat from it. Grill it slowly, making sure that the meat is well cooked throughout by turning the pieces over frequently and sprinkling them with salt and pepper. A sauce is served separately, usually tomato, *diable* or *piquante*.

FRIED LAMB

slices of leg of lamb
2 tablespoonfuls (2½ tablespoonfuls) each olive oil and vinegar
3 teaspoonfuls (3¾ teaspoonfuls chopped parsley
fat for frying

Get the butcher to cut you a slice or two of lamb from the leg, and cut these into strips 1 in. thick. Flatten them to ¾ in. and leave them for several hours (all night if you wish) in a covered dish with a mixture of 2 tablespoonfuls olive oil, the same of vinegar and 3 teaspoonfuls chopped parsley sprinkled over them. When ready to cook, wipe the pieces of lamb clean and dry and fry them in a heavy frying pan in as little fat as you possibly can, as they should have when finished the appearance of being grilled rather than fried.

MUTTON AND LAMB

FRIED BREAST OF LAMB

1 breast of lamb	Cook a breast of lamb in a stewpan with the bouquet, the onion stuck with half a dozen cloves, a teacupful of diced carrot and a quarter of a small turnip also diced. Add salt and a few peppercorns and just cover the meat with boiling water. Skim and cook gently till the bones slip out easily, then remove them and press the meat between two plates with a weight on top. When cold, cut in neat pieces for serving, egg-and-breadcrumb and fry them golden on each side. A tomato sauce goes well with them, especially if it is reinforced by some chopped or pickled gherkins, but some prefer just plain French mustard, and very good the combination is, too.
1 small onion	
cloves	
bouquet garni	
carrot	
turnip	
peppercorns	
egg	
salt	
breadcrumbs	

LAMB CHOPS WITH APRICOTS

Grill the chops in the usual way, and when they are half-done, turn them over sprinkle them with salt and pepper and place a stewed apricot or two on top. Brush this over with melted butter, and finish grilling when the fruit browns a little.

Alternatively, you can substitute for the apricots a pineapple ring or a slice of orange from which the skin, pips and pith have been removed.

LAMB CUTLETS MILANAISE

lamb cutlets	Dip the cutlets in melted butter and cover them with a half-and-half mixture of grated cheese and breadcrumbs, pressing it well on with the blade of a knife. Now gently shake off any crumbs that are not adhering, and dip the cutlets very carefully in beaten egg. Coat again with the cheese and crumb mixture and grill very gently and slowly. Serve tomato sauce with them.
butter	
grated cheese	
breadcrumbs	
egg	
tomato sauce	

MUTTON CUTLETS MURILLO

cutlets	Fry the cutlets on one side only, then coat the uncooked side with a purée of mushrooms bound with with thick white béchamel sauce, raising it to a slight dome above the meat. Put these cutlets into a buttered baking tin, sprinkle with a little grated cheese and a few drops of melted butter and bake quickly. Fried tomato slices should be served with this dish.
mushrooms	
thick béchamel sauce (p. 206)	
grated cheese	
butter	
tomatoes	

SOUVLAKIA (Greece)

2 lb. lean lamb
2 tablespoonfuls (2½ tablespoonfuls) olive oil
juice of half a lemon
oregano
bay leaves
salt, pepper

Cut the meat into small walnut-sized pieces and thread it on metal skewers with a piece of bay leaf in between each one. For this quantity of meat, beat 2 tablespoonfuls olive oil with the juice of half a lemon, season this with salt, pepper and oregano and leave the laden skewers in this marinade for 30 minutes, turning them once. Then grill over a hot fire (a charcoal grill is best), turning all the time so that while the surface gets well seared, the inside of the meat is tender and juicy. Serve immediately they are ready, preferably with a tomato and cucumber salad and quarters of lemon.

SHISH KEBAB (Middle East)

1 lb. lamb or mutton
salt, pepper
dried thyme and powdered bay leaf
milk
3 tomatoes
3 green sweet peppers
3 medium onions
3 bay leaves

Cut the meat into small cubes and rub the salt, pepper and herbs well into them. Now cover them with milk and let the meat soak for 3–4 hours, draining and drying the pieces afterwards. Impale the meat on metal skewers alternately with the sliced tomatoes, peppers and onions, and put a bay leaf in the middle of each skewerful. Grill over a good fire and serve with pilaff rice accompanied by spring onions.

Veal can be used in place of the lamb or mutton.

LAMB CUTLETS SUÉDOISE

4 lamb cutlets
butter
breadcrumbs
marinade:
minced onion
bouquet garni
juice of 1 lemon
olive oil
1 lb. cooking apples
white wine
fresh grated horseradish

Trim the cutlets and marinate for 30 minutes, turning once, in a sprinkling of minced onion, the juice of a lemon, a little olive oil and a bouquet garni. When ready, drain and dry, wiping off any traces of the bits in the marinade. Now brush over with melted butter and coat with fine breadcrumbs pressing these on with the flat of a knife. Grill gently, basting with butter and serve round a thick purée of apples.

This purée should be really thick, so that it makes a heap in the middle of the serving dish.

Use a little white wine in making the purée and when it is ready, stir in a tablespoonful or two of fresh grated horseradish.

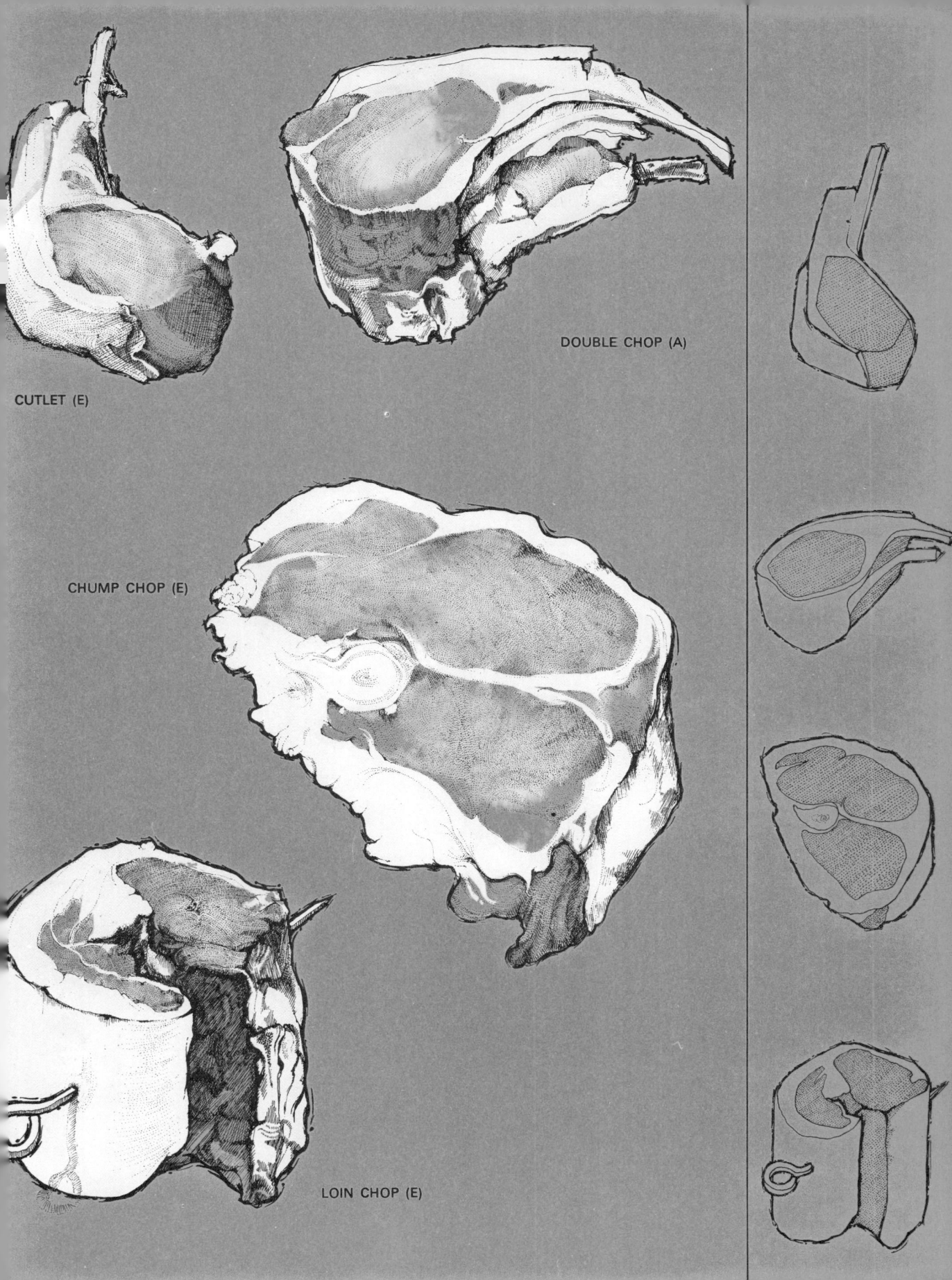

CÔTE (F)

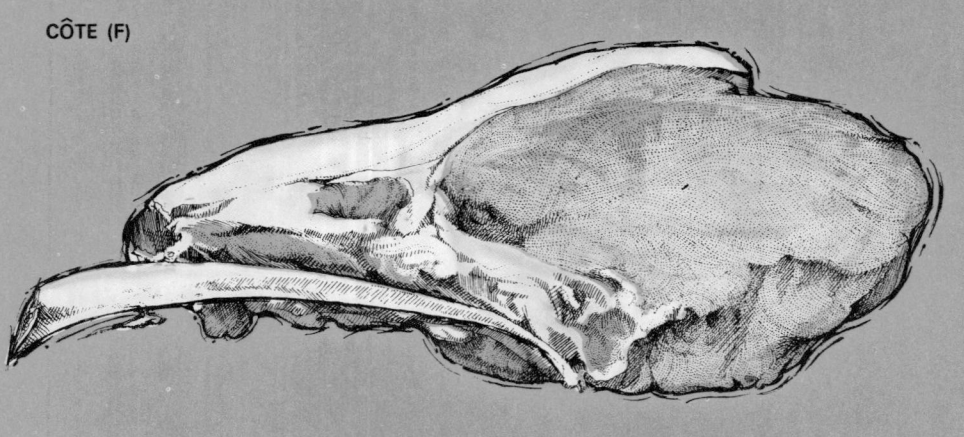
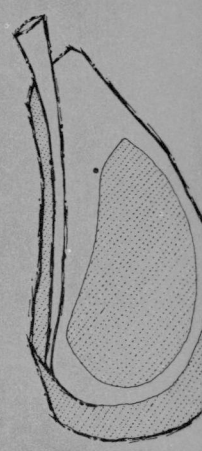

CÔTELETTES (F)

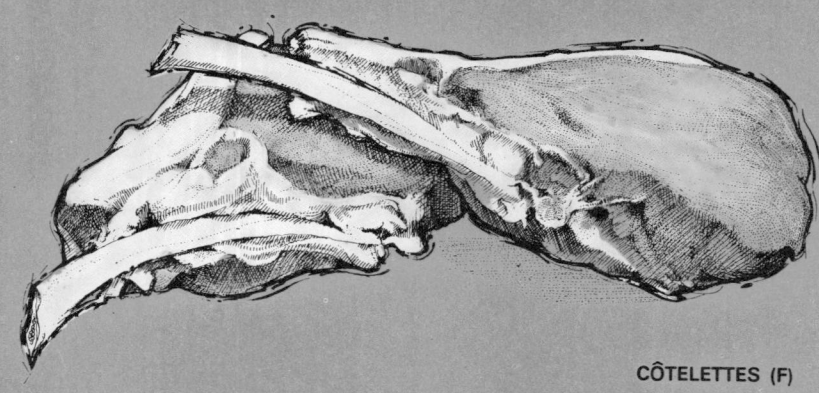

NOISETTE (F)

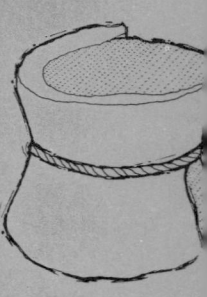

MUTTON AND LAMB

STEWED AND BRAISED MUTTON AND LAMB

BREAST OF LAMB À LA SAINTE-MÉNÉHOULDE

a breast of lamb
fattish mild or green bacon
2 carrots
4 onions
bouquet garni
2 tablespoonfuls (2½ tablespoonfuls) meat stock
breadcrumbs
salt, pepper

Put 2 good rashers of fattish mild or green bacon in the bottom of a casserole or stewpan, lay on them the breast of lamb and cover it with more bacon, diced this time, 2 sliced carrots, 4 chopped onions and the bouquet. Moisten with just a couple of tablespoonfuls only of good stock, cover with greased paper or kitchen foil and then the lid and cook slowly in the oven for 3 hours. Then take out the breast, bone it and season with salt and pepper. Sprinkle with breadcrumbs, put the breast back into the hottest part of the oven and let the crumbs get crisp and golden, basting all the time.

DAUBE AVIGNONNAISE (France)

Make in the same way as for *Daube provençale* (see p. 47), replacing the beef by pieces of mutton cut from the leg. Escoffier says that the most delicious accompaniment to this is a dish of small white Cavaillon haricot beans cooked with a piece of streaky bacon and a small garlic sausage.

JUGGED LAMB CUTLETS

1 lb. lamb cutlets
1 onion
½ oz. (1 tablespoonful) butter
2 tomatoes
flour
½ pint (1¼ cups) meat stock
salt, pepper
celery salt
juice of 1 lemon
1 teaspoonful (1¼ teaspoonfuls) redcurrant jelly
½ glass port wine
parsley

Brown a quartered onion in ½ oz. butter, take it out and in the same fat brown the lamb cutlets well trimmed on each side. Transfer the onion and cutlets into a casserole and add 2 medium-sized tomatoes and a little flour browned in the butter. Now moisten with a good meat stock seasoned with salt, pepper and celery salt, squeeze in the lemon juice and cook, closely covered, in a slowish oven with the lid on for 2 hours. Ten minutes before serving the dish, stir in the redcurrant jelly, some freshly chopped parsley and the wine. Garnish with triangular sippets of toast or fried bread, and, if you like, large fried or grilled mushrooms.

LAMB CATALANE (Spain)

1 thick slice from leg of lamb
salt, pepper
pork fat
1 clove garlic
1 red or green sweet pepper
1 glass dry white wine
1 tablespoonful (1½ tablespoonfuls) tomato purée
stock

A thickish slice from a leg of lamb, cut right across the bone, is what is wanted here, and it should be well seasoned with salt and pepper and then fried on both sides in pork fat. Then add a clove of garlic and a chopped red or green sweet pepper and cook on for a few minutes longer. Now transfer to a casserole, and swill and scrape the first pan after adding the wine. Pour this liquid over the meat in the casserole with a tablespoonful of thick tomato purée and just enough hot stock to cover the meat. Put on the lid as tightly as you can and stew gently till the piece is quite tender. Thicken the gravy before serving.

LAMB CHOP CASSEROLES (U.S.A.)

For this you really want a small casserole for each person, and the chops should be boned and tied round so that they will fit.

1 lamb chop for each serving
tomatoes
apples
onions
potatoes
1 tablespoonful (1¼ tablespoonfuls) water

Lightly brown the chops in very little fat in a heavy frying pan, and when browned on each side put them into the small heated casseroles with half a peeled tomato, half a peeled and cored apple, a very small blanched onion and 2 or 3 raw potato balls cut with a scoop. Season and add a good tablespoonful of boiling water, put on the lids and bake in a moderate oven for about 45 minutes.

MUTTON OR LAMB CURRY (India)

The method is the same as for beef curry (*see* p. 54) substituting mutton or lamb for the beef.

WELSH VENISON

loin of mutton
mixed herbs
pepper, salt
2 glasses port wine
redcurrant jelly

Have the loin boned and season it with a sprinkling of mixed herbs, salt and pepper. Roll it up, tie with tape and braise for 2½ hours. Keep it hot while you skim off the fat and reduce the braising liquor to a demi-glace, then add 2 glasses of port wine, glaze the joint with this mixture and serve with redcurrant jelly.

MUTTON AND LAMB

SHISH KEBAB (Greece)

2 lb. lean lamb
2 oz. (4 tablespoonfuls) butter
2 onions
4 ripe tomatoes
tomato paste
1 pint (1¼ pints) hot water
a little sugar
salt, pepper
pinch of cinnamon
1 wineglassful vermouth

Slice the onions finely and soften them in the butter in a heavy saucepan. Add the skinned and roughly chopped tomatoes, the sugar and cinnamon and the tomato paste diluted with a little water. Season with salt and pepper, and put the meat, cut in small pieces, into the pan and then stir in the hot water. Put on the lid and stew very slowly for about 1 hour, when the meat should be tender. At the last minute, add a wineglassful of vermouth, and serve very hot with a rice pilaff. It is commonly supposed that all Shish Kebabs are cooked on skewers, but this is not so – the word *kebab* means a small piece of meat.

LANCASHIRE HOTPOT (England)

A simpler hotpot can be made by omitting the oysters and mushrooms.

2 lb. middle neck of mutton
1 oz. (2 tablespoonfuls) dripping
1 onion
1 oz. (¼ cup) flour
¾ pint (1 pint) stock
salt, pepper
1 teaspoonful (1¼ teaspoonfuls) caster sugar
2 sheeps' kidneys
4 or 5 mushrooms
20 oysters
2 lb. potatoes

Have the meat cut into chops and brown these on both sides in the dripping. Transfer them to an earthenware hotpot and stew the onion, sliced, for a few minutes in the dripping. Sprinkle with flour and go on cooking till browned. Add the stock, as though making gravy, and season to taste with salt, pepper and a teaspoonful of caster sugar; skin and core the kidneys and cut them in thick slices, peel the mushrooms and cut in pieces and add these with the oysters in layers in the pot containing the meat. Peel and cut the potatoes in thick slices, arrange them in overlapping rings on top of the meat to cover the top completely. Now strain the thickened stock over the potatoes, put on the lid and stew in a moderate oven for a couple of hours, removing the lid for the last 20 minutes or so, for the top potatoes to brown.

IRISH STEW

1 lb. neck of mutton
salt, pepper
2 lb. potatoes
½ lb. onions

Cut the neck of mutton into neat pieces, wash them and put into a stewpan and cover with hot water. Add salt and pepper and boil up. Then remove all traces of scum. Meanwhile peel 2 lb. potatoes and cut up about one-third of them into slices. Add these to the contents of the pan, with the blanched and sliced onions. Stir up and add the rest of the potatoes, whole, on top and stew for 2–3 hours, stirring now and then. The point of slicing the potatoes is to effect a thickening of the broth when the meat is cooked. Serve very hot on hot plates, as the appearance of this dish deteriorates as it cools.

BOILED MUTTON AND LAMB

Care should be taken when preparing mutton or lamb for boiling that the joint has not been hung for too long or it will taste too muttony. Nor should too many vegetables be cooked with it or they may impart too much of their flavour to the cooking liquor, to the detriment of the taste of the meat. Put the leg into the water while it is boiling and allow, from the time when it comes to the boil again, 20–25 minutes to the pound. The joint should go into the water with the side which will be served downwards, as the upper surface may become spotted by the boiling action. Keep the water well skimmed during the cooking. Alternatively, the leg may be poached very slowly for several hours till it is tender enough to be cut with a spoon. In either case the cooking should be slow and thorough, and, in addition to the usual 'boiling' vegetables the water should be salted with 2 tablespoonfuls of salt to each gallon of water. Boiled lamb and mutton are invariably accompanied by caper sauce.

MUTTON HAM

Although long a delicacy in Scotland, mutton ham is seldom seen today, in spite of a brief spate of interest during the last war, when it was sold as an extra to supplement the bacon ration. The following note on it appears in Marian McNeill's *The Scots Kitchen* and gives the traditional way of curing it.

Cut the hind quarter of good mutton into the shape of a ham. Pound 1 oz. of saltpetre with 1 lb. of coarse salt and 4 oz. of brown sugar. Add 2 oz. of Jamaica pepper (allspice) and black pepper and ½ oz. of coriander seeds. Rub the ham well with this mixture, taking care to stuff some into the hole in the shank. Lay the hams in the trough, keep them carefully covered and baste them with the brine every other or even every day. Let it lie for a fortnight. Then take it out and press it with a weight for one day. Smoke it with sawdust for 10 or 15 days or hang it to dry in the kitchen. In the Highlands dried juniper berries are used in curing mutton hams. 'No sort of meat', says Meg Dods, 'is more improved by smoking with aromatic woods than mutton.'

If the ham is to be boiled soon after it is smoked, soak it for 1 hour, and if it has been smoked for any length of time it will require to be soaked for several hours. Put

MUTTON AND LAMB

it on in cold water and boil it gently for 2 hours. It is eaten cold at breakfast, luncheon or supper.

STUFFED, BREAST OF MUTTON WITH CAPER SAUCE

breast of mutton
2 tablespoonfuls (2½ tablespoonfuls) bread-crumbs
1 tablespoonful (1½ tablespoonfuls) suet
chopped parsley
mixed herbs
milk
salt, pepper
white stock
½ pint (1¼ cups) melted butter sauce
1 tablespoonful (1½ tablespoonfuls) capers
1 dessertspoonful (½ tablespoonful) vinegar
salt, pepper

Bone and trim the meat and spread it with a mixture of breadcrumbs, shredded suet, chopped parsley, mixed dried herbs and a seasoning of salt and pepper. Moisten with a little milk and spread this on the meat, rolling the joint up lightly and binding it with tape. Bring the stock to the boil and put in the meat, simmering gently for 2 hours. Serve with caper sauce, made as follows, poured over it. To make the caper sauce, make ½ pint (1¼ cups) melted butter sauce (p. 213), using some of the stock in which the meat was cooked instead of water, and add to this 1 tablespoonful of capers either cut in halves or coarsely chopped, 1 dessertspoonful of the vinegar from the capers and a seasoning of salt and pepper.

PIES

MUTTON PIES (Scotland)

¾ lb. lean mutton or lamb
salt, pepper
grated nutmeg
gravy
pastry:
4 oz. (½ cup) beef dripping
½ pint (1¼ cups) water
1 lb. (4 cups) flour

Mince the meat and season with salt, pepper and nutmeg.

To make the pastry, first sieve the flour into a bowl, making a well in the middle. Now boil the water with the dripping and pour into the flour. Knead lightly, turn onto a board and continue kneading till smooth. Roll out thinly and cut out rounds. Line straightsided individual pie cases with the pastry, reserving half for the lids. These pies are usually about 3–3½ in. in diameter and about 1–1½ in. in height. Fill the cases with mixture, moisten with gravy. Wet the rims of the piecases with water and press on the lid. Brush with egg yolk or milk and bake in a pre-heated oven at 350°F. (177°C.) for about 40 minutes. Serve hot or cold.

LAMB PIE

loin, neck or breast of lamb
sheeps' kidneys
stock
salt, pepper
shortcrust or puff pastry (p. 65)

Cut the meat from the bones, which can be used for stock or gravy, and divide it into pieces suitable for serving. Put them into a piedish, sprinkling each layer with salt and pepper and adding a few thin slices of sheeps' kidney. Half-fill the dish with stock, cover with the chosen pastry and bake in a moderate oven for 1½ hours. Use the strained stock from the bones for filling up the pie at the end of cooking. Eat hot.

LEFT-OVERS

DEVILLED MUTTON

cold roast mutton
lemon juice
salt, pepper
cayenne pepper
butter
browned breadcrumbs
watercress

Cut some thickish slices of roast mutton, season them with salt and pepper and cayenne pepper and sprinkle them with lemon juice. Leave them for 30 minutes, then dip into oiled butter, coat lightly with browned breadcrumbs and bake in a moderately hot oven for a few minutes till well heated through. Serve in a circle with sprigs of watercress, seasoned with salt and pepper and lemon juice, in the middle.

DEVONSHIRE SQUAB PIE

The present-day name of squab pie is a misnomer, the mutton or lamb being a modern substitute for the squabs, or young pigeons. This pie was originally made, it is said, by a husband and wife, one of whom liked sweet food and the other savoury, hence the mixture of onion and apple.

cold mutton or lamb
apples
onions
potatoes
8 fl. oz. (1 cup) water
dripping
salt, pepper

Fry in dripping some peeled, cored and chopped apples and an equal quantity of chopped onions. Grease a piedish well and line it with raw potato cut in very thin slices. Season with salt and pepper and fill up with alternate layers of apple and onion and thin slices of the meat, seasoning further as you go. Pour in a cupful of water, add a dab or two of dripping, and cover with a final layer of potato slices. Bake in a moderate oven.

MUTTON AND LAMB

MOUSSAKA (Greece)

2 lb. aubergines (egg-plants)
1 lb. (2 cups) minced lamb or mutton
1 tablespoonful (1¼ tablespoonfuls) grated onion
1 tomato
1 tablespoonful (1¼ tablespoonfuls) chopped parsley
good pinch of cinnamon and nutmeg
1 oz. (2 tablespoonfuls) butter
1 wineglassful red wine
1 lb. (5 cups) grated cheese
¾ pint (1 pint) béchamel sauce (p. 206)
2 small eggs
olive oil
salt, pepper

Fry the sliced aubergines in olive oil till brown on each side, drain them and keep them hot. In another pan fry, this time in the butter, the meat, onion, tomato and parsley, adding the spices and seasoning of salt and pepper, and then the wine diluted if preferred with a little water. Cook all together for about 20 minutes and fill a buttered fireproof dish with alternate layers of aubergines and the minced meat mixture, sprinkling each layer with a grated cheese. Finish with a final layer of aubergines. Now mix the béchamel sauce with the beaten eggs and season with a little nutmeg, pour it into the dish and complete with a sprinkling of the rest of the cheese. Bake in a moderate oven till the top is golden brown, which should take about 45 minutes.

The long purple aubergines are the ones to use for this dish, but it can also be made with baby marrows or even potatoes.

MUTTON HASH (Turkey)

1 lb. cold roast mutton
4 oz. (⅔ cup) rice
tomato sauce
2 aubergines (egg-plants)
olive oil
breadcrumbs
parsley

Cook the rice as for a pilaff, cut the meat in small pieces and mix it with the tomato sauce. With a fork, mix the meat with the rice and keep hot. Cut the aubergines in halves lengthways, score the cut sides criss-cross with a sharp knife and fry them lightly in a little olive oil. Now scoop out the flesh, chop it up finely and add it to the meat mixture. Arrange the aubergine halves in the serving dish, fill them with the meat and sprinkle with breadcrumbs. Add a few drops of olive oil and put into a moderate oven for 10 minutes or so, till the crumbs brown. Scatter a little chopped parsley over them just before serving.

A QUICK CURRY
cooked lamb
2 onions
2 oz. ($\frac{1}{4}$ cup) butter
garlic
1 tablespoonful ($1\frac{1}{4}$ tablespoonfuls) curry powder
salt
8 oz. tomatoes

Make a curry sauce in this way. Fry a couple of small onions, finely sliced, in the butter, adding a clove or half a clove of garlic. Stir in a good tablespoonful of good curry powder, and season with salt. Now add the peeled and quartered tomatoes and a little water to make a thickish sauce, and simmer together a little. Then add your pieces of cooked meat and simmer very gently for 15 minutes. The sauce can be used as it is or sieved before the final simmering.

MUTTON HASH
1 lb. lean roast mutton
1 oz. (2 tablespoonfuls) butter
2 tablespoonfuls ($2\frac{1}{2}$ tablespoonfuls) finely chopped onion
salt, pepper
nutmeg
3-4 tablespoonfuls ($3\frac{3}{4}$-5 tablespoonfuls) tomato-flavoured demi-glace sauce (p. 209)
parsley

Fry the onion in the butter till it begins to brown, then add the mutton cut in very small pieces, season with salt, pepper and nutmeg to taste and heat through, stirring now and then. Finally, moisten with the sauce and serve sprinkled with chopped parsley. Fried or poached eggs may accompany this, and the sauce can be seasoned with a pinch of tarragon.

SHEPHERD'S PIE
8 oz. cold lamb or mutton
1 lb. (2 cups) mashed potato
butter
onions
salt, pepper
$\frac{1}{2}$ pint ($1\frac{1}{4}$ cups) gravy
cream or yolk of egg or melted butter

Line the bottom of a piedish with rather buttery mashed potato then add thin slices of cold lamb or mutton, sprinkling each layer with salt, pepper and sliced parboiled onion. Pour in the gravy and cover with the rest of the mashed potato. You can decorate this top by drawing the tines of a fork across it to make ridges or you can smooth it and imitate a pie cover by notching the edges as one does with pastry. Brush over with cream or yolk of egg or with a little melted butter. Bake for 1 hour in a moderate oven.

MUTTON AND LAMB

MINTED LAMB CUTLETS (U.S.A.)

2 lamb cutlets for each serving
mint sauce
gelatine

Thicken some mint sauce (p. 213) with gelatine and when it is on the point of setting dip the trimmed cold cutlets into it. Let the jelly coating set and serve the cutlets round a green salad or a mould of cold cooked green peas.

RISSOLES

lean cooked lamb
salt
black pepper
flour
yolks of eggs
breadcrumbs

Mince the meat finely or put in an electric blender at high speed. Season rather highly and mix to a firm but not heavy consistency with some of the egg yolk and a little flour. Shape into small cakes. Egg and breadcrumb the cakes and fry in deep fat.

This recipe can also be used for left-over beef or ham.

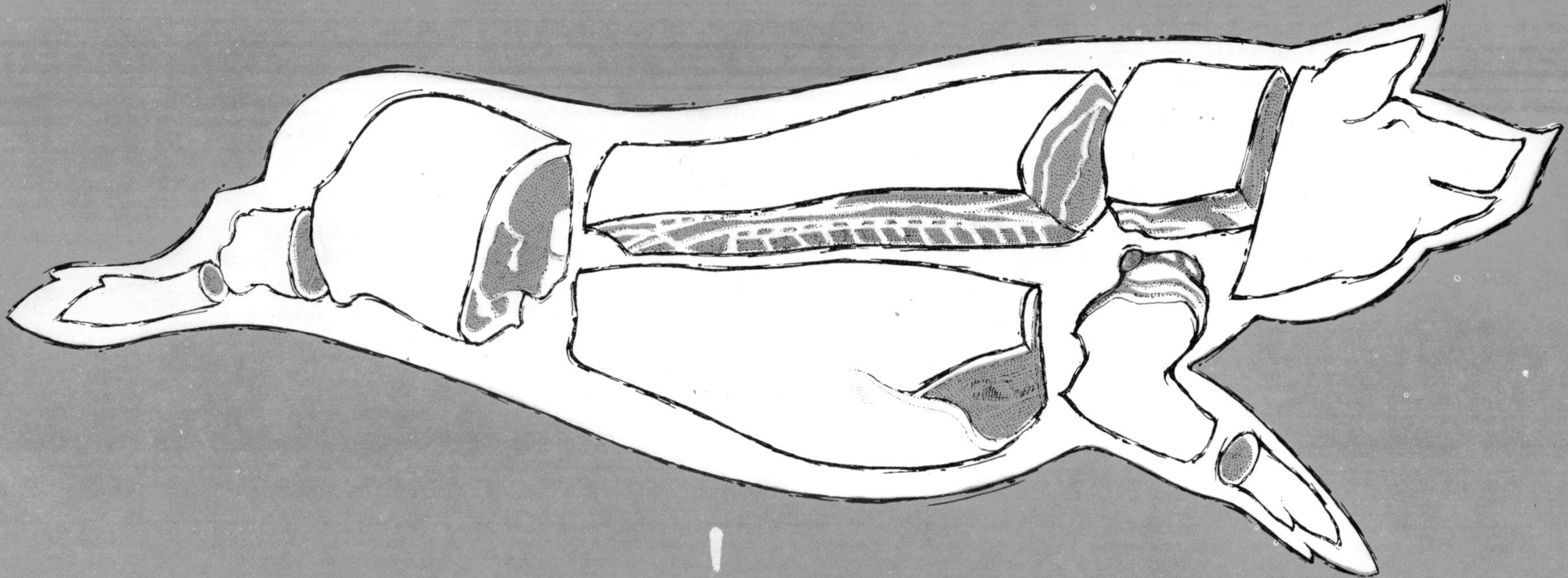

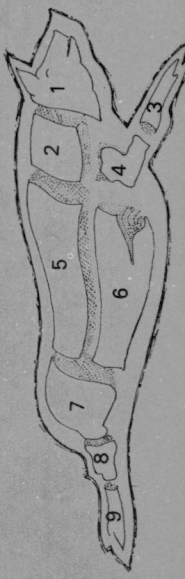

PIG

1 HEAD
2 NECK END
3 FORE END
4 FORE LOIN
5 BEST LOIN
6 BELLY
7 W LEG
8 K LEG
9 KNUCKLE

PORK

For many years pork was the Cinderella of the kitchen, and fifty years ago was never seen in my mother's kitchen, save very occasionally in winter as a roast leg of pork. Enormous joints of pickled pork, however, used to be consumed by the maid-servants. Kettner must have been thinking of something like this when he wrote in 1887 in his *Book of the Table*:

> Pork is so little to be seen at good tables, save in the form of ham and bacon, that it would seem to be a work of supererogation to refer to it. It is, however, eaten – indeed largely consumed – on the sly, and must have a word or two.

Among these words he gives the following piece of advice.

> Pork is scored to make the crackling, and is in the first instance put before the fire at a long distance, that it may be well heated through before the skin hardens. The reason of this is that pork takes more of the fire than any other meat, and there is danger of the outside being burnt before the interior is cooked.

It was at one time thought dangerous to eat pork in summer-time and, as in the case of oysters, the directive was an 'r' in the month for safety, but today owing to the progress of refrigeration we can eat it all the year round, and this has contributed in no small degree to its present popularity. The lean of pork should be pale pink, smooth and finely grained and the fat white and firm. It should have no smell. Pickled, or salt pork, is more indigestible than fresh and cannot be roasted. The brine in which it has been pickled necessitates its being soaked in cold water before use for varying lengths of time according to its saltiness.

Pork should never be undercooked, and, unlike beef, should be seasoned before cooking. The plain and heavy vegetables are the best to go with pork: boiled cabbage (especially savoy), Brussels sprouts and, in the European fashion, sauerkraut.

Chicory, braised celery and lettuce are also favourites, while the English usually plump for carrots, turnips (and turnip tops), carrots, French beans, tomatoes and of course boiled potatoes (roast potatoes make the whole dish too rich). In France one may sometimes come across redcurrant jelly with pork, and in America cranberry sauce, grilled apricots, stuffed baked apples and pickled peaches.

Cuts of Pork

Leg: roast leg of pork is one of Britain's traditional dishes. The skin is scored by the butcher so that there are ample supplies of crisp crackling. If the leg is to be boiled, it must first be pickled or salted. The leg is occasionally boned and rolled.

Fillet: slices taken from the upper part of the hind leg are usually grilled or fried. Fillet corresponds to the escalope of veal.

Tenderloin: this is the same cut as the fillet of beef and is cut from the carcass and sold separately. Small butchers very often do not recognize this joint, but it is very tender.

Loin: an excellent joint for roasting, whether on the bone (which is better) or boned and rolled. Sometimes divided into hind and fore loin, with half of the kidney left in each.

Chops: excellent fried or grilled, but trim well. Chump chops and loin chops (often with a piece of kidney in them) are cut from the hind loin, while chops with fat and lean interspersed come from the fore.

Short ribs: when the ribs of the loin shorten, these are sold separately. Their popularity has increased recently with the craze for barbecues, for which they are specially suitable.

Bladebone: very good when boned and stuffed and then roasted or braised.

Spare rib: one of the tenderest and most delicious joints of pork. Leave on the bone if possible, but it can be boned and rolled, braised or stewed. It can also be divided into rather awkward-shaped cutlets.

Shoulder (Hand): can be boned, rolled and roasted or braised, but is far better when pickled or salted and boiled in the same way as the leg.

Approximate equivalent cuts of Pork

ENGLISH	FRENCH	AMERICAN
Hind loin	*Pointe de filet*	Tenderloin
Middle loin	*Filet*	Loin
Best end of neck	*Carré*	Fore loin
Chop, cutlet	*Côte, côtelette*	Chop, cutlet
Shoulder	*Epaule*	Shoulder butt
Spare ribs	*Echine*	Spare ribs
Blade bone	*Palette*	Shoulder slice
Hand and spring	*Jambon de devant*	Picnic shoulder, pork hock
Belly	*Poitrine*	Bacon
Pig's trotter	*Pied*	Front foot
Head	*Tête* or *hure*	Head
Fat back pork	*Lard gras*	Fat back

ROAST PORK

In England, where the eating of the crackling is traditional, the skin should be scored in narrow strips about ¼ in. wide, and salt and pepper rubbed in. The surface is brushed with oil and the joint cooked in a moderate oven (380°F. or 195°C.) for a good 30-35 minutes per pound. If you are using a meat thermometer, when the pork is done it should register 185°F. (85°C.)

In the U.S.A. pork joints are sold without the skin. The oven thermometer for such joints should be slightly lower, but the cooking time is unchanged.

Normally the pork is roasted plainly and served with apple or sage and onion sauce, but in France herbs and crushed garlic are sometimes rubbed in, and cloves may be inserted in incisions so that their heads do not protrude.

More elaborately the joint can be rubbed, just before being put into the oven, with a mixture of caster sugar or honey, moist sugar and dry mustard, and basted with vinegar, dry white or red wine, cider, or orange, pineapple or tomato juice.

LOIN OF PORK WITH PRUNES

3 lb. loin of pork
1 lemon
6-8 prunes
cream

Rub the joint and do this thoroughly with half a lemon till there is no juice left. Parboil the prunes, stone, and cut them in quarters. Make close rows of holes in the loin with a skewer and stuff each with a piece of prune. Grease a baking tin and allow the loin to brown in a

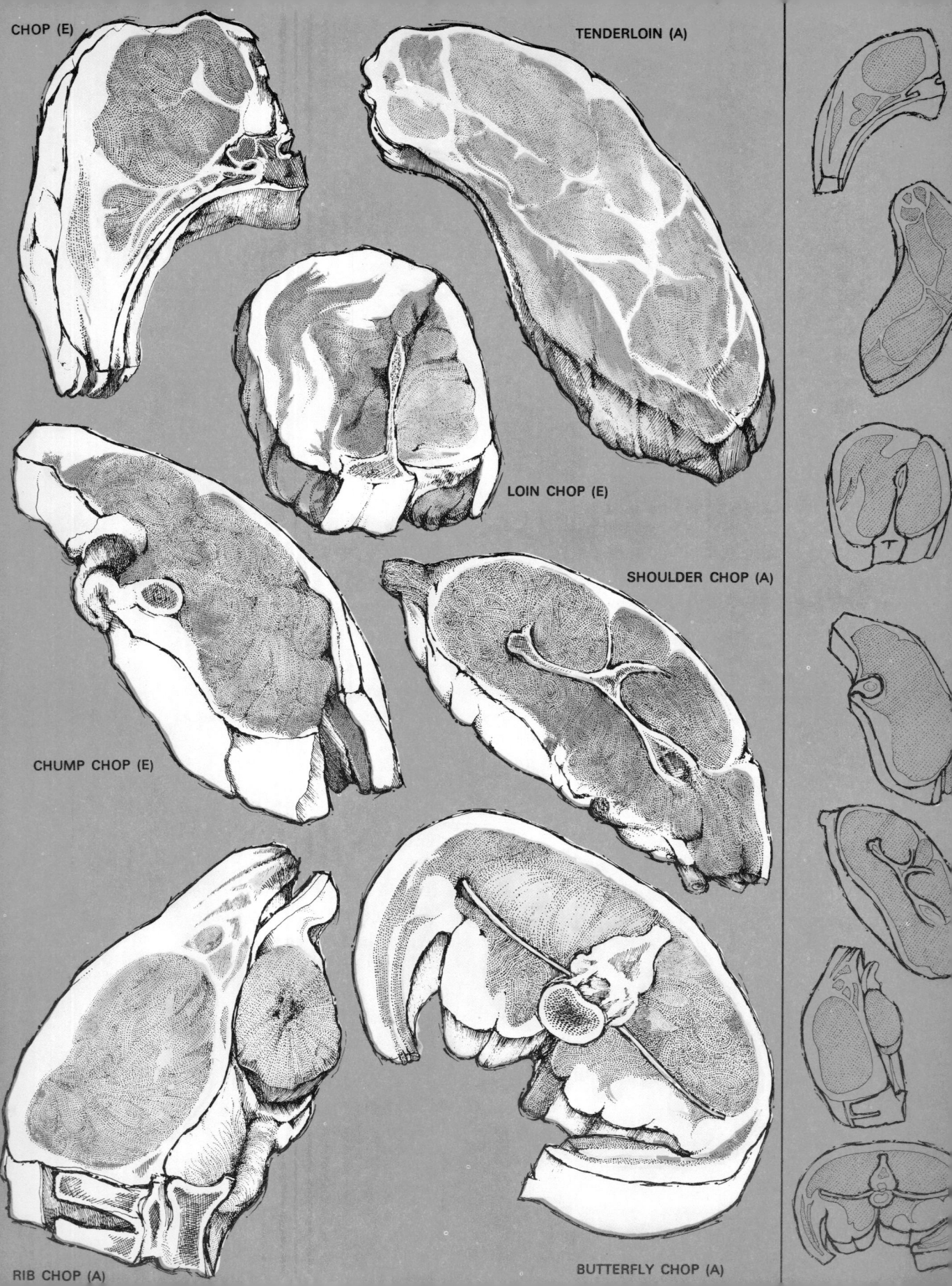

PORK

hot oven, then sprinkle it with salt and pour over it the hot liquid from the prunes' parboiling. Roast in the oven in the usual way, basting every 10 minutes. When it is done, make a thick gravy from the liquid in the tin, adding a little cream.

MOCK GOOSE
leg of pork
butter or pork dripping
breadcrumbs
powdered sage
onion
black pepper, salt
minced onion
sage and onion stuffing

Parboil a leg of pork and skin it. Then roast the joint in the usual way, basting it with butter or pork dripping. Make a savoury mixture of fine breadcrumbs, powdered sage, black pepper and salt, with a very little minced onion, and sprinkle this over the joint when it is nearly done, so as to brown and crisp it nicely. Garnish with forcemeat balls made of sage and onion stuffing, and serve with apple sauce.

PORK CHOPS AND CRANBERRIES (U.S.A.)
6 pork chops
salt
4 breakfastcupfuls cranberries
1 teaspoonful (1¼ teaspoonfuls) ground cloves
12 oz. (1½ cups) honey

Brown the chops quickly on each side in a heavy frying pan, then sprinkle them with salt and put 3 of them in a greased baking dish. Mix together the cranberries put through a sieve with the ground cloves and the clear honey. Spread half of this mixture on the chops in the dish, lay the other 3 chops on top, put the rest of the mixture on top again and bake with the lid on in a moderate oven for 1 hour.

PORK CHOPS WITH MUSTARD AND CREAM
4 pork chops
flour
1 teaspoonful (1¼ teaspoonfuls) dry mustard
1 teaspoonful (1¼ teaspoonfuls) vinegar
1 teacupful (1 cup) water
sour cream
salt

Rub the chops well with salt, grill them quickly on each side till browned, then sprinkle them with flour and transfer them to a baking tin. Mix together the dry mustard, vinegar and water, and when smooth, pour over the chops. Cook for 15 minutes in a hot oven, then pour over some sour cream seasoned with a dash of salt and bake for another 10 minutes, basting twice.

PORK CUTLETS AU GRATIN

pork cutlets
butter
onion
garlic
parsley
breadcrumbs
stock
lemon juice

Fry some pork cutlets (or, if preferred, some fillet of pork) in butter, and when browned on both sides, move to a baking tin and sprinkle with a mixture of salt, pepper, minced onion and garlic, chopped parsley and breadcrumbs. Now put the pan into a moderate oven, scatter a few more plain breadcrumbs over the meat and when these are browned, add $\frac{1}{4}$ pint ($\frac{1}{3}$ pint) stock and bake on till the meat is done. Some like to add a little lemon juice with the stock, which diminishes the richness of the pork.

ROAST PORK PÉRIGOURDINE

This recipe, given to me by Marcel Boulestin, provides one of the most delicious ways of serving cold pork that I know. It can, of course, also be served hot.

6 lb. leg or fillet of pork
salt, pepper
garlic

Skin and bone the pork and flatten it on a board. It should be well seasoned on both sides with lots of pepper and salt. Add 2 or 3 small pieces of garlic (this can be omitted, but it would be a mistake not to try it at least once, as the flavour it gives the meat is incomparable and the smell almost unnoticeable). Roll the meat and tie it well with string. Sprinkle again with salt and pepper and put it into a fireproof dish with $\frac{1}{2}$ tumblerful water. Cook in a very moderate oven for 2 hours, basting occasionally. Remove the skin and serve in the same dish, cutting thin slices. When served cold, spread on each slice a little of the fat and gravy produced during the cooking.

STUFFED PORK CHOPS (U.S.A.)

4 pork chops
savoury forcemeat or sausagemeat
flour
salt, pepper
lard
apples

Cut the thick chops through horizontally to the bone and stuff the pocket thus formed with the chosen stuffing. Press together and fasten with short wooden skewers, sprinkle with salt and pepper, dredge lightly with flour and brown each side quickly in a heavy frying pan. Then transfer them to a baking dish and bake them in a moderate oven for about 45 minutes.

Dressed Saddle of Mutton or Lamb and some of the ingredients for Roast Saddle of Mutton or Lamb

PORK   139

Put half a cored (but not peeled) small tart red apple, cut side down, on top of each chop when the dish goes into the oven.

ROAST PORK WITH VEGETABLES AND APPLE SAUCE

leg or loin of fresh pork
2 onions
2 carrots
1 turnip
1 stick celery
2 dozen button onions
mixed herbs
1 oz. (2 tablespoonfuls) butter
2-3 oz. (4-6 tablespoonfuls) dripping
gravy
salt, pepper
apple sauce:
1 lb. cooking apples
1 oz. (2 tablespoonfuls) butter
2 oz. ($\frac{1}{4}$ cup) sugar
1 quince, if desired

Slice up the onions, carrots, turnip and celery, and put them into the bottom of a baking tin. Sprinkle with salt and pepper and add the mixed herbs and 2-3 oz. of dripping. Lay the scored meat on this bed, and cook in a moderate oven for 30-40 minutes per pound, basting frequently. Half an hour before the meat is ready to serve, fry the peeled button onions in 1 oz. butter till browned. These are used as a garnish to the meat, and gravy made from the sediment in the baking dish is served in a sauceboat. Apple sauce is also served. To make this, peel, core and slice 1 lb. cooking apples, put them in a pan with 1 oz. butter and a very little water, and cook carefully and slowly till tender. Rub through a hair or nylon sieve and reheat, adding the sugar. A slice or two of ripe quince may be added to the apple and cooked with it.

PORK CUTLETS MARSEILLAISE

pork cutlets
salt, pepper
French mustard
butter
browned breadcrumbs
pickled gherkins
potatoes
mustard sauce (p. 206) or piquante sauce (p. 210)

Season the cutlets with salt and pepper and smear each with a little French mustard. Let them lie for a time in warm butter, turning once, and then grill them on the unsmeared side. Put them again in the butter and then coat them on both sides with browned breadcrumbs, put them on a grid in a baking tin. Bake in a moderate oven for about 10 minutes, then serve sprinkled with chopped pickled gherkins round a border of mashed potato, the centre of which is filled with crisply fried potatoes. Serve a mustard or piquante sauce with them.

Roast Saddle of Mutton or Lamb

CROWN ROAST OF LAMB

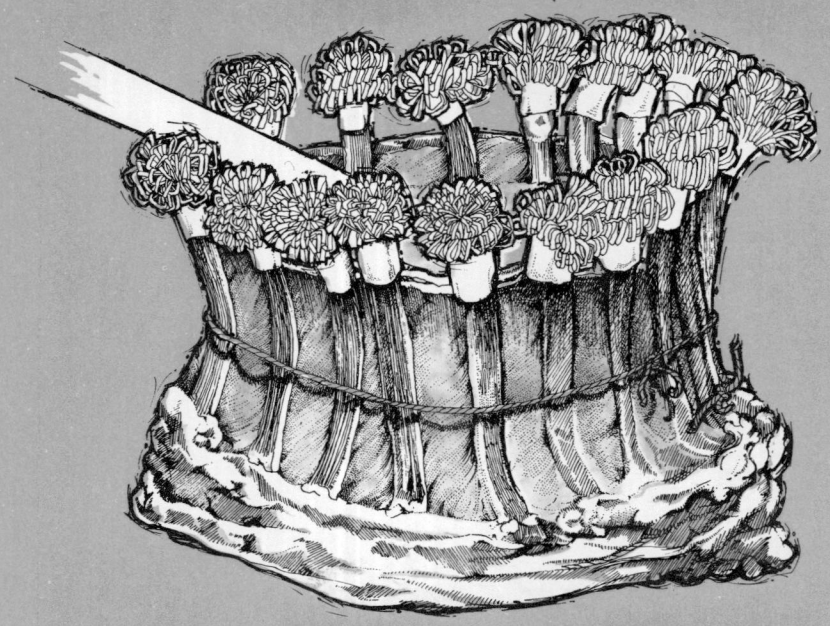

ROAST RIB OF PORK

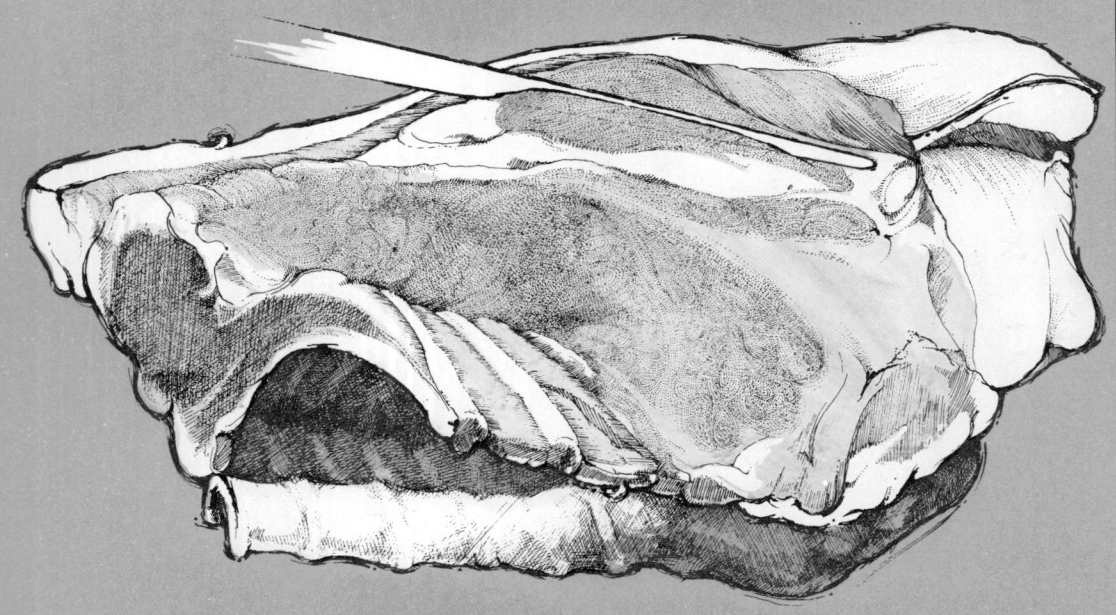
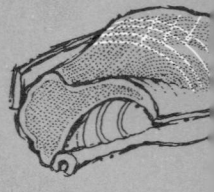

PORK

ROAST SUCKING PIG

The sucking pig should be cooked whole. However, if it is too big for the domestic oven, the butcher will cut it in halves after he has cleaned and prepared it for you. It can weigh from 8–15 lb. and should be cooked as soon as possible after it has been killed. It is usually stuffed with sage and onion stuffing and is accompanied by apple or prune sauce.

The sucking pig is well seasoned before it is stuffed and then brushed over with olive oil and sprinkled with salt. It is roasted for 35 minutes to the pound at a temperature of 355°F. (180°C.), and should be basted frequently. Fifteen minutes before it is ready, dredge it with flour, increase the heat a little, continuing to baste to obtain golden crackling. Serve with mashed potatoes and apple sauce to which you have added a few swollen currants.

A good alternative stuffing can be made from sausages and chestnuts or from a herb stuffing flavoured with a few drops of brandy in which the cooked chopped liver of the pig has been incorporated.

Instructions for carving sucking pig will be found on p. 21 and a drawing on p. 141.

PRUNE SAUCE

Boil 1 lb. soaked prunes in ½ pint (1¼ cups) water till they are soft, then add 1 tablespoonful moist sugar and 1 tablespoonful rum or brandy. Rub through a fine sieve, heat up and serve.

GRILLED AND FRIED PORK

Grilled pork should always be over rather than under done. The cooking times should be longer than those given for steaks (*see* p. 37).

PAN-FRIED PORK CHOPS

pork chops	The chops (1 to each serving) should be ¾–1 in. thick,
salt, pepper	sprinkled with salt and pepper and dusted lightly with
flour	flour. The heavy frying pan is greased as lightly as
fat	possible and the chops quickly browned on each side
apple	when it is very hot. Any fat is then poured off, the pan covered and the chops cooked slowly for about 25 minutes. Serve with thin slices of fried apple.

PORK CHOPS WITH APRICOT, ORANGE OR PINEAPPLE

See the entries for similar dishes under Lamb (p. 117).

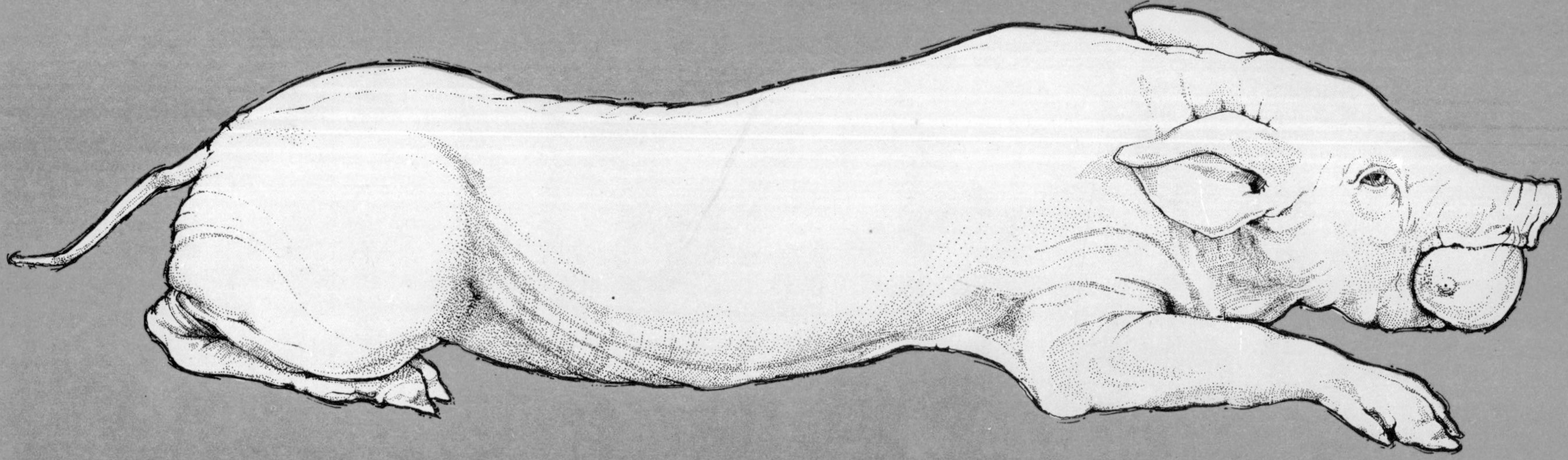

SUCKING PIG

PORK

PORK CHOPS A L'AUVERGNATE

pork chops
white cabbage
salt, pepper
milk
butter
sage
dry white wine
grated cheese

Cook some cabbage, then run the cold tap over it, drain it well and squeeze out as much of the moisture as possible, and chop it up roughly. Simmer for 30 minutes, seasoned with salt and pepper, in a little creamy milk. Meanwhile fry the pork chops, which should be cut thin, in a little butter, and when they are done remove them from the pan and add a good pinch of fresh chopped or diced sage and ½ glass dry white wine to the fat in it. Mix the cabbage with this and put a layer of it in a shallow fireproof dish. On this lay the chops and over them the rest of the cabbage. Now scatter grated cheese over the top, sprinkle this with a little melted butter and let the dish cook very gently at a low temperature in the oven for 30-45 minutes.

PORK CHOPS À LA MARÉCHALE

Grill the chops, allowing one to each serving, and just before serving them make a few gashes on each side and spread on them a mixture of butter, chopped parsley, salt and pepper. Serve an orange sauce with them.

PORK CHOP SANDWICHES (Germany)

2 pork chops
apples
prunes
butter
sugar
flour
egg
breadcrumbs
sauerkraut

Flatten the pork chops a little, and spread one with a layer of finely chopped apples and prunes first cooked till soft with butter and sugar. Put the other chop on top to make a sandwich, dredge on both sides with flour, brush with beaten egg and coat with breadcrumbs. Then fry slowly in butter till each side of the sandwich is cooked right through. Serve garnished with sauerkraut.

PORK CUTLETS WITH HORSERADISH

Grill the cutlets, plainly or coated with melted butter and breadcrumbs, and while they are cooking mix a little flour by degrees with some good stock, seasoning with salt and pepper to taste. When nicely bound and smooth, add grated horseradish to taste, cook for 4 minutes only, without allowing it to boil, and then take off the heat immediately. Arrange the cutlets on a dish, and pour the sauce over them.

PORK CUTLETS VILLAGEOISE

4 boned pork cutlets
½ oz. (1 tablespoonful) lard
1 clove garlic
3 dessertspoonfuls (1½ tablespoonfuls) olive oil
chopped parsley
French mustard
salt, pepper

Fry the cutlets in lard for 5-6 minutes on one side, then lower the heat for 15 minutes on the other. Now rub the dish in which they are to be served with a cut clove of garlic and add the olive oil, chopped parsley, French mustard and salt and pepper, and mix these together with a fork. When the cutlets are done, put them into the dish, turning them in the seasoning and keeping them hot. Drain off the fat from the pan, add 2-3 tablespoonfuls hot water, and stir to dissolve the congealed juices from the meat to serve as sauce.

PORK FILLET WITH RED PEPPERS

fillet of pork
butter
sweet red peppers
tomato sauce or purée
garlic

Fry some ¼ in. slices of pork fillet in a little butter till nearly done, then add some skinned sweet red peppers cut in thin strips. When meat and pepper are slightly browned, serve them with a tomato sauce or purée, flavoured with a little garlic.

STEWED, CASSEROLED, AND BRAISED PORK

BASQUE PORK FILLET (France)

3-4 lb. fillet of pork
lard
salt, pepper
milk

Brown the piece of pork in a little lard, seasoning it with salt and pepper. Then just cover it with warm milk, and simmer for 2-3 hours till tender. Serve with a sauce made from the milk.

BAKENOFF (Alsace)

1 lb. pork
1 lb. mutton
2 lb. potatoes
1 lb. onions
salt, pepper
bay leaf
4 fl. oz. (½ cup) stock
4 fl. oz. (½ cup) dry white wine

Put into a large deep greased earthenware dish a layer of thinly sliced potatoes and on them equal parts of fresh pork and mutton cut up as if for a stew. Cover these with a layer of chopped onions and season with salt and pepper. Finish with another layer of potato, embed a bay leaf in the middle and pour in a breakfast-cupful of half stock half dry white wine. Put on the lid and start off cooking on the top of the stove till the liquid just boils, then transfer the dish, still covered, to a moderate oven for a couple of hours.

CARCASSONNE CASSOULET (France)
One of the most famous of French farmhouse dishes.

1 lb. small haricot beans
1 lb. sparerib pork
5-6 oz. salt pork or bacon in a piece
1 onion
1 carrot
bouquet garni
1-2 cloves garlic
1 lb. breast or leg of lamb
½ lb. garlic sausages
1 partridge ⎫
1 small duck ⎬ **optional**
preserved goose ⎭
breadcrumbs

Soak the beans overnight in cold water. Remove the skin from the pork, salt pork or bacon. If these have been bought without skin and rind, try to buy at least ½ lb. separately, as it is an essential part of a *cassoulet*. Cut the rind into small cubes and put them in a pan together with the beans, onion, carrot, bouquet garni, garlic. Add the salt pork or bacon. Cover with water and boil for about 1 hour, topping up the water as necessary.

Meantime roast the pork and the lamb. The sausages may be either roasted for 20 minutes with the meat or boiled with the beans. If one or more of the birds are included, they should be partly roasted and then jointed.

When the beans are nearly cooked, drain them and put aside the liquid. Cut the lamb, pork, salt pork and the birds into small pieces. Put half the beans and rind in a deep casserole, cover with the meats and cover them in turn with the rest of the beans. Add a cupful of the bean liquid. Spread a layer of breadcrumbs on top and then cook in a very slow oven for 1½ hours. If the *cassoulet* dries out during cooking, add some more liquid.

MOCK GEESE

12 slices lean raw pork
1 dessertspoonful (½ tablespoonful) salt
equal quantity of white pepper and ground ginger
3 small apples
6 prunes
butter
stock

Flatten 12 thin slices of lean raw pork and sprinkle them with the mixture of salt, white pepper and ground ginger. Now put on each a quarter of an apple and half a parboiled prune, roll up each slice and tie firmly. Brown the little rolls all over in butter, then add enough stock to come half-way up their sides and stew gently for 2-2½ hours or till they are quite tender, turning them over and basting them now and then. Serve masked with a gravy made from the stock and the liquid in which they cooked.

DEVILLED PORK FILLET (U.S.A.)

1 lb. pork fillet
salt, pepper
butter
3 teaspoonfuls (3¾ teaspoonfuls) chilli sauce
3 teaspoonfuls (3¾ teaspoonfuls) walnut ketchup
Worcester sauce
mustard
a little minced onion, salt and paprika
2½ fl. oz. (⅓ cup) water

Cut the fillet into 6 slices, flatten them and sprinkle with salt and pepper. Fry them in butter till browned and almost done, then put them into a baking tin. To the fat in the frying pan add the chilli sauce (American style), walnut ketchup, Worcester sauce, mustard, minced onion, salt and paprika. Bring the water to the boil and add to the fat mixture. Stir well together over the heat, pour this sauce over the meat and bake in a moderate oven for 15 minutes.

PORK CHOPS (Mexico)

4 pork chops
1 large onion
4 tablespoonfuls (5 tablespoonfuls) rice
1 cup (1¼ cups) tomatoes
salt, pepper

Arrange the chops closely together in a casserole or stewpan and add a single slice of a large onion. Now put a level tablespoonful of uncooked rice on top of each chop, and pour over them stewed or tinned tomatoes after seasoning with salt and pepper. Cover and bake in a moderate oven or 1¼–1½ hours.

PORK CURRY

2 lb. lean pork
1 large onion
1 clove garlic
1 cooking apple
1 oz. (2 tablespoonfuls) butter
1 tablespoonful (1¼ tablespoonfuls) curry powder
flour
1 pint (1¼ pints) water
salt
juice of 1 lemon

Cut up the pork into small cubes half the size of walnuts, then put the onion, cut in small dice, into a stewpan with the garlic and a sliced, peeled and cored cooking apple. Stir with 1 oz. butter over a moderate heat till lightly browned, then stir in a good tablespoonful of mild curry powder mixed with half as much flour, and mix well. Now add the water, let it just boil up and put in the pork, stirring round to mix well with the curry, and then put the pan on a slow heat or in a very slow oven for 1½ hours. When done, add the juice of a lemon and a little salt and serve, with plain boiled or steamed rice.

PORK CHOPS WITH CAPERS (Italy)

6 pork chops
butter
salt, pepper
1 tablespoonful (1¼ tablespoonfuls) each of capers and pine kernels
¼ pint (⅓ pint) dry white wine
½ pint (1¼ cups) stock

Brown the chops on both sides in butter and put them into a shallow fireproof dish. Season them with salt and pepper and sprinkle them with the capers and pine kernels. Moisten with dry white wine and cook them in a brisk oven so that the wine reduces. Then add the stock and cook on till the chops are done.

PORK CUTLETS À L'ÉTUVÉ

pork cutlets
olive oil
butter
salt
poivrade sauce (p. 210)

Get the cutlets rather fat and a good inch thick, brush them over with olive oil on both sides and leave them for a few hours in a cool place. Then melt ½ oz. clarified butter in a stewpan, and when it is hot, but not yet beginning to colour, put in the cutlets and close the pan tightly. After 10 minutes cooking, turn the cutlets over, sprinkle the cooked side with salt, cover and cook for 10 minutes and salt the newly-cooked side. Now cook, still with the lid on, for 25 minutes or so according to thickness, and when they are quite done, serve coated with a *poivrade* sauce.

PORK CUTLETS WITH TURNIPS

pork cutlets
butter
small turnips
salt, pepper
caster sugar

Brown the cutlets in a little butter in a frying pan, then take them out and in the same pan brown some small turnips cut in halves. Put the cutlets back into the pan with the turnips on top and add enough water just to cover them. Boil for 10 minutes and then simmer for 45 minutes. The browning of the turnips can be hastened – and improved – by sprinkling them very lightly with caster sugar.

PORK FILLET WITH CREAM

Cut a pork fillet across into 2 in. slices, flatten them well, sprinkle with flour seasoned with salt and pepper, and fry in butter till browned on both sides. Now transfer them to a baking dish. Pour 1 teacupful single cream into the fat in the frying pan, mix together well and bring to the boil, pouring it immediately over the meat. Then put the lid on and simmer, or bake in a moderate oven for 30 minutes or so till the pork is quite tender. French beans are excellent with this.

PORK AND KIDNEY STEW

6 small pork chops	Peel and slice the potatoes and onions, and put them
2 pigs' kidneys	in layers in a stewpan with the chops and 2 skinned and
1½ lb. potatoes	sliced pigs' kidneys. Sprinkle each layer with a little
1 lb. onions	chopped apple and powdered sage and season with
chopped apples	salt and pepper and a few drops of tomato sauce.
sage	Finish with a layer of the potatoes, pour over the water,
salt, pepper	cover closely and cook slowly for 2–3 hours.
tomato sauce	
8 fl. oz. (1 cup) water	

PORK STEWED IN RED WINE (Italy)

3-4 lb. loin of pork	Season the pork with salt and pepper and brown all
salt, pepper	over in olive oil, adding several cloves of garlic and a
olive oil	little chopped parsley. Now moisten with the Chianti,
garlic	put on the lid and simmer in the oven till the meat is
parsley	tender and the wine reduced by half. Make a gravy
½ flask red Chianti	with the cooking liquor.

PORK WITH PINEAPPLE

lean pork	Put a 1½ in. slice of pork into a lightly-buttered cas-
flour	serole and rub the top with flour, salt and pepper. Cut
salt, pepper	3 slices of pineapple in halves and arrange them on the
pineapple	meat. Cover the casserole and cook for about 1½ hours
	in a moderate oven, by which time the pork should be
	tender.

PORK SPARE RIBS WITH SAUERKRAUT

3 lb. pork spare ribs	Put the spare ribs, cut in pieces, into a large stewpan,
salt	add ½ level teaspoonful salt, cover with boiling water
4 cups (5 cups)	and simmer with the lid on for 30 minutes. Then add
sauerkraut	the drained sauerkraut, bring to the boil and cook on,
	uncovered this time, for another 30 minutes.

BOILED PORK

BOILED PORK WITH PEASE PUDDING

The joint generally chosen for this form of cooking is the leg or hand, and it must invariably be pickled; it is accompanied by pease pudding. This is a classic recipe for boiled pork.

leg or hand of pickled pork
1 onion
1 carrot
½ turnip
1 stick celery
12 peppercorns
1 cabbage
6 parsnips (optional)
pease pudding:
2 pints (5 cups) split peas
1 oz. (2 tablespoonfuls) butter
salt, pepper
2 egg yolks

Put the pork into a pan and cover it with warm water (unless it is very salt, in which case use cold). Bring to the boil, skim well, boil for 10 minutes and add the thickly sliced onion, carrot, turnip and celery. Add the peppercorns and simmer gently for 25–30 minutes per pound and 30 minutes over. Boil the parsnips and cabbage separately and when they are done cut the cabbage into quarters. The old English fashion was to press the cabbage well, season it with pepper and serve it cut into 2 in. squares, and although this has too often been derided, it is by no means to be despised, especially when served with a rich dish.

Serve with pease pudding. To make this soak the split peas for 12 hours and then tie them in a cloth and boil in the pan with the pork for about 1½ hours. Rub them through a fine sieve, dry a little over the heat till the right thickness is obtained, and then mix in the butter, salt and pepper. To make the pudding more interesting, mix in the yolks of eggs as well, tie up again in the cloth and put back with the pork for another 40 minutes. If preferred, the mixture can be turned into a buttered mould or basin and either steamed or baked for 45 minutes.

PICKLED SALT PORK AND CABBAGE (Denmark)

white cabbage
pickled pork
peppercorns

Slice some white cabbage finely, run cold water over it and put it into a thick-bottomed stewpan. Lay slices of slightly salted pork over this, and then fill up the pan with more cabbage. Do not add any water; the drops clinging to the shreds of cabbage will provide sufficient moistening. Sprinkle a few peppercorns among the cabbage and simmer with the lid tightly on for 3 hours or more.

PORK CHEESE

pickled hock of pork
salt, pepper
chopped fresh sage
water

Soak a hock of pickled or salt pork all night in cold water, then put it into a pan with enough cold water just to cover it. Boil till the meat leaves the bone, then take out the bones and put them back into the cooking liquor to simmer on. Season the meat with salt and pepper, adding a little chopped fresh sage if you like, and cut it up finely. Now strain the cooking liquor, reduced to $\frac{1}{2}$ pint ($1\frac{1}{4}$ cups), on to the meat in a basin, mix well together, correct the seasoning and turn out when cold. Serve with a green salad and spring onions.

BOILED PORK WIENERWALD (Austria)

leg of pork
2 carrots
1 large onion
2 or 3 cloves
1 small turnip
bouquet garni
8 peppercorns
salt
tomato sauce:
2 lb. tomatoes
$\frac{3}{4}$ pint (2 cups) dry white wine

Put the pork into a pan of warm water, bring to the boil and skim. Then add the carrots (sliced lengthways), the onion (stuck with cloves), turnip, bouquet garni, peppercorns and salt. Bring to the boil again and cook gently, allowing 30 minutes to the pound. Serve carved in thin slices masked with tomato sauce and garnished with macaroni or dumplings. To make the tomato sauce boil 2 lb. tomatoes in $\frac{3}{4}$ pint (2 cups) dry white wine till reduced to a pulp, then rub them through a fine sieve and reduce the ensuing purée to the proper consistency by rapid boiling.

PIES OR PUDDINGS

PORK AND ONION PUDDING

2 lb. fresh pork
suet crust pastry (p. 66)
$1\frac{1}{2}$ lb. onions
salt, pepper
sage (optional)
$\frac{1}{4}$ pint ($\frac{1}{3}$ pint) water

Line a greased pudding basin with suet crust; cut up the pork into suitable pieces and chop the onions roughly. Put these in alternate layers in the pudding, seasoning each layer with salt and pepper and perhaps a little dried sage if desired. Pour $\frac{1}{4}$ pint ($\frac{1}{3}$ pint) water in, put on the top crust and steam for 4–5 hours.

PORK CHOP PIE

3 rashers fat pickled pork or green bacon
4 potatoes
2 onions
5 fresh pork chops
salt, pepper
1 pint (1¼ pints) water
breadcrumbs

Put the pork or bacon in the bottom of a deep fireproof dish, and then add alternate layers of sliced raw potatoes, medium-sized onions and thinnish fresh pork chops, seasoning each layer with salt and pepper and making the last one of chops. Add 1 pint of water, sprinkle the top with ½ teacupful breadcrumbs and dot these over with little pieces of fat taken off the chops when trimming them. Bake, covered, for 1½ hours in a moderate oven, then take off the lid and bake on for 30 minutes longer till the crumbs are golden brown.

TOURTE LORRAINE (France)

lean raw pork
lean raw veal
onion
garlic
parsley
peppercorns
salt
cloves
½ glass dry white wine
shortcrust pastry (p. 65)
2 or 3 eggs
cream

Cut some pork and veal into thin strips, and let these lie for 24 hours in a marinade of onion, garlic, parsley, peppercorns, salt, cloves and ½ glass dry white wine, turning them every now and then. When you are ready, make some of your best shortcrust pastry and line a dish or flan case with it. In this lay your drained and well-wiped strips of meat, and put a lid on the pie, making a hole in the top. Bake it for 25 minutes in a hot oven, then take it out and pour into the hole through a little funnel 2 or 3 eggs beaten well with a breakfastcupful of slightly salted cream. Bake for 10 minutes longer, and the pie is ready to be eaten.

RAISED PORK PIE

1½ lb. lean fresh pork
pork bones
small onion
1 lb. (4 cups) plain flour
6 oz. (¾ cup) lard
¼ pint (⅓ pint) water
salt, pepper
cayenne pepper
yolk of egg

Cover the bones with cold water, add the onion and some more salt and pepper and simmer for at least 3 hours so that the stock will jellify when cold. Cut the meat into dice and season it well with salt, pepper and cayenne pepper. Make a hot water paste by putting the flour into a basin with a good pinch of salt; in a separate pan boil the lard and water together, then add it to the flour, stirring it thoroughly till cool enough to be kneaded. The art of raising a pie crust can only be learned by experience, but meanwhile the tyro may try placing a small jar in the middle of the paste and moulding the paste over it. This is then the receptacle in which the pie is cooked, and when it is filled with the meat, a few spoonfuls of the gelatinous stock are poured in, the top put on and the pie baked in a moderate oven for at least 2 hours. When it is three-quarters cooked, it may be gilded with yolk of egg.

SAUSAGES

Few can compete with the exciting savoury mixtures in which European *charcutiers* excel; British sausages have always been simple but excellent; although their standard declined after two world wars they are showing signs of improvement today on both sides of the Atlantic. For a really good sausage dish make your own sausagemeat.

Allow 4–6 oz. sausagement or 3–4 sausages for each serving.

SAUSAGEMEAT

Mix together $3\frac{3}{4}$ lb. minced lean pork and $\frac{1}{4}$ lb. minced fat pork. Stir in 2 level tablespoonfuls salt, 3 level teaspoonfuls black pepper and 3 level dessertspoonfuls powdered sage. Keep in a refrigerator for at least 12 hours before using.

BLACK PUDDINGS

These pleasant sausages are generally only obtainable commercially, and are not particularly exciting in flavour, but if anyone has the desire (or the facilities) to make one's own, this Irish recipe shows the way.

2 pints ($2\frac{1}{2}$ pints) pig's blood
1 teaspoonful salt
$\frac{1}{2}$ pint ($1\frac{1}{4}$ cups) milk
$1\frac{1}{4}$ lb. (3 cups) lard
$\frac{1}{2}$ lb. onions
$1\frac{1}{2}$–2 lb. (4–$5\frac{1}{3}$ cups) oatmeal
mixed spices

Take the blood when the pig is killed and stir it till it is almost cold. Then add salt, stirring till this dissolves. Strain the blood, adding the milk. Chop up the leaf lard, chop and parboil the onions, and mix them with toasted coarse oatmeal. Stir all this into the blood, seasoning to taste with mixed spices. Put the sausage-meat into skins, prick them all over with a darning-needle and boil for 30 minutes, pricking again after the first 5 minutes. Hang them up in a cool dry place; they are then grilled or fried when wanted.

In 1850, Soyer wrote about this product of the pig: 'I should recommend those who are fond of black puddings (for breakfast) to partake of no other beverage than tea

PORK

or coffee, as cocoa or chocolate would be a clog to the stomach. In France they partake of white wine for breakfast, which accounts for the very great consumption of black pudding. Now really this is a very favourite dish with epicures, but I never recommend it to a delicate stomach'.

BOILED SAUSAGES

Prick the sausages well, put them into a frying pan of hot water and bring gently to the boil. Let them simmer very gently indeed for 40–45 minutes; slowness of cooking is the secret of success here.

EPPING SAUSAGES (England)

1 lb. young pork	Put the pork through a mincing machine and then
2 sage leaves	pound it in a mortar. Spread the meat out on a board.
grated lemon rind	Scatter the finely shredded sage leaves over it and add
thyme	a little grated lemon rind with some thyme, savory and
marjoram	finely chopped marjoram. Sprinkle with a little pepper
savory	and grated nutmeg and some salt. Now mince the suet
salt, pepper	finely and scatter it on top, mix all well together and
grated nutmeg	press into a basin till wanted. Then bind with a little
1 lb. (2 cups) beef suet	egg and make into sausages. Grill or fry them.
1 egg	

OXFORD SAUSAGES (England)

1 lb. young pork	Chop very finely or put through the mincing machine
1 lb. veal	the pork, lean veal and suet. Add the breadcrumbs,
1 lb. (2 cups) beef suet	the grated rind of half a lemon, grated nutmeg, sage
8 oz. (2⅔ cups) bread-	leaves, finely minced with a little thyme, savory and
crumbs	marjoram, pepper and salt. Mix all well together and
rind of ½ lemon	press down in a basin till wanted. Then – and only
1 nutmeg	then – roll with floured hands into sausage shapes. It is
6 sage leaves	better, however, to chop the veal rather than mince it.
thyme	
savory, marjoram	
pepper and salt	

SAUSAGES WITH BANANAS

Follow the recipe for sausages with apples (*see* p. 154) but use bananas sliced lengthways instead of apples and dispense with the sage.

SAUSAGES WITH APPLES

sausages
cooking apples
milk
flour
powdered sage
  (optional)

Fry the sausages and keep them hot, while in the same fat you fry some rings of cooking apples, cored but not peeled and dipped first in a little milk and then in flour. Serve the sausages in a heap with the overlapping rings of apple round them. The apple may be sprinkled at the last moment with a very little powdered sage.

SAUSAGES WITH CABBAGE

sausages
cabbage
pickled pork
bouquet garni
butter
pepper
grated nutmeg
beef stock
juniper berries
  (optional)

Cut a cabbage into fairly small pieces and half-cook them in the liquor in which you have previously boiled a piece of pickled pork with a bouquet garni. At the same time grill some sausages and put half the drained and chopped cabbage mixed with a little butter and fat from the grilled sausages, pepper and grated nutmeg, into a fireproof dish. Lay the sausages on top and cover them with the rest of the chopped cabbage. Pour over this some good beef stock, put on the lid and bake in a moderate oven for 30 minutes. See that the cabbage is well drained again before serving: this dish must on no account be watery.

Any meat stock will do, though beef seems to give the most satisfactory depth of flavour. Juniper berries can be added to this dish.

SAUSAGES WITH PINEAPPLE

Grill the sausages and serve them with pineapple rings drained, dried and lightly floured and fried a delicate brown in a little butter.

SAUSAGES WITH WHITE WINE

sausages
white wine
butter
flour
stock
egg

Use the thinner type of sausages for this and first blanch them for a moment or two in boiling water. Then prick lightly and fry them, straining off the fat. For every 12 sausages pour into the frying pan a glass of dry white wine. Let this reduce slowly while, in another saucepan, you make a sauce with butter, flour and good stock. Add the white wine from the pan, bind with an egg yolk and pour it over the sausages.

Dressed Best End of Neck of Lamb

SAUSAGES IN BEER

sausages
butter
1 bay leaf
peppercorns
salt
1 pint (1¼ pints) ale
1 tablespoonful (1¼ tablespoonfuls) potato flour
mashed potatoes

Blanch the sausages for a minute by pouring boiling water over them, then drain and dry them and brown all over in butter with a bay leaf, a few peppercorns and a little salt. Add half the ale, bring quickly to the boil and boil for a few minutes to reduce it a little. Then add the rest of the ale, enough to cover the sausages, and simmer them in it for 15 minutes. Thicken the strained sauce with the potato flour, pour this over the sausages in a border of mashed potato and serve.

SAUSAGE HOTPOT

1 lb. sausages
2 onions
potato
1 cooking apple
2 tomatoes

Brown the sausages and sliced onions in lard or other suitable fat, and fill a hotpot with alternate layers of sausages, onions and thinly sliced potatoes till the pot is nearly full. On the last layer of potatoes lay a peeled, cored and sliced cooking apple and on that 2 tomatoes in halves, cut side uppermost. Add no liquid, but put on the lid and bake in a slow oven for about 1 hour.

SAUSAGE ROLLS

sausages
puff pastry

Skin the sausages and wrap them in thin puff pastry, moistening the join and ends to encase the meat properly. Bake in a hot oven for 20 minutes or so.

SAUSAGE TOAD-IN-THE-HOLE

sausages
Yorkshire pudding batter (p. 27)
dripping or lard

Make a Yorkshire pudding batter. Heat some dripping or lard in a shallow baking dish, pour in enough batter just to cover the bottom, let this barely set in the oven and use it as a bed on which to set your sausages. Pour the rest of the batter over them and bake for about 1 hour in a moderate oven. Some people like to mix finely chopped or dried mixed herbs with the uncooked batter.

Crown Roast of Lamb

SKINLESS SAUSAGES (France)

pork
garlic
thyme
marjoram
basil
rosemary
breadcrumbs
egg
salt, pepper

Mince equal parts of lean and fat pork, putting them through the machine with a little garlic to taste, a sprig of thyme, marjoram, basil and rosemary. Season with salt and pepper and mix with sufficient breadcrumbs to give the mixture the proper consistency when bound with beaten egg. Form into small sausages on a floured board, and fry, grill or poach them in a little water.

SCOTCH EGGS

eggs
sausagemeat
breadcrumbs
fat for frying
parsley

Boil some eggs hard, shell them when cold and roll lightly in flour. Now wrap up each in a thin coating of raw sausagemeat, egg-and-breadcrumb them and fry them golden brown in deep fat or oil for about 10 minutes. Serve cut in halves lengthways.

LEFT-OVERS

FORT LINCOLN (U.S.A.)

1 lb. (2 cups) cold pork
3 oz. (6 tablespoonfuls) pork fat
2 tablespoonfuls (2½ tablespoonfuls) flour
½ pint (1¼ cups) milk
salt, pepper

Heat the pork (or salt pork) fat and add the flour and milk to make a sauce. Season with salt and pepper and add the sliced or dried cooked pork. Heat through and serve in a border of mashed potato. A dish of turnips is suggested with this.

PORK CAKE

1 lb. cooked pork
shortcrust pastry (p. 65)
3 small onions
1 large cooking apple
salt, pepper
1 teaspoonful (1¼ teaspoonfuls) caster sugar

Grease and line a baking dish with shortcrust pastry and spread over it the cooked pork cut in small pieces. Cover these with the parboiled onions, finely chopped, and then cover again with a peeled and cored large cooking apple cut in thin slices. Season well with salt and pepper throughout and sprinkle over it 1 teaspoonful caster sugar. Cover with a thin pastry top and bake in a hot oven for 45 minutes. Serve hot or cold.

HAM AND BACON

BACON

Bacon is made by curing the whole sides of specially bred pigs in dry salt or salt dissolved in water. After preserving, the bacon is matured for about three weeks when it will be ready for sale in a pale state usually referred to as 'green' bacon and will be much milder than the kinds generally eaten in England and America. For a smoky flavour, the bacon is simply hung for a couple of days above smouldering sawdust.

The quality of bacon varies according to breed, age, the feeding of the pig and the way in which it has been cured. It also varies according to the cut which is being used. When bought it should be an appetizing pink colour with the fat a clear white. Bacon should be stored in a cool place and should keep for 10–12 days in winter. In summer it will not last more than 4–5 days in the larder but it will, of course, last longer in a domestic refrigerator if kept well wrapped. Vacuum packed bacon will keep up to about 10 days. It is always marked with the latest dates by which it is wise to use the packet. It should on no account be kept in a deep freeze as the drying action of freezing is intensified by salt and the meat becomes dehydrated and hard.

English cuts of bacon are given below. Scottish bacon, of which Ayrshire bacon is perhaps the best known, is cut differently. The most obvious difference is that Scottish bacon is always sold without the rind, this being left on solely in the case of boiling joints. Ayrshire bacon is rolled and sliced.

Canadian bacon is cut from the eye of the loin and is in consequence very lean.

English cuts of Bacon

Fore hock: whole or split in three (butt, small hock and fore slipper) for boiling, or boned and rolled. Inexpensive.

Top streaky: economical when cut thinly into rashers for frying or grilling. The whole cut, weighing about 1¼ lb., can be boned and boiled.

Prime streaky: the best cut of streaky bacon. Fry or grill in rashers, or boil in one piece.

Thin streaky: best for those who prefer their fried or grilled rashers crisp.

Flank: economical for boiling or frying. A good cut for liver and bacon.

Long back: very lean. Should be sliced thinly and fried gently or grilled quickly for best results.

Oyster: like long back but slightly fatter and used in the same way. If baked makes a nice small joint (1½ lb.) for two.

Short back: rivals prime streaky for frying or grilling. The setting No. 6 or 7 on the bacon machine is recommended.

Back and ribs: similar to short back but leaner. Streaky towards the end of the rasher. Grill.

Top back: a good lean cut for boiling or braising in one piece, or can be cut into thin rashers and grilled.

Prime collar: boil whole (6 lb.) or in smaller pieces, or cut into rashers and fry.

End of collar: small 2 lb. joint for boiling or braising. Skin and press lightly after cooking. Inexpensive.

Bacon chops: ¼–½ in. thick slices taken from the short back cut.

Bacon joints

Gammon: gammon of bacon, though almost precisely the same cut of bacon as ham, lacks the latter's delicacy of flavour owing to the method of curing. It can be used in the kitchen in the same way as ham, and in all the recipes given for ham. For boiling gammon (*see* p. 162). The gammon can be divided in the following way, in which the joints are perhaps more suitable for one treatment rather than another:

HAM AND BACON

Gammon slipper: provides a small family joint which normally appears as the traditional boiled bacon, whether cooked with beans or not, or served hot or cold. It may also be cut into rashers for frying or grilling. Gammon rashers are usually about ¾ in. thick.

Corner of gammon and **middle gammon**: the best joints for boiling, with a preponderance of lean, but by no means lacking in fat. They can also be cut into thick rashers specially for grilling and these are particularly succulent when served accompanied by green peas or a purée of spinach. Instructions for carving corner of gammon will be found on p. 21 and a drawing on p. 163.

Gammon hock: best when it is first parboiled and then baked.

Gammon steaks: they are cut right across the leg, and should be about 1 in. thick, weighing about 1½ lb. each. Soak them in cold water for about 1 hour, then dry and cut off the skin. The fat should then be nicked round the edge of the whole steak to stop it curling up when it is grilled; the centre bone should be taken out and the steak brushed over with melted butter before being placed under the grill.

Cooking Bacon joints

ROASTED BACON
(Best cuts: collar, gammon, forehock, rolled shoulder, and thick streaky).

Soak for 24 hours or overnight, then put into fresh water and bring to the boil. Simmer gently for half the cooking time given for boiling, then take the joint out, carefully remove the skin and put it into a roasting tin. If it is very lean, dot with bacon fat and roast for the rest of the cooking time, basting frequently. The oven temperature for this second half of the cooking should be 350 °F. (175 °C.), increasing for the last 15 minutes to 425 °F. (220 °C.) so that the fat becomes a beautiful golden brown.

BAKED BACON
(Best cuts: whole gammon, gammon hock, middle and corner gammon, fore hock, rolled shoulder and collar)
Calculate the cooking time as for boiling, simmer the joint for half this time, then wrap it in kitchen foil and bake it in the oven at 350 °F. (175 °C.) till 30 minutes before the end of the given time. Take it from the foil, and remove the skin neatly and carefully. Score the fat in squares or diamonds and stud each square with a spice

clove. Cover the surface with brown sugar, put into the oven at 425°F. (220°C.) till the top is golden brown.

BOILED BACON
(Best cuts: collar, hock and gammon)
Soak the piece of bacon in cold water overnight, then put it into a saucepan with fresh water to cover and gradually bring this to the boil, removing any scum that may rise. Simmer gently till the bacon is cooked, then take it from the water, strip off the skin and sprinkle with browned breadcrumbs. Cooking time should be 20–25 minutes to the pound after boiling point is reached for joints below 10 lb. in weight.

BOILED GAMMON
For boiling, a whole gammon should first be soaked overnight, and after this it should be well scraped and any rusty parts cut off. In the same way as cooking ham (*see* 168), it should then be simmered with black peppercorns and a bay leaf, and when it is done, left for a couple of hours in the water in which it was cooked, when the skin can be removed and any other procedure followed. If you like, the cut end may be rubbed over with brown sugar before boiling, but to my mind this does not make a really appreciable difference to the finished article, especially if it is to be subjected to further culinary treatment. If, however, it is to be served cold, it should not be cut before 24 hours have elapsed.

If a whole gammon is being cooked to eat cold, the cooking time should be 15–20 minutes to the pound and 15 minutes over, and the joint should be allowed to get cold in the water in which it was cooked, before any breadcrumb covering is sprinkled on.

BRAISED BACON
(Best cuts: collar, fore hock and gammon)

1 oz. (2 tablespoonfuls) bacon fat
onion
carrot
turnip
leek
stock
bouquet garni

Proceed as for boiling but for only half the time given. Slice the vegetables and brown them lightly in the fat. Just cover them with stock and lay the half-cooked piece of bacon on them. Put on the lid and bake in the oven at 350°F. (175°C.) for the rest of the time. Half an hour before this is up, remove the rind and the bouquet of herbs. Then put the bacon back in the casserole and keep the lid off so that the top browns. If you wish, thicken the braising liquor before serving.

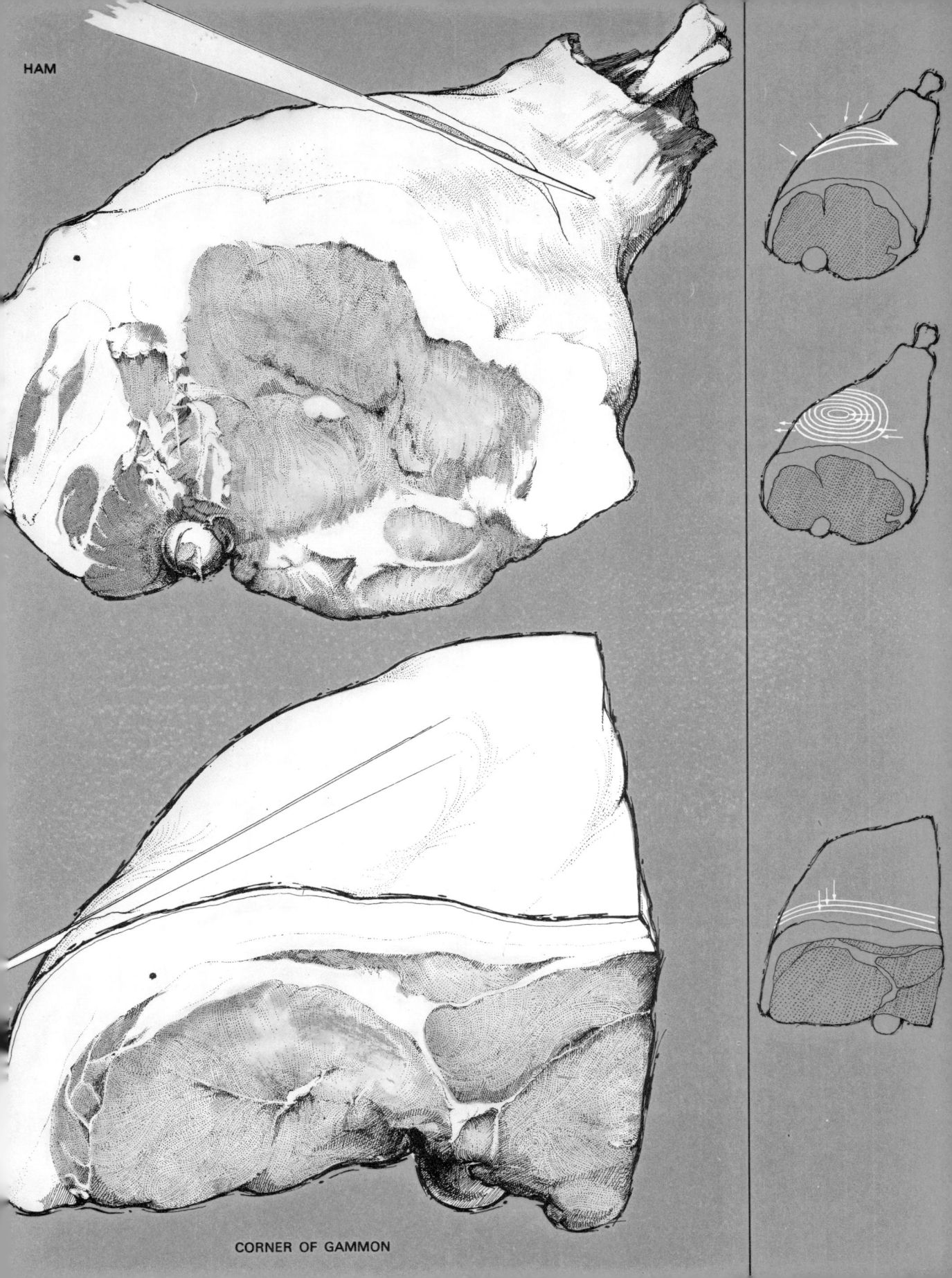

HAM

CORNER OF GAMMON

Bacon recipes

BACON FROISE (Old English)

bacon
Yorkshire pudding batter (p. 27)

Cut some streaky bacon into strips or dice, and fry them gently in their own fat in a frying pan. When cooked, pour over some Yorkshire pudding batter, fry on both sides and fold over to serve.

BACON GAMMON STEAKS WITH WINE AND CREAM

gammon
garlic
thyme
red wine
cream

Have the gammon steaks from green bacon (unsmoked) and cut about 2 in. thick. Marinate them overnight in red wine with a little garlic and thyme. Drain them, wipe free from the marinade and cook them gently in it for $1\frac{1}{2}$ hours or longer. Finish by binding this delicious sauce with cream.

BACON AND EGG PIE

cooked bacon
pastry
eggs

Line a piedish or shallow dish with shortcrust pastry, and spread a layer of thinly sliced bacon on it. Break some eggs over it so that the whites cover the meat entirely and the yolks are fairly evenly spaced apart. Cover with a thin top of pastry and bake in a moderate oven for 30 minutes.

BACON AND ONION TART

4 rashers streaky bacon
pastry flan case
4 eggs
$\frac{1}{2}$ pint ($1\frac{1}{4}$ cups) milk
salt, pepper
spring onions

Fill a baked pastry flan case with the following mixture: 4 eggs beaten into $\frac{1}{2}$ pint ($1\frac{1}{4}$ cups) milk with salt and pepper to taste, 4 very thin rashers of streaky bacon fried very crisp and broken into small pieces, and a few spring onions finely minced and browned in the fat from cooking the bacon. Bake in a moderate oven till the top is nicely browned, then serve at once.

BACON AND MUSHROOMS IN PASTRY

bacon
mushrooms
butter
shortcrust pastry (p. 65)

Cook some smallish flat mushrooms in butter and fry some pieces of thin streaky bacon of the same size as the mushrooms. When both are cold, sandwich a mushroom between two pieces of bacon, wrap in very thin shortcrust pastry, and bake in a moderate oven till the pastry is cooked. Serve hot.

BACON ROLY-POLY PUDDING

8 oz. cold boiled bacon
3 onions
salt, pepper
thick brown gravy
suet crust pastry:
8 oz. (2 cups) flour
4 oz. ($\frac{1}{2}$ cup) suet
1 teaspoonful ($1\frac{1}{4}$ teaspoonfuls) baking powder
milk
salt, pepper

Make a suet crust with 8 oz. flour, 4 oz. suet, a pinch of salt and pepper, 1 teaspoonful baking powder and milk to moisten. Roll out to about $\frac{1}{4}$ in. thick and spread with a mixture of 8 oz. cold boiled bacon and 3 onions minced together and seasoned with a little pepper. Roll up in a pudding cloth and boil for 2 hours. Serve with thick brown gravy.

FIDGET PIE (Old English)

bacon
potatoes
apples
sugar
4 oz. onions
$\frac{1}{2}$ pint ($1\frac{1}{4}$ cups) stock
shortcrust pastry (p. 65)
salt, pepper

Put a good layer of sliced peeled potatoes on a piedish, then a layer of finely chopped lean bacon, a layer of thinly sliced peeled and cored apples, a little sugar and a layer of 4 oz. onions cut in thin rings. Season as you go with salt and pepper and repeat the layers till the dish is full. Then pour in $\frac{1}{2}$ pint ($1\frac{1}{4}$ cups) stock, cover with pastry and bake in a moderate oven for just over an hour.

FRIED BACON

(Best cuts: back, streaky and gammon)

Cut the rind off each piece of bacon and remove the little bits of gristle which may appear in the lean of the rasher. Put each rasher on a board and flatten it with the blade of a kitchen knife. This will make it easier to fry.

Lay the rashers in a frying pan so that the fat side of each is overlapped by the lean side of the next. Fry gently and, half-way through the cooking, turn them over. If too much fat exudes from them during frying, pour it away when you turn the rashers over so that the frying is as dry as possible. If the bacon will have to wait some time before being eaten – and this applies especially to breakfast time – it is a good idea partly to fry the bacon and to put it in a low oven or warmer till required.

GRILLED BACON
(Best cuts: back, streaky and gammon)

The rashers are prepared as for frying, but this time when they are placed on the grid of the grill, the fat side of the rashers should overlap the lean side so that it is protected from the fierce heat.

Lean cuts, such as gammon, should be brushed over with a little melted bacon fat or olive oil before they are put under the grill. This will prevent them drying during cooking.

HAM

Ham, like gammon, comes from the hind leg of the pig, but it is cut off round the bone at the fresh pork stage and cured separately which ensures its special flavour and delicacy.

The following are the types of ham available today. In past centuries similar cuts of beef, mutton or lamb were cured and cooked in the same manner.

English hams

York ham: a firm and tender ham, famous the world over – indeed, the name York is synonymous with all that is best in cooked ham. It is mild, but by no means insipid in flavour, its pink meat appetizing and delicate.

Wiltshire ham: this type of ham is, in effect, a gammon, as it is cured like bacon while still on the side of the pig. It is mild, but lacks the distinctive flavour of a ham cured separately. One of its virtues, however, is its mildness. It does not keep so long as other separately cured hams.

Bradenham ham: this noble ham, distinguished by its black skin and pinkish flesh within, also comes from Wiltshire, and is produced by a firm in Chippenham. It has a sweet and mild cure which dates back to the end of the eighteenth century, and must be hung for many months after pickling so that its delicate and characteristic flavour can mature and develop. This ham is expensive and becoming scarcer, but no reasonable price can be too dear for a ham which surpasses any that I know.

Suffolk (or Seager) ham: this ham depends also upon its secret sweet cure and maturity. It is even scarcer than the Bradenham and equally expensive, and its flavour is full yet at the same time delicately mild.

Irish hams

Irish hams are dry-salt cured, and after being boned, are peat-smoked.

American hams

Virginia ham: the true Virginia hams come from razor-back pigs, fed on peanuts and peaches, and cured after secret recipes and then smoked over apple and hickory wood fires and left in the smokehouse till the proper flavour has been reached.

A variation of these hams is known in America as the Smithfield ham (this name has no connection with Smithfield market in London but belongs to a small town in Virginia). The pigs feed in the woods on acorns and beech and hickory nuts for the first nine months, and after being turned into the peanut fields are fed on corn. The hams are dry-salted and spiced with black pepper, then heavily smoked with hickory, oak and apple, and matured for at least a year.

Kentucky ham: these hams are taken from Hampshire hogs instead of from razor-backs and fattened on wild acorns, beans and clover. Towards the end of their lives they are penned and fed on grain. The hams are then dry-salted for about a month, smoked over apple and hickory for another month then matured for 10-12 months.

European hams

In Britain the best-known foreign hams are those which are eaten raw as an hors d'oeuvre; there is nothing which replaces smoked salmon, trout or eel so well where the first course of the meal is fish. Such hams should be cut in almost transparent slices. The best known are: *Jambon d'Ardennes* from Belgium; *Jambon de Bayonne*, which is actually made at Orthez which lies just north of the Pyrenees in Navarre; *Prosciutto di Parma*, from Parma in Italy and Westphalia ham from Germany.

All these can be eaten in the Italian fashion, that is with an accompaniment of melon or fresh figs, but to my mind a supply of very small pats of fresh butter (and nothing else) offers the finest partnership of all. These hams are never boiled, but may be eaten hot in the form of slices heated up in butter to eat with eggs, etc. They are often used, cut up, in cooked dishes.

French Jambons de campagne are locally cured hams for eating hot or cold. They tend to be rather coarser than the other hams, but often have an interesting flavour derived from a treasured family recipe for curing.

Jambon glacé (or **Jambon de Paris**) is smoked either very lightly or not at all.

Prague ham is salted and cured in brine for several months, when it is smoked with beech wood and kept in a cool cellar to mature till it is marketed. In the opinion of many this is the finest ham of all.

Danish hams: these are a subsidiary product of Danish bacon factories and are shipped green. Like some American hams, they are also boned and tinned for export.

German hams: apart from the Westphalia ham, the best known is that from Mainz, which may be eaten raw but is sometimes boiled whole and served in thin slices as a cold hors d'oeuvre.

Spanish ham: the best known is the famous *jamon serrano*, a raw ham from the region of Huelva where traditionally the hams are left in the snow to mature. It has a very delicate flavour and should be a rosy pink at its best. A dark *jamon serrano* will be dry and tasteless.

Zampino: though not strictly a ham, is an Italian commercial product. It is actually a leg of pork, boned and stuffed. It should be soaked for 3 hours in cold water and then have the skin scraped thoroughly. It is pricked in a few places with a trussing needle, wrapped in butter muslin, with both ends tied, put in a pan of cold water and simmered for 3 hours. It can be served either hot, with sauerkraut, boiled cabbage or haricot beans, or cold in thin slices with a salad.

Cooking ham

A ham must always be soaked before cooking, or it will be too salt. The time depends upon how long it has been hung, and no one but the purveyor can tell you this. Normally 12 hours or so will be enough so long as the water is changed several times, but a very dry ham may need twice as long. After soaking, the ham should be scraped and brushed to remove the rust, and coloured parts should be trimmed away.

When the ham has been soaked, weigh it, put it into a pan and cover it with cold water. Bring it to the boil, and while you are doing this heat up enough fresh water to cover the ham and add a teaspoonful of whole cloves and half a dozen or so black peppercorns. Some like to add half a bottle of dry white wine; it is a matter of personal taste. As soon as the first water round the ham boils, throw it away and substitute for it the liquid with the spices, bring it to a gentle boil again and let it simmer with the lid on for 25 minutes to the pound. The skin will respond easily to stripping

HAM AND BACON

when the ham is done. Then let it cool in this liquid, drain it, and only then remove the skin and, if necessary some of the fat.

In England it is then traditionally covered with browned breadcrumbs.

BOILED HAM (France)

1 whole ham
½ pint (1¼ cups) Madeira, port or other sweet wine

Boil the ham in the usual way, and 30 minutes before it is cooked, take it out and drain it well. Take off the skin and a little of the fat and put the ham into a stewpan or casserole just large enough to hold it. Then pour the wine over it, cover the pan closely and put in a slow oven for 1 hour. Use the liquor in the pan for making the sauce.

BOILED VIRGINIA HAM (U.S.A.)

1 whole ham
1 pint (1¼ pints) vinegar
2 onions
1 clove garlic
8 cloves
3 bay leaves
celery leaves
2 tablespoonfuls (2½ tablespoonfuls) molasses
3 tablespoonfuls (3¾ tablespoonfuls) Worcester sauce
1 teacupful dry biscuit (cracker) crumbs
mustard
a little brown sugar
yolk of 1 egg

Soak the ham for 24 hours in enough cold water to cover it, then scrub it well and put into a pan, skin side down with fresh water to cover it well. Add the vinegar, onions, garlic, cloves, bay leaves, some celery leaves, molasses and 2 tablespoonfuls Worcester sauce. Cover and simmer till tender, allowing 20 minutes to the pound from the moment when the water boils. Leave the ham to cool in the liquid, when the skin must be removed, the ham put into a baking pan with the following mixture spread on it: mix together well the biscuit (cracker) crumbs, mustard, 1 tablespoonful Worcester sauce, brown sugar and the yolk of 1 egg. Put the ham into a hot oven and let this crust brown quickly.

BOILED BRADENHAM HAM (England)

1 whole ham
water
1 lb. (2 cups) black treacle

The producers of this lovely and famous ham give the following directions for its cooking: after soaking for 48 hours, put the ham into cold fresh water, add the black treacle, bring to the boil and allow to simmer (do not boil fast) for 4 hours if under 14 lb., for 30 minutes longer up to 18 lb. and, if over 18 lb., for 5 hours. Unless you are going to eat it hot, allow it to remain in the liquid in which it has been cooked till it is quite cold.

BAKED HAM IN PASTRY

1 whole ham
shortcrust pastry
mirepoix of vegetables
shallots
mushrooms
onions
salt, pepper

Boil ham till three-quarters cooked. Drain, skin and glaze the cut surface. Roll out pastry and on this spread the mirepoix, sautéed in butter, and mixed with the remaining ingredients all chopped and lightly cooked in butter. Place the ham on this bed, with the glazed side down; seal, decorate with pastry leaves; brush with egg yolk. Bake in moderate oven for 45 minutes.

BAKED ALSACE HAM (France)

Soak the ham for 12 hours, then drain and dry it and cover completely with a crust of bread dough. Then bake in a moderate oven, allowing 25 minutes to the pound. The crust is of course, in this case, inedible. A shortcrust cover may be substituted for the bread dough; this has a curious charm but is rather salty for some people.

BAKED AUVERGNE HAM (France)

ham
Madeira
bread dough
Madeira sauce (p. 209)

Boil a small ham till almost done, then take off the skin and carve the upper side in slices, but leave them still adhering to the bone of the ham. Sprinkle the whole ham well with Madeira, and cover it completely with bread dough $\frac{1}{2}$ in. thick. Bake in a moderate oven for $1-1\frac{1}{2}$ hours, and when the crust is coloured a light gold, serve the ham in it, accompanied by a Madeira sauce.

BAKED MISSOURI HAM (U.S.A.)

1 whole ham
cloves
1 large cupful each molasses, vinegar and cider
1 tablespoonful ($1\frac{1}{4}$ tablespoonfuls) Worcester sauce
2 bay leaves

Soak a 12 lb. ham for 24 hours in cold water, then take it out and scrub well. Now remove the skin carefully, taking off as little of the fat as possible, and stick cloves all over the top at $1\frac{1}{2}$ in. intervals. Put the ham into a baking dish with a cover, and pour over it a mixture of the molasses, vinegar, cider and Worcester sauce; add the bay leaves, cover and bake in a slow oven for $5\frac{1}{2}$ hours, basting every 30 minutes. Then take off the cover and bake for a final 30 minutes. When the ham

HAM AND BACON

is done, take the dish out of the oven, put the cover on again and allow the ham to cool in the baking dish for 3 hours.

BAKED HAM (U.S.A.)

1 whole ham
carrots
onion
2 sticks celery
3 sprigs parsley
1 teaspoonful (1¼ teaspoonfuls) cloves
1 teaspoonful (1¼ teaspoonfuls) allspice
peppercorns
1 breakfastcupful breadcrumbs
1 breakfastcupful brown sugar
1 teaspoonful (1¼ teaspoonfuls) dry mustard
vinegar or pineapple juice
cider
cider sauce:
½ pint (1¼ cups) cider
¾ pint (1 pint) brown sauce
salt, pepper
1 bay leaf
2 cloves

Boil the ham in the usual way (*see* p. 168), with 6 slices each of carrot and onion, the celery, parsley, cloves, whole allspice and peppercorns. Let the ham cool in the water, then take it out, strip off the skin and spread the fat with a mixture of soft breadcrumbs, brown sugar, dry mustard and enough vinegar or pineapple juice to bind the mixture together. Pour 2 breakfastcupfuls cider or pineapple juice over this and bake for 1 hour in a slow oven, basting every 10 minutes. Make a cider sauce by mixing the ingredients; stir them well together and simmer quietly till the sauce reaches the desired consistency. Do not forget to add the scrapings of the baking pan to it.

BRAISED HAM

whole cooked ham
Madeira, sherry or dry white wine

Put the skinned ham into a large heavy stewpan or casserole and pour in half a bottle of sherry, Madeira or dry white wine. Cover the pan closely and cook in a very moderate oven (355°F. or 180°C.) for 45 minutes.

It is then ready. Do not forget to keep the fat from the top of the braising liquid. It can be marvellous for enriching various other dishes.

PARSLEY HAM
1 whole ham
water
dry white wine
1 calf's foot
a few veal bones
carrots
onions
salt
shallots
peppercorns
bouquet garni
garlic
wine vinegar
parsley

Cook the soaked ham in enough water and dry white wine (in equal parts) to cover it, with a calf's foot, a few veal bones, a few carrots and onions cut in slices, a dozen shallots, salt, coarsely broken black peppercorns and a bouquet garni.

When the ham is cooked, skin it, remove the bone and gristle and mash the lean and the fat together with a heavy fork, pressing it all eventually into a large bowl. Now reduce the cooking liquor on a low heat, strain it and add a very little minced garlic, a few drops of wine vinegar and a port wineglassful of the dry white wine already used in the cooking. Pour this fragrant stock, reinforced by plenty of chopped parsley, over the ham in the bowl, and let it set in a cool place.

GLAZED HAM
whole cooked ham
Madeira, sherry or port
moist brown sugar

Put the drained cooked ham on a baking dish, and pour over it a glass of Madeira, sherry or port. Cover the fat with plenty of moist brown sugar and put it into a very hot oven (445°F. or 230°C.) and let it remain there for 15 minutes or so, when it will be found to be coated with a lovely golden glaze. Then lower the heat to 355°F. (180°C.) and let it go on cooking for another 15 minutes, when the ham will be ready to carve (*see* p. 21).

GLAZED HAM (U.S.A.)
whole cooked ham
cloves
Barbados sugar
water, vinegar, orange or pineapple juice

Remove the skin from a cooked ham cooled in its cooking liquor; put the ham, fat side uppermost, in a baking-tin in a moderate oven (355°F. or 180°C.) and bake it for 30 minutes. Then trim the fat evenly so that it is about ½ in. thick, and criss-cross the surface with ¼ in. deep incisions. Many like (as I do) to stick a clove in the middle of each diamond. Now spread over the whole surface of the ham a glazing mixture of 5–6 tablespoonfuls of Barbados sugar which has been mixed to a paste with a little water, vinegar or orange or pineapple juice according to your fancy. Put the ham back into the oven now at 445°F. or 230°C. and baste it with the syrup to ensure its glazing evenly. Carefully done, it makes an entrancingly appetizing dish.

DISHES WITH HAM

CREOLE HAM GRILLADES (U.S.A.)

2 or 3 onions
butter
8 oz. tomatoes
salt, pepper
chopped chilli pepper
raw ham
¼ pint (⅓ pint) water

Chop the onions and brown them lightly in a little butter. Then add chopped skinned tomatoes, mix well and cook for about 10 minutes, adding salt, pepper and a very little chopped chilli pepper. Now put in some ¼ in. slices of raw ham, add ¼ pint (⅓ pint) water, cover the pan and simmer for an hour or so, turning the slices of meat now and then adding a little more water if the sauce shows signs of boiling away. Serve the slices of ham with the sauce poured over them, and accompany with plain boiled rice, boiled hominy or fried hominy cakes.

HAM BAKED WITH APPLES (U.S.A.)

1 slice raw ham 1 in. thick
7 oz. (1 cup) brown sugar
½ teaspoonful (full ½ teaspoonful) ground cloves
½ teaspoonful (full ½ teaspoonful) cinnamon
3 apples
6 fl. oz. (¾ cup) pineapple juice or syrup

Gash the fat on a 1 in. slice of raw ham to prevent it from curling up in the cooking, and mix 1 breakfastcupful brown sugar thoroughly with ½ level teaspoonful each of ground cloves and ground cinnamon. Rub a quarter of this mixture into one side of the slice, and put it into a greased fireproof dish, sugared side down. Now rub half of the remaining sugar mixture into the exposed side. Arrange ½ in. slices from 3 peeled and cored medium-sized apples over the ham, and sprinkle the rest of the spiced sugar over them. Heat a teacupful of pineapple juice, fresh or tinned, to boiling point, pour it over the apples and bake with the lid off in a moderate oven for about 45 minutes, by which time the ham should be cooked. Serve the ham with the apple rings round it, and pour the liquid from the dish over them.

DEVILLED HAM
cooked ham
½ pint (1¼ cups) milk
a little made mustard
1 teaspoonful (1¼ teaspoonfuls) ketchup
1 teaspoonful (1¼ teaspoonfuls) Worcester sauce
1 dessertspoonful (½ tablespoonful) Parmesan cheese
1 dessertspoonful (½ tablespoonful) mango chutney
salt
cayenne pepper
¼ pint (⅓ pint) cream
butter

Make a thin white sauce of the same consistency as cream with milk, and add to it the made mustard, ketchup and Worcester sauce, grated Parmesan or similar cheese, mango chutney, salt, a little cayenne pepper and cream. Cook gently for a minute or two and then strain. Arrange some thin slices of cooked ham in a shallow fireproof dish, pour the sauce over them, dot with a few thin flakes of butter and sprinkle over some more grated cheese. Bake till the top is browned, and serve with hot dry toast.

HAM BAKED IN MILK (U.S.A.)
2 lb. raw ham steak
2 oz. (⅔ cup) breadcrumbs
3 teaspoonfuls (3¾ teaspoonfuls) brown sugar
1 teaspoonful (1¼ teaspoonfuls) mustard
1 teaspoonful (1¼ teaspoonfuls) Worcester sauce
yolk of 1 egg
milk

Cover the piece of raw ham with cold water, bring to the boil and boil for 10 minutes. Dry it and put into a baking tin. Now mix together into a paste the breadcrumbs, brown sugar, mustard, Worcester sauce and the yolk of 1 egg. When well amalgamated, spread this evenly over the top of the ham and pour over it enough milk to come three-quarters of the way up the side. Bake in a moderate oven for 40 minutes, and if the milk gets too much reduced, add a little more during the cooking.

HAM AND BACON

HAM BAKED WITH PINEAPPLE

1 raw ham steak
mustard
tin of pineapple slices
7 oz. (1 cup) brown sugar
6 cloves

Soak a 1 in. piece of raw ham in lukewarm water for 1 hour, then drain it and put into a shallow fireproof dish. Smear it over with made mustard and pour over ½ pint (1¼ cups) of the syrup from a tin of pineapple slices. Now sprinkle with 1 teacupful brown sugar and stick it with half a dozen cloves. Arrange the slices of pineapple on the ham and bake till they become a delicate brown, basting frequently with the syrup.

HAM COUNTRY STYLE (U.S.A.)

raw ham steak
butter
onion
6 sliced carrots
3 dessertspoonfuls (1½ tablespoonfuls) raisins
6 thin strips orange peel
8 fl. oz. (1 cup) water
6 fl. oz. (¾ cup) orange juice
3 level teaspoonfuls (3¾ level teaspoonfuls) flour

Brown a 1½ in. piece of raw ham on both sides in butter, then add a large chopped onion, the sliced carrots, raisins, orange peel and water. Put on the lid and simmer for 1½ hours. Mix smoothly together the flour and orange juice and add this to the ham and its cooking liquor. Stir over the heat and in about 3 minutes it will thicken and the dish is ready to serve.

HAM AND EGG PIE

8 oz. (1 cup) cooked lean ham
6 eggs
onion juice or chopped parsley
shortcrust pastry
pepper

Line a pie plate or flan case with shortcrust pastry, and fill it with a mixture of 6 slightly beaten eggs and the cooked ham cut in very small dice, seasoned with pepper and either onion juice or finely chopped parsley. Put on a pastry crust, prick it with a fork and bake for 10 minutes in a hot oven and then at a moderate heat for another 10 minutes.

VEAL AND HAM PIE
(*See* under Veal on p. 99.)

HAM AND MUSHROOM PIE

1 raw ham rasher
1 teaspoonful (1¼ teaspoonful) sugar
1 lb. mushrooms
milk
bacon fat
salt, pepper

Put a fairly large ½ in. rasher of ham into a buttered frying pan and sprinkle it with 1 teaspoonful sugar. Put a cover on the pan and cook the ham for 15 minutes on each side. Meanwhile stew the mushrooms in enough milk to cover. Grease a piedish with melted bacon fat and put in half the drained mushrooms, adding a little salt and plenty of pepper. Lay the ham on top, and pour on the rest of the mushrooms. Cover with a closely-fitting lid and bake in a hot oven for 20 minutes.

The flavour of nutmeg consorts well with both ingredients of this homely dish.

HAM WITH NOODLES (U.S.A.)

1 lb. slice of raw ham
olive oil
2 onions
1 clove garlic
1 small carrot
1 tablespoonful tomato paste or purée
¾ pint (2 cups) stock
salt, pepper
noodles
Parmesan cheese

Cut the ham into long narrow strips, fat and lean, and fry them in olive oil with the onions, carrot and garlic, the vegetables having been put through the mincing machine. When the contents of the pan have browned, add the tomato paste or purée dissolved in stock, and simmer gently for 10–15 minutes. Season with salt and pepper if necessary, and serve the ham strips in a border of cooked noodles, pouring the sauce over all. Serve grated Parmesan cheese separately.

HAM PANCAKES

2 oz. (½ cup) cooked ham
½ oz. (1 tablespoonful) butter
6 small mushrooms
salt, pepper
2 eggs
2 oz. (½ cup) flour
1 tablespoonful (1¼ tablespoonfuls) milk
cheese or tomato sauce

Chop the cooked ham small, and fry it in ½ oz. butter with the mushrooms, peeled and cut in quarters. Season with salt and pepper and keep hot. Make a batter with the yolks of 2 eggs, the flour and 1 tablespoonful milk, beat it for 10 minutes and then add the stiffly-whisked whites of the eggs. Fry pancakes of this mixture in butter, and as each is cooked put a spoonful of the mixture inside, and roll it up. Arrange side by side in a long dish and serve coated with cheese sauce (p. 206) or tomato sauce (p. 211) and browned.

HAM AND EGG COCOTTES

cold ham
pepper, salt
parsley
butter
eggs
1 teaspoonful (1¼ teaspoonfuls) cream

Chop up some cold ham finely and mix it with a little pepper and chopped parsley. Butter some *cocottes*, and sprinkle them with this mixture. Break an egg into each, season with salt and pepper, put a thin flake of butter on top of each, and add 1 teaspoonful cream. Bake in a hot oven in a pan of water for about 10 minutes or till the white is just set.

HAM HOTPOT

1 raw ham steak
1 chopped onion
1 dessertspoonful (½ tablespoonful) brown sugar
2 medium apples
1 lb. potatoes
½ pint (1¼ cups) stock

Soak the ham in warm water for 1 hour, then cut it in neat pieces. Put the chopped onion and brown sugar in the bottom of an earthenware hotpot, and add the pieces of ham. Cover them with the peeled, cored and sliced apples, and sliced, peeled potatoes. Pour in the stock, and bake slowly for 1 hour or so, taking off the lid for the last 20 minutes of the cooking, for the top of the potatoes to brown.

OFFAL (VARIETY MEATS)

BRAINS

Brains are one of the most delicious of all light foods and are the basis of many succulent dishes. They are nourishing and rich in phosphorus and, notes Escoffier, 'form the most wholesome and reparative diet for all those who are debilitated by excessive headwork'. Calf's and sheep's brains are preferable to those of the ox, but the recipes that follow can be applied to all three. Allow 4–5 oz. brains for each serving.

Preparation of brains

In the first place brains must be freed from all traces of blood, and this is done by soaking them in cold water, frequently changed or renewed under the cold tap, till they are perfectly white. This will take not less than 2 hours, and a little salt in the water will help matters so far as the extraction of the blood is concerned. The skin and fibres should then be carefully removed, the brains are then put into a saucepan and enough boiling water is poured over to cover them; they must then be blanched by poaching for 3 minutes and then plunged into fresh cold water. When they have become quite cold, boil, or rather poach, for about 20 minutes either in water, or stock seasoned with onion, bay leaf, salt and pepper, or in a *court-bouillon* (*see* opposite page).

BRAINS WITH BLACK BUTTER (*Cervelles au Beurre Noir*) (France)

a set of brains
2 oz. (4 tablespoonfuls) butter
parsley
vinegar

Slice the cooked brains and season them with salt and pepper. Heat some butter in a frying pan till it becomes dark brown (not really black or it would be burnt). Add immediately a small sprinkling of chopped parsley. Do not cook it, but pour at once with the butter over the

OFFAL (VARIETY MEATS) 179

brains. Now quickly swill the frying pan with a few drops of good vinegar and pour this, too, over the brains.

One of the very best accompaniments to this dish is a plate of noodles, and some spinach *en branches* if a vegetable is wanted. Some like a few capers with the butter.

FRIED BRAINS

a set of brains
lemon
olive oil
salt, pepper
chopped parsley
deep hot fat or oil
tomato sauce
batter:
2 oz. (½ cup) flour
pinch salt
1 egg white
1 dessertspoonful (½ tablespoonful) oil
about 2 fl. oz. (¼ cup) warm water

Cut the cooked brains in small slices and let these lie for an hour in a marinade of a little lemon juice, olive oil, salt and pepper, and chopped parsley. Now prepare the batter. Mix the flour with the salt, make a well in it and add the oil and water. Mix to a smooth batter and beat till light. Leave in a cold place till wanted, then just before use add the very stiffly-beaten egg white. Dip the brains in this and fry in deep fat or oil and serve a tomato sauce with them if desired. 1 set of sheep brains is sufficient for each person.

COURT-BOUILLON FOR COOKING BRAINS

onion
1 clove
bouquet garni
several black peppercorns
3-4 tablespoonfuls (¼ cup) wine vinegar
4 pints (5 pints) water

Bring the *court-bouillon* to the boil and boil it for 20 minutes. Remove the peppercorns. When you are ready, bring to the boil again and poach the brains in it; about 30 minutes for the ox brains, but only about 20 minutes for the others.

Escoffier points out helpfully that brains cannot really be overcooked. Prolonged cooking only succeeds in stiffening and not in toughening them, and, he adds, they may cook for 2 hours longer (i.e. than 20 minutes) without harm, seeing that the process only makes them firmer. They are invariably cooked in this way before being used in the following recipes, of which the first is probably the most popular.

BRAINS À LA RAVIGOTE (France)
Fry the brains as above, slice them and serve them masked by a hot *ravigote* sauce.

RAVIGOTE SAUCE

¾ **pint (1 pint) white sauce** **4 tablespoonfuls (¼ cup) each dry white wine and white wine vinegar** **1 tablespoonful (1¼ tablespoonfuls) finely chopped shallot** **chives** **chervil** **tarragon** **½ oz. (1 tablespoonful) butter**	Put the wine, vinegar and shallot into a small saucepan, and reduce the liquid by rapid boiling to 3 tablespoonfuls. Add the hot white sauce to this, simmer together for 5–6 minutes and then, off the heat, add a spoonful of the mixed chopped herbs and ½ oz. butter cut into little pieces.

FEET

Sheep's and pig's trotters must be cleaned and blanched before cooking. Calves' feet are only used in the kitchen to make a stock or gravy more gelatinous. A clear jelly made from calves' feet was a great delicacy several decades ago particularly for invalids. It is still obtainable as a commercial product.

LANCASHIRE SHEEP'S TROTTERS

sheep's trotters **stock** **bouquet garni** **milk** **flour** **salt, pepper** **1 or 2 yolks of eggs** **lemon juice or vinegar**	Put the prepared trotters from the butcher into some cold stock with a bouquet garni. Bring to the boil and cook for 2 or 3 hours till the bones slip out easily. Remove the herbs and reduce the stock if necessary, and thicken with milk and flour. Put back the meat from the trotters, season with salt and pepper and thicken with 1 or 2 egg yolks beaten in a little lemon juice or vinegar.

OFFAL (VARIETY MEATS)

SHEEP'S TROTTER SALAD

cooked sheep's trotters
vinegar
olive oil
button or spring onions
shallots
parsley
salt, pepper
made mustard
hard-boiled egg
anchovy fillets
blanc:
1 tablespoonful (1¼ tablespoonfuls) flour
4 pints (5 pints) water
rock salt
3 tablespoonfuls (full ⅓ cup) vinegar
bouquet garni
suet or fat from white stock

First, prepare a *blanc* like this. Mix gradually a good tablespoonful of flour with cold water so that there are no lumps, make the water up to 2 quarts and add the rock salt and vinegar or lemon juice. Bring to the boil stirring all the time, and put in the meat to be cooked. Now add a bouquet garni and, lastly, either finely chopped or shredded suet or fat taken from the top of white stock. Draw the pan to the side of the fire, put the lid on three-quarters, and boil gently without intermission as directed.

Now let the trotters get cold and put them into a salad bowl bound with the following dressing: 2 tablespoonfuls good vinegar, 4 of olive oil, a few tiny button onions or spring onions, 2 chopped shallots, a teaspoonful or so of chopped parsley, salt, pepper and 1 dessertspoonful made mustard all well mixed together. Garnish with hard-boiled egg and anchovy fillets, and serve either as an hors d'oeuvre or as an accompaniment to a green salad.

PIG'S TROTTERS AND PEAS (Holland)

2 pig's trotters
4 pints (5 pints) water
½ pint (1¼ cups) split peas
4 leeks
8 sticks celery
2 oz. (4 tablespoonfuls) butter
salt

Soak the split peas all night in the water, and the next morning cook them in the same water, adding salt, till they are done, which will take about 2 hours. Pass them, with the liquid, through a fine sieve and cook the pig's trotters for 1 hour in this soup. Then add the white part of the leeks and the sticks of celery cut in small pieces. Add the butter and cook till the vegetables are done. Serve as a meat broth with the trotters in it.

HEADS

A sheep's head would not be looked on nowadays as anything particularly exciting, but a brawn and broth made from it was formerly highly appreciated in Scotland. The brawn later fell out of favour; more attention was given to the broth.

BOILED CALF'S HEAD

Remove all the meat from a calf's head and boil it very gently with an onion and salt to taste for 2½ hours. Then cut into portions for serving with a white sauce made from the cooking liquor and a little milk, to which chopped button onions have been added.

FRIED CALF'S HEAD

cooked calf's head
deep fat or oil
batter
marinade:
2 tablespoonfuls (2½ tablespoonfuls) olive oil
1 tablespoonful (1¼ tablespoonfuls) lemon juice or vinegar
chopped parsley
chopped onion or shallot
minced herbs
salt, pepper

Cut the remains of a boiled calf's head into strips 2½ × 1 in. and soak them in the marinade for at least 1 hour. When ready to cook, drain and remove any bits of the marinade, wipe the pieces and fry till golden in deep fat or oil after dipping them in batter. Serve with fried parsley, mashed potato and spinach purée.

HEARTS

Ox hearts, like those of the calf and sheep, provide some very savoury dishes with the added merit of cheapness. They are generally stuffed before cooking, but a French ragoût makes attractive eating. Allow 6–10 oz. of heart for each serving.

Ox hearts are usually baked or braised, but they respond very well to potroasting. Here are two simple English stuffings which will provide a pleasant family dish.

STUFFING (1)

1 minced onion
2 tablespoonfuls (2½ tablespoonfuls) breadcrumbs
sage
salt, pepper and paprika

Having stuffed and sewn up the hearts, you can either braise them on a bed of vegetables, potroast them in a little stock after first browning them all over in dripping, or roast them in the oven, seeing that they are well basted to avoid any dryness. If you are prepared to take the trouble they can, of course, be larded first.

OFFAL (VARIETY MEATS)

STUFFING (2)

3 tablespoonfuls (3¾ tablespoonfuls) breadcrumbs
1 dessertspoonful (½ tablespoonful) chopped cooked ham
chopped parsley
grated rind of ½ lemon
salt, pepper
celery salt
beaten egg to bind
a few stoned raisins

The times for roasting and stewing are about the same, but braising will take a little longer. A stuffed ox heart will take 1½–2 hours at least, calf's heart 1–1½ hours and sheep's heart about 40 minutes. The temperature should be moderate. Hearts will be spoiled if the temperature is high.

CALF'S HEART À L'HONGROISE

1 calf's heart
butter or dripping
glass or red or white wine (Hungarian, if possible)
12 button onions
24 small carrots
bouquet garni
veal stock
salt, pepper

Brown the heart all over in the dripping or butter, season it with salt and pepper and pour the wine, preferably Hungarian, over it. Then add the button onions and baby carrots, the bouquet garni and enough good veal stock to cover the contents of the pan. Put on the lid and simmer for 1½ hours, thickening the sauce before serving.

OX HEART CASSEROLE

ox heart
green bacon or pickled pork
flour
red wine
stock
bouquet garni
button onions

Cut the heart into cubes and colour them in the fat from some chopped green bacon or pickled pork. Sprinkle them with flour, brown and moisten with red wine or half stock and half wine. Add a large bouquet garni, and halfway through the cooking add some button onions which have previously been fried lightly in the same fat. 3 hours cooking, preferably in the oven and with the lid on, should be enough. Serve garnished with triangles of fried bread and accompanied by red or black currant jelly.

KIDNEYS

Sheep's kidneys are one of the most delicious morsels the offal of this animal provides. Calves' kidneys are even more delectable, especially for those who find sheep's kidneys too strong for their taste.

Unless it is directed to cook them whole with some of their skin still round them, kidneys should be cleared of their fat and membrane before cooking. They should not be cut too thinly or the slices will toughen. For grilling, see that a thin layer of fat is left round them and kidneys cut in halves lengthways and skewered so that they do not lose their shape in the cooking. The cut side should be grilled first. Kidneys should be eaten as fresh as possible and not kept in the refrigerator for more than 24 hours. If too great a heat is applied to them, or they are cooked for too long they tend to be tough and coarse in flavour.

Owing to their strong and sometimes rather unpleasant smell ox kidneys demand certain precautions that are unnecessary with the kidneys of other animals. Skin them first, and then cut them in halves and remove all trace of fat. Cut the halves in two again, and then into slices. Plunge these, *for a second only*, into boiling water, and then drain them in a cloth, and dry them well.

Ox kidneys can be cooked by any of the methods suggested for veal kidney, but remember to throw away the fat in which they are fried and never add to any sauce the blood or juices that have come from them while they have been keeping hot.

Ox kidney is mostly used in steak-and-kidney pudding or pie, though it can be quite good cooked *en casserole* or stewed as suggested for heart. Here is another recipe which is suitable for pig's kidneys as well.

Allow 4–5 oz. ox or calves' kidneys for each serving, one sheep's or pig's kidney or two of lamb.

CREOLE VEAL KIDNEY (U.S.A.)

veal kidneys
6 thin rashers bacon
2 small chopped onions
1 chopped green sweet pepper
8 fl. oz. (1 cup) tomato juice
salt, pepper
bay leaf
flour

Soak 4 veal kidneys, split in halves, for 30 minutes in cold water, then drain them and cut each into ½ in. slices. Cut the rashers of bacon into small squares and fry them for a minute or two in a heavy and barely greased frying pan. Then flour the kidney slices and add them to the bacon with the chopped onions and green sweet pepper. Stir all together on a low heat till the kidney is seared, then add the tomato juice, salt, pepper and bay leaf. Cover, simmer for 30 minutes, thicken the sauce and serve with boiled rice.

OFFAL (VARIETY MEATS)

DEVILLED SHEEP'S KIDNEYS

Skewer the sheep's kidneys flat and grill them. Serve on toast sprinkled with lemon juice and parsley and with a pat of devil or cayenne butter on each. Cayenne butter is made by creaming a little butter and mixing it thoroughly with about a teaspoonful cayenne pepper and devil butter by creaming a little butter with a good teaspoonful of curry powder, some pounded shallot and a drop of Tabasco sauce.

OX KIDNEYS EN CASSEROLE

$1\frac{1}{2}$ lb. ox kidney
fat
1 oz. (2 tablespoonfuls) butter
10 mushrooms
1 small onion
$\frac{1}{2}$ glass each of red or white wine and good stock
2 tablespoonfuls ($2\frac{1}{2}$ tablespoonfuls) cream parsley

After blanching the kidneys chop them up coarsely and fry quickly in fat. Drain and put aside. Slice the mushrooms and brown them in the butter, adding the minced onion, the flour, and then the wine and stock, warmed. Season with salt and pepper and simmer for 15 minutes or so. Now add the chopped kidney, having first carefully drained off any fat or exudation from them. Add the cream and heat gently. Serve sprinkled with chopped parsley.

SHEEP'S KIDNEYS EN BROCHETTE

sheep's kidneys
stock
mushrooms
bacon
buttered toast

First cook the kidneys for 10 minutes in a little stock, then drain them and cut into slices. Have a skewer ready for each person and slip on a small mushroom, the rounded side towards the end of the skewer. Then add alternate pieces of kidney and thinly sliced fattish bacon ending with another mushroom also rounded side outwards. Grill till the bacon is crisp, and serve on strips of buttered toast. If a sauce is wanted, the stock from the preliminary cooking of the kidneys could be used in making it.

SHEEP'S KIDNEY IN POTATO

potato
sheep's kidney
salt, pepper

Take a very large potato, cut a good slice off the top and scoop out a hole inside big enough to hold a whole sheep's kidney on which you have left a little of the fat. Put the kidney into the potato, seasoning it with salt and pepper, and then put the top slice on as a lid, tying it on firmly. Now bake the stuffed potato in the oven very slowly, and when the potato is cooked, the kidney will be ready.

VEAL KIDNEY ALI-BAB

veal kidney
butter
1 liqueur glassful brandy
1 glass dry sherry
6 mushrooms
12 fl. oz. (1½ cups) thick cream
freshly grated horseradish to taste

Cut some trimmed raw veal kidney in slices, and brown these quickly in a little butter. As soon as the raw look has disappeared, pour the brandy over and set it alight. When the flames have died down, add the sherry and then the mushrooms, peeled and sliced. Cook all together for 10 minutes, then add the cream and a seasoning of grated horseradish to taste. Bring to just on boiling point and serve at once.

VEAL KIDNEY CROQUETTES

veal kidney
frying oil or fat
beef marrow
flour
fresh breadcrumbs
salt, pepper
4 eggs
sauce tartare (p. 212)

Cut up and chop finely a raw veal kidney. Melt a little fat in a frying pan, and fry the kidney till done, then put it into a bowl with some chopped cooked beef marrow, a little flour, some white breadcrumbs and plenty of salt and pepper. Bind with 3 eggs and shape into croquettes. Egg-and-breadcrumb these, fry them crisp and golden in deep fat or oil and serve them with a separate *sauce tartare*.

VEAL KIDNEY EN COCOTTE

veal kidney
butter
diced bacon
mushrooms
small potatoes
small glazed button onions
veal gravy

Trim the kidney so that there is only a very little fat left in it, and fry it all over in a little butter for a few minutes. Put it into an oval *cocotte* and add the small dice of bacon first blanched and tossed in butter, raw quartered mushrooms also tossed; small blanched potatoes cut in the shape of small long olives; and very small glazed button onions. Put on the lid and cook gently for about 30 minutes and serve with a little veal gravy.

VEAL KIDNEY FLAMBÉ

veal kidney
salt, pepper
butter
brandy
French mustard
cream
half a lemon
cayenne pepper

Trim and skin the kidney, season it with salt and pepper and cook it for about 3 minutes in foaming butter till it is browned all over. Now quickly cut the kidney, which will be found to be still red and juicy inside, into slices, and toss these in a little butter for a few seconds, with the juices which have come out of the kidney. Now pour in a little brandy, set it alight, and when the flames have disappeared add a little mustard and some thick cream, both at your discretion, and cook for 2 or 3 minutes more. Have the cut side of the half-lemon sprinkled with cayenne pepper, and at the last minute before serving squeeze this over the dish. An opportunity to show your skill with a chafing-dish.

VEAL KIDNEY LIÈGEOISE (France)

veal kidney
1 oz. (2 tablespoonfuls) butter
1 small wineglassful burned gin
2 juniper berries
veal gravy

Leave a very thin layer of fat all round the kidney. Heat the butter in a stewpan or *cocotte* just large enough to hold the kidney, then put the seasoned kidney in, and cook it gently for about 30 minutes, turning it often. One minute before serving, pour in a small wineglassful of burned gin and add the crushed, dried juniper berries. Finally add a tablespoonful or so of strong veal gravy, and serve just as it is.

SHEEP'S KIDNEY ROLLS

sheep's kidneys
parsley
onion
fresh breadcrumbs
egg
bacon
hot buttered toast

Make a stuffing with finely chopped parsley and onion and breadcrumbs, and bind with a little beaten egg. Spread this lightly on very thin rashers of streaky smoked bacon, and wrap one round each whole or half skinned sheep's kidney. Bake for 20 minutes in a hot oven, and serve on hot buttered toast.

VEAL KIDNEY SOUFFLÉ

Take a veal kidney for each person, skin, remove the fat and mince very finely. Mix with a slice of bread first soaked in milk, salt, pepper and a whole egg. Steam in a border mould for 1 hour and serve with creamy mushroom sauce poured over.

LIVER

Calves' liver is acknowledged to be the finest for cooking though some prefer the somewhat tenderer flesh of the lamb. Liver from lamb and sheep can equally well be used in all the calves' liver recipes.

Pig's liver is an important ingredient of European country pâté and liver pâté owes nothing to anything but this strongly flavoured liver. Ox liver, however, although it might possibly be used by the ingenious for making a pâté, is really hardly worth bothering about as it is coarse in texture and flavour.

Allow about 4 oz. of liver for each serving.

CALVES' LIVER CASSEROLE

1 lb. calves' liver
flour
salt, pepper
dripping
1 large onion
1 turnip
1 carrot
8 oz. (1⅓ cups) rice
a dash of Worcester sauce (optional)
1½ pints (just under 2 pints) water

Cut the liver in slices, dip them in seasoned flour and fry on both sides for a minute or two in dripping. Slice a large onion, a carrot and turnip and put them into a casserole with the liver, rice and, if desired, the Worcester sauce. Add 1½ pints water, put on the lid and cook in a very slow oven for 2 hours.

CALVES' LIVER DUMPLINGS

a good slice of calves' liver for each serving
2 eggs
3 tablespoonfuls (3¾ tablespoonfuls) flour
fried onions
parsley
breadcrumbs
milk
croûtons
butter
salt, pepper

Mince up the liver with a sharp knife (*not* through the mincing machine); season well and add the 2 egg yolks, the flour, some chopped parsley and onions fried golden and then the well-whisked egg whites. Soak some breadcrumbs in milk, squeeze them fairly dry and make into a paste with the liver and egg mixture. Shape into little balls, and poach them in boiling water for about 25 minutes. Drain and arrange them on a dish, and pour over them some butter and the little bread croûtons that have been fried in it.

Loin of Pork and some of the ingredients for Roast Loin of Pork

CALVES' LIVER LYONNAISE

½ oz. (1 tablespoonful) butter
2 large sliced onions
1 lb. calves' liver
a little vinegar
salt, pepper

Put the butter into a frying pan and in it brown the sliced onions. Cut the liver into slices about 3 in. long by ½ in. thick, season these well with salt and pepper and stir them in with the fried onions. Put a lid on the pan and cook for about 3 minutes, then turn the liver slices over and give them another 3 minutes. Now add the vinegar, fry for 3–4 minutes more, and serve as hot as possible with mashed potatoes.

CALVES' LIVER LOAF

1 lb. calves' liver
3 oz. (1 cup) breadcrumbs
2 teaspoonfuls (2½ tablespoonfuls) grated onions
2 teaspoonfuls (2½ teaspoonfuls) chopped parsley
1 tablespoonful (1¼ tablespoonfuls) finely minced celery
salt, pepper
2 eggs
⅓ pint (½ pint) milk
bacon rashers
brown gravy

Have ready 1 lb. calves' liver in one piece, pour enough boiling water over it to cover and leave it for 5 minutes; then drain it, cut it up and put it through the mincing machine.

Now add the breadcrumbs, a seasoning of 2 teaspoonfuls each grated onion and chopped parsley, 1 tablespoonful finely minced celery, and salt and pepper to taste. Mix well together and bind with 2 eggs beaten in about 1 cup milk. Grease a cake tin and line it, sides and bottom with thin rashers of streaky bacon. Pack the liver mixture into this and bake in a slow oven till the loaf is firm, which will take about 1 hour. Serve hot with thick brown gravy or cold with a green salad.

CALVES' LIVER AND BACON

calves' liver
2 oz. (4 tablespoonfuls) butter
flour
chopped parsley
salt, pepper
streaky bacon

Have ready some flour seasoned with salt and pepper and roll thinly cut slices of the calves' liver in it. Fry these slowly in butter till they are a rich brown on both sides, then arrange them on a dish, pour over them another ½ oz. melted butter to which the parsley has been added, and surround them with very crisply grilled streaky bacon rashers.

Roast Loin of Pork

CALVES' LIVER EN PAPILLOTES

calves' liver
olive oil
bouquet garni
onion
peppercorns
fat bacon
mushrooms
sauce poivrade (p. 210)

Slice the liver rather thickly and marinate the slices for a few hours in olive oil seasoned with a bouquet garni, onion and peppercorns, turning them now and then. When wanted, drain them, wipe dry and wrap each slice up in little sheets of oiled paper or kitchen foil with a little minced fat bacon, mushrooms and parsley. Twist the ends of the paper or foil together so that the little bags are as airtight as possible, and bake them gently for about 30 minutes. Serve in their *papillotes*, with a *sauce poivrade*.

CALVES' LIVER WITH MUSHROOMS

calves' liver
mushrooms
shallot or garlic
parsley
chives
tarragon
butter
olive oil
lemon
flour
salt, pepper

Cut thin slices of the liver and chop up finely a mushroom for each slice with parsley, chives, tarragon and the shallot or a little garlic. Season and flour the liver lightly, and fry it quickly on each side in a mixture of butter and olive oil. When the liver is nicely coloured, throw in the mushrooms and herb mixture and cook gently for another 5 minutes, shaking the pan to prevent the liver from sticking to the bottom. Serve very hot with a little lemon squeezed over it.

CALVES' LIVER, STUFFED AND BAKED

calves' liver
hard-boiled egg
breadcrumbs
stock
salt, pepper
parsley
garlic
a pig's caul

Buy the liver in one piece and make some fairly deep incisions in it at regular intervals, stuffing these with a mixture of finely chopped hard-boiled egg, breadcrumbs soaked in stock and then pressed dry, salt, pepper, chopped parsley and a very little chopped garlic. Cover the liver completely with a pig's caul and bake in a moderate oven for about 30 minutes. (Not much longer, as it should still be faintly pink inside when cut.) It is done when there is no sign of blood when it is pricked with a skewer and exudes only a very pale pink juice.

French beans are admirable with this unusual dish.

OFFAL (VARIETY MEATS)

DEVILLED CALVES' LIVER

calves' liver
mustard
chutney
salt and black pepper
cayenne pepper
butter or olive oil
mushrooms or tomatoes

Cut some calves' liver in slices, and brush each slice over with a mixture of made mustard and chutney. Now sprinkle with a mixture of equal parts salt, freshly ground black pepper and cayenne pepper, dip in melted butter or olive oil, and grill. Serve in a ring with mushrooms or thickly sliced tomatoes which have been spread with mustard butter, and sprinkled with the mixed pepper already described and grilled or baked in the oven.

GRILLED CALVES' LIVER

Wipe small ½ in. slices of liver with a damp cloth. Dry them well, brush with melted butter and sprinkle with salt and pepper. Lay them on a greased grid and grill for about 5 minutes, turning them once. Brush again with butter before serving.

A so-called Spanish style demands that the slices should be brushed with maître d'hotel butter after grilling and served with grilled slices of tomatoes and onions.

MOCK TERRAPIN

1 lb. calves' liver
1 oz. (2 tablespoonfuls) butter
2 hard-boiled eggs
1 teaspoonful (1¼ teaspoonfuls) dry mustard
2 tablespoonfuls (2½ tablespoonfuls) dry sherry
⅓ pint (½ pint) water
salt
cayenne pepper

Rub the liver with salt and a little cayenne pepper, and fry it in the butter till a dark brown on both sides, then dredge with flour and cut into small pieces. Add the mustard dissolved in the water, and the chopped eggs too, and cook gently till the liver is quite tender. Then add the sherry and cook on for 2 minutes longer. Serve on crisp pieces of buttered toast.

PORK LIVER PÂTÉ

There are innumerable different ways of making and seasoning this popular hors d'oeuvre. This is a simple and satisfactory one. A pâté can be varied according to taste and need by the addition of a little sherry or brandy, herbs or chopped truffles. A simple substitute for truffles is to use chopped pickled walnuts.

1 lb. pigs' liver
¾ lb. fat green bacon
salt, pepper
nutmeg
streaky smoked bacon
bay leaf (optional)
lard

Mince the liver, free from skin and gristle, and mix it thoroughly with the minced fat green bacon. Season well with salt, pepper and grated nutmeg and when well amalgamated pass it through a sieve. Line the bottom and sides of an earthenware terrine with very thin rashers of streaky smoked bacon, and fill up with the mince. Arrange some more thin rashers on top and cover with buttered paper or kitchen foil. Stand the terrine in a baking tin containing water, and bring this to the boil over the heat. Then transfer it to a moderate oven and cook for just a little over 1 hour, testing with a skewer to see when it is done. This will be when nothing is exuded from the pâté and the skewer comes out quite clean; if it sticks at all, or any blood comes out, further cooking is needed.

Leave the pâté to cool with a weight on top, actually pressing the meat hard down, and when cold, pour over a layer of melted lard and let it set. Do not turn the pâté out to serve, but cut slices straight out of the terrine. If you like the taste, a single bay leaf may be placed in the middle of the bottom of the terrine before the bacon lining is put in.

PIGS' LIVER AND SAUSAGE PIE

¾ lb. pigs' liver
¾ lb. sausagemeat
shortcrust pastry

Boil the liver for about 5 minutes then mince it up very finely and mix thoroughly with an equal amount of pork sausagemeat. Line a dish with shortcrust pastry made with lard, fill with the mince, cover with more pastry and bake. Serve hot or cold, but better hot.

MARROW

The spinal marrow of ox, sheep and lamb is known as *amourette* in France and can all be treated in any of the ways suitable for brains. In England, however, beef marrow is enjoyed in a special way, either eaten from the bone itself with long silver spoons specially made for the purpose or extracted from the bone and served as a savoury on toast. In the U.S.A. it is also made into *quenelles* and served as an hors d'oeuvre.

OFFAL (VARIETY MEATS)

MARROW BONES

Mrs Rundell, a famous 19th-century cook, gives the following instructions. 'Saw the marrow bones in half if very long. Cover the end of each bone with a very stiff flour-and-water paste, so as to prevent the marrow from escaping while it cooks and then tie a cloth over each bone. Put them in a large saucepan full of boiling salted water, and let them boil for 3 hours. Then take them out of the pan, remove the cloths and all the paste and pin a clean napkin round each. Serve upright on a hot dish accompanied by dry toast in a toast-rack'. Proper marrow spoons must be provided to scoop the marrow from the bones; if these are unobtainable, the marrow must be served as in either of the two following recipes.

MARROW PATTIES

beef marrow bones
cold water
puff pastry
parsley
chives
thyme
1 tablespoonful ($1\frac{1}{4}$ tablespoonfuls) cream
salt, pepper
lemon juice

Have the bones broken so that the marrow can be got out in walnut-sized pieces, and put these into a pan with a pinch of salt and cover them with cold water. Then boil for a minute or two, and pass through a nylon or hair sieve. Have ready 6 pattypans lined with puff pastry and beat 1 tablespoonful cream with a finely minced tablespoonful of parsley, chives and thyme mixed together. Season with lemon juice, salt and pepper and put a little of this with the pieces of marrow in the pattypans. Bake in a moderate oven for 15 minutes and serve at once.

MARROW TOASTS

Get the marrow taken from the bone in fairly large pieces, blanch them for 5 minutes, then drain and let them get quite cold. Cut into small pieces, put them on a fireproof dish, season with salt and pepper and brush them over with liquid meat glaze (*see* p. 213). Warm the marrow and keep it hot, and when the toast has been made, brush the marrow rather quickly over it.

If preferred, the little pieces of the cooked marrow can be set on buttered fingers of toast and brushed over with the glaze just before serving.

PALATES

'Ox palate, which was very much used in *ancienne cuisine*', says Escoffier in his *Ma Cuisine*, 'is almost completely neglected in modern cookery. This, in my opinion, is a pity'. He used to cook the palates for about 4 hours in a thin white sauce after first soaking and blanching them and then removing the white skin, but in my own opinion they want a more savoury preparation. Blanch them for 10 minutes in boiling salted water. Drain them and let them get cool, and then scrape off all the white skin and trim them. Put them into a stewpan with 2 pints (2½ pints) stock, a large bouquet garni, and some pieces of ham or bacon. Bring to the boil and let them simmer gently but steadily on a very low heat for 3–4 hours. Then drain, let them get cold and split in halves lengthways.

FRIED OX PALATES

As above, but egg-and-breadcrumb them or dip them in batter and fry them in deep fat or oil. Serve with tomato sauce (*see* p. 211).

GRILLED OX PALATES

Divide the cooked palate into pieces 2–2½ in. across, dip them in melted butter and then in breadcrumbs and grill gently. Serve with a rémoulade or tartare sauce (*see* p. 212).

SWEETBREADS

Calves' and lambs' sweetbreads are a great delicacy and all the recipes I have given for calves' sweetbreads apply equally to lambs'. Sweetbreads must always be blanched before cooking. Allow 4–5 oz. for each serving.

Escoffier says 'Veal sweetbreads may be looked upon as one of the greatest delicacies in butchers' meats, and may be served at any dinner, however sumptuous. Select them very white, entirely free of bloodstains, and leave them to soak in fresh water, which should be frequently changed, for as long as possible or, better still, place them under a running tap.

'To blanch them (an operation the purpose of which is to harden the surface) put them into a saucepan with enough cold water to cover them completely, and bring to the boil gently. Let them boil for 10 minutes; withdraw them and plunge them into a basin of fresh cold water. When the sweetbreads are cold, trim them; that is to say, cut away all cartilaginous and connective tissue, lay them between two pieces of linen and put them under a light weight for 2 hours. Veal sweetbread consists of two parts as unequal in quality as in shape. They are the "kernel" or true sweetbread, which is the round and most delicate part, and the "throat" sweetbread, which is the elongated part and not of such fine quality as the former'. The throat sweetbread is in fact the thyroid gland, while the true sweetbread is the pancreas. The former should be considerably cheaper to buy.

BRAISED VEAL SWEETBREADS

sweetbreads
1 small onion
1 small carrot
1 stick celery
6 peppercorns
½ turnip
bouquet garni
veal stock
meat glaze (optional)
bacon bones (optional)

Prepare the sweetbreads by blanching them as above. Cut up the onion, carrot, turnip and celery and put them in a stewpan just large enough to contain the sweetbreads, adding half a dozen peppercorns, a bouquet garni and enough good stock nearly to cover the vegetables. Wrap the sweetbreads in buttered paper, lay them on the vegetable bed and cook them gently, with the lid on, for 45 minutes. Before serving, with the thickened strained braising liquor handed separately, they may be brushed over with a little melted meat glaze. Some like to add a few small bacon bones with the vegetables, but although the idea is pleasant enough, I think their additional flavour detracts from that of the sweetbreads.

GRILLED SWEETBREADS

sweetbreads
butter

Escoffier recommends an extremely delicate and delicious way of cooking these and here is his recipe. 'Blanch and poach the sweetbreads and when they are cold cut them in halves across, dip each half in melted butter and grill very gently, basting with melted butter'. They may, of course, be grilled whole; if so they will take a little longer and the heat must not be so great.

SWEETBREAD SALAD

sweetbread
lettuce
mayonnaise
cucumber
cream (optional)
chervil (optional)

Shred up some lettuce and toss it in a light mayonnaise, adding a little thin cream to it if desired. Arrange this in a dish and lay on it some thin slices of cooked sweetbread. Spread some more mayonnaise, but thicker this time, over the sweetbreads and garnish with cucumber slices. If liked, garnish with chopped chervil.

VEAL SWEETBREADS IN BACON

sweetbreads
butter
bacon rashers
salt, pepper

Cut each blanched sweetbread into quarters; season these pieces with salt and pepper and roll up in a very thin rasher of streaky smoked bacon. Impale on a skewer and fry, grill or bake them for 10-15 minutes till the bacon is crisp and golden-brown. Some nicely buttered broad beans will do admirably as an accompaniment.

VEAL SWEETBREADS À LA CRÈME

sweetbreads
4 fl. oz. (½ cup) brandy
1½ cups (2 cups) double cream
butter
meat glaze
a little lemon juice
French mustard
salt
black pepper
fried bread croûtons

Blanch the sweetbreads as directed on p. 196 and cook in butter in a casserole over a low heat for 20 minutes. Now add the brandy, set it alight and, when the flames have died down, pour in the thick double cream. Mix with this a little meat glaze, the lemon juice, a suspicion of French mustard, and salt and pepper to taste. Reduce this sauce over a slow heat till the cream has thickened suitably, and serve garnished by a few croûtons of bread fried in butter.

VEAL SWEETBREADS, COUNTRY STYLE (U.S.A.)

sweetbreads
salt, pepper
flour
butter
fat pickled salt pork

Sprinkle the blanched sweetbreads with salt and pepper and shake a little flour over them. Arrange them in a buttered shallow fireproof dish, brush them over with melted butter and cover with thin slices of fat pickled salt pork. Bake for 25 minutes in a hot oven, basting twice during that time, and remove the pork for the last 5 minutes so that the sweetbreads can brown.

VEAL SWEETBREAD FLAN

1 veal sweetbread
white sauce
mushrooms
salt, pepper
brandy
shortcrust pastry flan case
cream

Blanch a sweetbread weighing about ½ lb. and simmer it in salted water for 20 minutes. Then skin it and cut it up into small pieces. Make a thickish white sauce in the usual way, adding just a very little of the water in which the sweetbread was cooked and some small white mushrooms (preferably cooked yourself, but in any case cut in halves); season the sauce with salt and pepper and add just a touch of brandy. Use this mixture to fill a cooked shortcrust pastry flan, pour a little thick cream over the top and brown the top very lightly. A purée of spinach would be very good with this.

OFFAL (VARIETY MEATS)

VEAL SWEETBREADS AU JUS

braised sweetbreads
stock
tomato
1 tablespoonful tomato purée
Madeira

Clear the strained braising liquor of as much fat as possible, and pour into it a small glass of Madeira. Reduce this by boiling quickly, scraping and stirring the bottom of the braising pan to release what juices have coagulated there. When the liquid is reduced to half, add the tomato purée, a tomato skinned and cut in pieces, and a sufficiency of good veal stock to bring the sauce to the consistency you desire. Mix well and reduce a little more to thicken it, and strain it over the sweetbreads. Green peas with this or, if you prefer, some fresh green *flageolet* beans.

VEAL SWEETBREADS WITH MUSHROOMS (U.S.A.)

3 veal sweetbreads
½ small carrot
½ onion
2 thin slices bacon
mushrooms
8 fl. oz. (1 cup) espagnole sauce (p. 209)
½ glass sherry

Blanch the sweetbreads and put them into an earthenware baking dish on the slices of bacon. Pour the sauce over them and sprinkle on top the sliced mushrooms mixed with the chopped onion and carrot. Put the lid on tightly, and cook in a moderate oven for 20 minutes. Then add the sherry and cook on for 15 minutes longer. Serve in the dish it was cooked in and accompany with fresh green peas.

VEAL SWEETBREADS À LA NANTUA

sweetbreads
chicken or veal stock
crayfish meat
white sauce
breadcrumbs
croûtons of bread
thick cream
salt, black pepper

Blanch the sweetbreads in the usual way and then braise or poach gently in well seasoned stock. Drain and then cut off the top third of the sweetbreads. Pile on the shellfish meat, reserving some of the choicer pieces for garnish. For a less luxurious dish but one with a delicious flavour use shrimps or prawns instead of the crayfish, although this is then not a classical recipe *à la Nantua*. Coat with a béchamel sauce, sprinkle with breadcrumbs, and glaze lightly in the oven. Serve on croûtons, decorate with pieces of shellfish meat, and serve with more sauce to which you have added some thick cream and a little pounded shellfish meat, reserved for this purpose. Seasoning of salt and pepper is added to taste before serving.

TAILS

Stewed oxtail is a splendid dish but it is not generally known that a particularly delicious stew can also be made with lambs' tails. Although they are seldom come by except in the sheep country at lambing time; I give a recipe in case you ever come across them. Although the Russians make a dish from pigs' tails, elsewhere they are normally only used to make a stock more gelatinous. In the Arab world, however, tails of the fat-tailed variety are much used in stews, in *cous-cous* and other delicacies.

Above all perhaps, oxtail is known for its use as the basis of a particularly rich and nutritious soup, a meal in itself on a cold winter's evening.

STEWED OXTAIL

oxtail
dripping or butter
onion
flour
1 pint (1¼ pints) stock
bouquet garni
2 cloves
1 blade mace
12 peppercorns
salt
lemon juice

Brown the sections of oxtail in dripping or butter, add a little flour and brown that too, and then a sliced onion. When all are well browned, add a bouquet garni, 2 cloves, a blade of mace and 12 peppercorns in a muslin bag and a seasoning of salt. Cover with stock, put on the lid tightly, and simmer, preferably in the oven, for at least 3 hours. If preferred use half stock and half red wine. When done, put the pieces of tail on a dish, remove the fat from the gravy, add a teaspoonful of lemon juice to it, and strain it over the meat. Garnish with carrots and onions, little toast triangles or fried bread, and a few mushrooms lightly fried in butter.

LAMBS' TAILS STEW

lambs' tails
onion
carrot
bouquet garni
peppercorns
bacon rashers
stock
salt, pepper

Blanch the tails and dry them, and put a sliced onion and carrot into a stewpan with the bouquet of herbs and the peppercorns. Lay the tails on this bed, season them with a little salt and pepper, bearing in mind the saltiness of the bacon, and cover them with bacon rashers. Add enough stock nearly to cover the vegetables, put the lid on tightly and cook gently for 2 hours, adding a little more stock now and then. Strain the sauce and reduce, if necessary. Serve the tails in a border of mashed potato and pour the strained and reduced sauce over the meat.

TONGUES

The meat of an ox tongue is quite incomparable, and the tongues of smaller animals cannot hold a candle to it. It can be obtained in a fresh, smoked or salted state, although the last two must be soaked for 12 hours or so before being cooked. In its fresh state, it should be soaked for 2 or 3 hours only, but it is sometimes left for 24 hours covered with salt, which is said to enhance the flavour. Salted tongue is cooked in plain unsalted water, but the fresh tongue is usually braised. The tongues of small animals, however, are always better braised. Allow about 4-6 oz. tongue for each serving.

Instructions for carving tongue will be found on p. 21 and a drawing on p. 202.

ASPIC FOR COLD TONGUE

2 pints (2½ pints) jellied veal stock (see p. 73)
1 oz. (¼ cup) gelatine
½ glass dry sherry
⅛ pint (⅙ pint) wine vinegar
the shells and whites of 2 eggs
bouquet garni
2 strips of celery

See that the stock is quite cold so that you can take off every vestige of fat, and then put it into a stewpan with the gelatine, the bouquet garni, the celery cut in large pieces, the broken egg-shells and the slightly beaten egg whites. Whisk over a good heat till nearly boiling, then add the sherry and vinegar. Go on whisking till the liquid actually does boil, then draw the saucepan off the heat and let simmer for about 10 minutes. Strain till quite clear and set aside for use.

BOILED OX TONGUE

ox tongue
onions
cloves
bouquet garni
garlic
salt
peppercorns
water

Put the soaked tongue into a saucepan and cover with fresh water. Add 2 onions, each stuck with a clove of garlic and the bouquet garni, doubling the usual amount of herbs. Add the peppercorns in a muslin bag and salt at the rate of ½ teaspoonful for each 2 pints of water. Bring to the boil, cover and simmer for 1½ hours. Then take out the tongue and skin it, put it back into the pan and continue cooking till it is quite tender when pierced with a metal skewer. To skin the tongue without damaging the meaty part, it is advisable to slit the skin on the underside when it is cool. For salt tongues to be served cold, fit into a round dish, put a plate with a weight on top and leave till set.

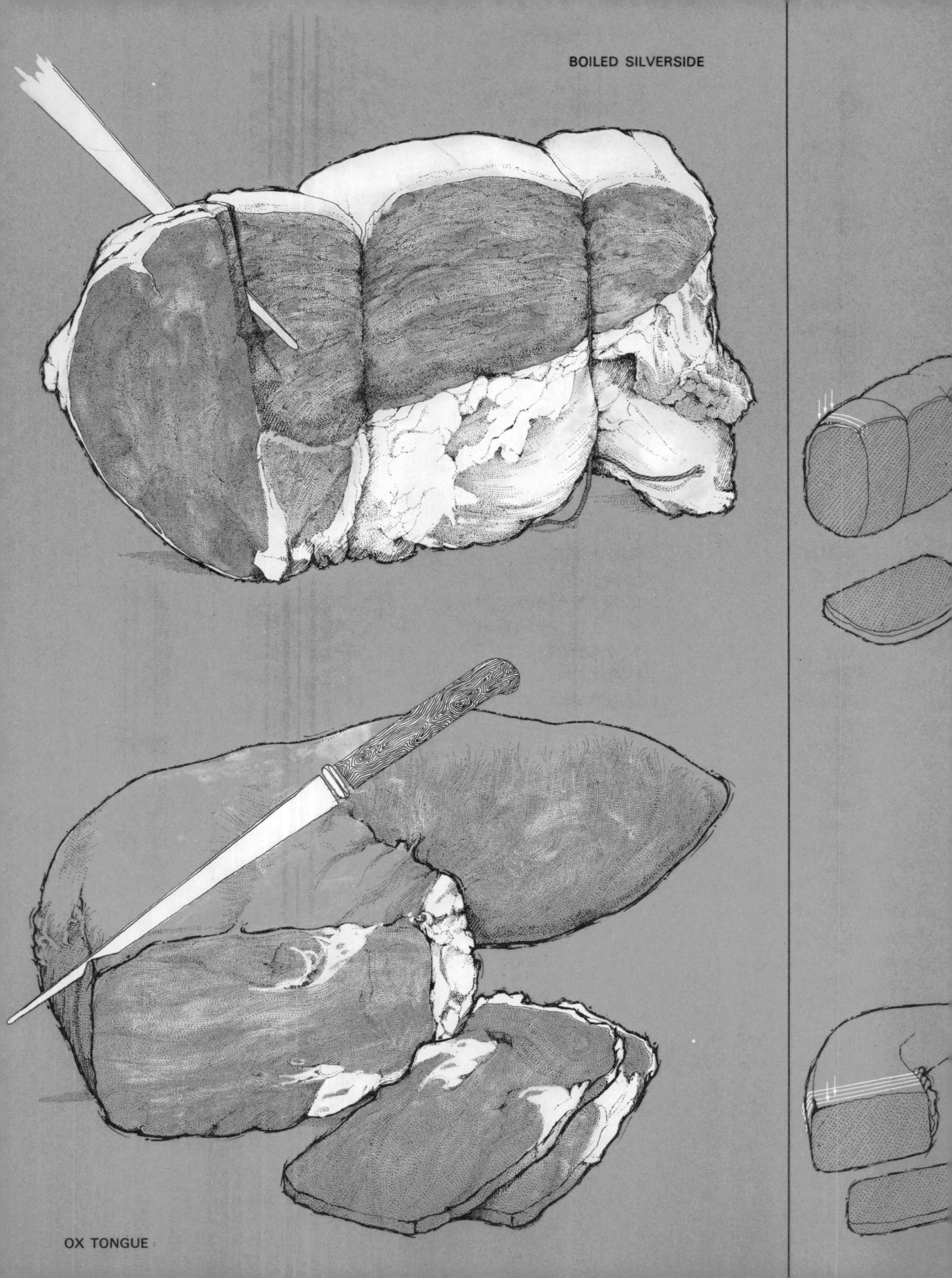

BOILED SILVERSIDE

OX TONGUE

OFFAL (VARIETY MEATS)

BRAISED CALVES' TONGUES

calves' tongues
bacon
carrots
onions
bouquet garni
stock
dry white wine
salt, pepper

Put the tongues in cold water, bring them to the boil, simmer for 10 minutes then drain. Put some pieces of fat bacon, with a thinly sliced onion and carrot into the stewpan, add the tongues and pour in enough stock and dry white wine (about half and half) to come halfway up their sides. Add a little salt and pepper and boil this liquid away till it has completely disappeared. Now cover the tongues with fresh lightly seasoned stock, add a bouquet garni, put on the lid and simmer till the tongues are nearly tender. Then take them out and skin them, put them back into the pan and go on cooking till the liquid almost sets in a jelly. Strain this over the tongue to serve either whole or cut in halves lengthways. A tomato or *piquante* sauce goes well with them, and a vegetable purée of some kind.

BRAISED OX TONGUE

ox tongue
carrots
onions
green bacon rinds
bouquet garni
1 pint (1¼ pints) dry white wine
beef stock
demi-glace sauce (p. 209)

Start off by cooking the tongue according to the recipe for boiled tongue (*see* p. 202) for the first 1½ hours. Then skin it and put it on a bed of thinly sliced onions and carrots, bouquet garni and bacon rinds. Pour on the wine and cook with the lid off till it is reduced by one-third. Next add enough beef stock (two-thirds) and cooking liquor from the tongue (one-third) so that the tongue is two-thirds covered, put on the lid and cook in the oven till tender. Arrange the skinned tongue on a dish and make a smooth thick sauce with the reduced cooking liquor bound with 6 tablespoonfuls of the demi-glace sauce.

VIRGINIA BOILED TONGUE (U.S.A.)

ox tongue
cranberries
brown sugar
½ lemon
1 teaspoonful (1¼ teaspoonfuls) cloves

Boil the tongue in the usual way, and when it is done skin and trim it and simmer it for 15 minutes with a mixture of a cupful of the cooking liquor, the same of cooked cranberries, a firmly-packed teacupful of brown sugar, a sliced lemon and 3 teaspoonfuls cloves. Serve this with it as a sauce.

It must not be forgotten that the liquor in which ox tongue has been cooked makes very excellent and savoury stock.

OX TONGUE IN SWEET-SOUR SAUCE

slices of cold ox tongue
1½ oz. cooked ham
celery
clove garlic
parsley
lard
2 tablespoonfuls (2½ tablespoonfuls) caster sugar
2 tablespoonfuls (2½ tablespoonfuls) grated chocolate
½ bay leaf
4 fl. oz. (½ cup) vinegar
raisins
pine kernels
glacé cherries
4 fl. oz. (½ cup) water

Chop up an onion with 1½ oz. fat ham, a small stick of celery, a clove of garlic and a few sprigs of parsley and brown in a little lard. Then add 2 tablespoonfuls of caster sugar, the same of grated chocolate and half a bay leaf. Mix well together and add just over ½ cup of good vinegar and ½ cup of water, a few raisins, some pine kernels and glacé cherries, all chopped and simmer very gently till the sauce is fairly thick and pour it over the slices of cold ox tongue.

Unsweetened or bitter chocolate is best used by those to whom this peculiar sweet-sour flavour is unfamiliar.

TRIPE

In this country the preliminary preparation is carried out by the butcher, and after that only 1½–2 hours' cooking is generally necessary, though some elaborate recipes call for longer.

TRIPE AND ONIONS

2 lb. dressed tripe
½ pint (1¼ cups) water
½ pint (1¼ cups) milk
2 onions
salt, pepper and nutmeg
flour

Cut 2 lb. dressed tripe into 3 in. squares, cover with cold water, bring to the boil and drain the water off. Now add ½ pint milk, ½ pint water and 1 teaspoonful salt. Bring to the boil and add 2 large onions, thinly sliced, and simmer tightly covered for 3 hours, preferably in the oven. About 15 minutes before serving, bind the liquor with flour and grate in a very little nutmeg.

OFFAL (VARIETY MEATS)

The French distinguish between all four stomachs of the ox, which they call the *tripes*, and the three stomachs as we know them in England which they call *gras-double*. The most elaborate and delicious recipe for cooking it comes from Normandy but is seldom attempted by the housewife or amateur cook.

TRIPES À LA MODE DE CAEN (France)

2 lb. tripe
ox-foot
calf's foot
fresh pork rind
2 carrots
4 onions
bouquet garni
tarragon
celery
garlic
4 cloves
salt
cayenne pepper
1 liqueur glassful Calvados or grape brandy
cider

Blanch the tripe for 30 minutes, then drain it and cut into smallish squares. Cut also into squares the meat from an ox-foot and a calf's foot. In the bottom of a large casserole, preferably of earthenware, put 2 or 3 pieces of fresh pork rind, the bones from the feet, 2 carrots and 4 onions cut in small pieces, a bouquet garni, tarragon, celery, and a clove of garlic tied in a little bundle, a seasoning of salt and cayenne pepper and 4 cloves in a muslin bag. Add the pieces of meat from the bones and the squares of tripe, and moisten with a liqueur glassful of Calvados and enough dry still cider to cover the meat. Now put on the lid and seal it down with a flour and water paste so that it is quite airtight. Cook in a slow oven for 8 hours. It is remarkable beyond belief.

BASIC SAUCES AND VARIATIONS

The making of meat stock is an elementary process in modern household kitchens, but is all too often supplanted by the various bouillon cubes which, although convenient, are not of course as good as the real thing. There are, however, a number of sauces which crop up over and over again and which are based on one or other of the mother sauces, or *sauces mères*, as the French call them.

WHITE SAUCES

BÉCHAMEL SAUCE

4 oz. (1 cup) light brown roux
2 pints (2½ pints) milk
salt, pepper
nutmeg
½ medium-sized onion
bouquet garni
butter

Whisking all the time, add to the light brown roux the boiling milk and then bring to boiling point again. Now add a good pinch of salt, a pinch of coarse white pepper, a little grated nutmeg, and half a medium-sized onion with the bouquet, and simmer for 30 minutes or so. Then strain the sauce through butter muslin, and cover the surface with a little melted butter to prevent a skin from forming.

CHEESE SAUCE

This is an ordinary white or béchamel sauce to which grated cheese has been added at the last minute and stirred till it melts. The usual proportions are a tablespoonful of cheese to ¾ pint (2 cups) of sauce, but more may be added according to taste. Some like to add a touch of made mustard as well, and a dash of cayenne pepper.

MUSTARD SAUCE

This is a white or béchamel sauce mixed with made English or French mustard in the proportions which appeal to the cook.

Uncooked Ham and some of the ingredients for Glazed Ham

BROWN SAUCES

ESPAGNOLE SAUCE (Brown sauce)

4 oz. (1 cup) brown roux
2 pints (2½ pints) brown stock
parsley, thyme, bay leaf
1 oz. (2 tablespoonfuls) diced onion
1 diced carrot
1 oz. (2 tablespoonfuls) butter
1 oz. (2 tablespoonfuls) bacon fat

Make the brown roux and dilute it with the brown stock by degrees, seeing that it is free from lumps and whisking all the time. Still whisking, bring it to the boil and add the herbs, diced onion and diced carrot, both previously browned in a mixture of 1 oz. each of butter and bacon fat. Simmer for 3 hours on a low heat, adding a little cold stock now and then, which will help to clear the sauce. Then rub through a sieve, and stir it now and again as it cools.

DEMI-GLACE SAUCE

This is nothing more than an espagnole sauce to which has been added strong brown veal stock or meat jelly at the last moment before using. This becomes *demi-glace tomatée*, with the addition of a third of its volume of tomato sauce (*see* p. 211).

DEVILLED SAUCE

½ pint (1¼ cups) dry white wine
3 sliced shallots
½ pint (1¼ cups) demi-glace sauce
cayenne pepper
1 tablespoonful (1¼ tablespoonfuls) mustard

Put the shallots in a saucepan with the dry white wine and reduce by two-thirds. Then add the *demi-glace* sauce and boil for a little longer. Finally add a pinch of cayenne pepper and a tablespoonful of made English mustard.

MADEIRA SAUCE

1½ pints (under 2 pints) demi-glace sauce
½ glass Madeira

Reduce the *demi-glace* sauce (*see* p. 209) till it is stiff, then remove it from the fire and add the Madeira, which should bring it back to its original consistency. Strain. It may be kept warm without allowing it to boil for a few minutes, but serve as soon as possible.

Glazed Ham

BORDELAISE SAUCE

½ glass red or white Bordeaux wine
1 shallot
coarsely ground pepper
8 fl. oz. (1 cup) demi-glace sauce
tomato sauce
fresh beef marrow

Put into a saucepan the red or white Bordeaux with a chopped shallot and a pinch of coarse pepper. Boil briskly till half its volume has disappeared. Then add the *demi-glace* sauce and a little tomato sauce to taste. Boil together for a few minutes, then strain through a fine sieve. This sauce, finished with some poached beef marrow cut in rings, is marvellous with beef.

SAUCE PIQUANTE

6 tablespoonfuls (½ cup) wine vinegar
2 finely chopped shallots
1 pint (2½ cups) demi-glace sauce
2 tablespoonfuls (2½ tablespoonfuls) chopped pickled gherkins
parsley
tarragon

Put the wine vinegar in a pan with the finely chopped shallots and boil till reduced by half. Now add the *demi-glace* sauce, and simmer for 10 minutes. Then, off the heat, add the chopped pickled gherkins, chopped tarragon and parsley. This sauce is notably good with boiled fresh beef or pork and with pigs' trotters.

SAUCE POIVRADE

2 oz. (4 tablespoonfuls) butter
2 oz. (4 tablespoonfuls) diced onion
2 oz. (4 tablespoonfuls) diced carrot
bouquet garni
1¾ pints (2½ cups) wine vinegar
1 pint (2½ cups) demi-glace sauce
a few tablespoonfuls marinade (optional)

Brown the diced onion and carrot in butter and add a bouquet garni and wine vinegar. Reduce to half and then add the *demi-glace* sauce and reduce further. Then strain through a fine sieve and add another ½ oz. (1 tablespoonful) butter.
(If the sauce is used with meat that has been marinaded, a few tablespoonfuls of the marinade may be added.)

BASIC SAUCES AND VARIATIONS

CHASSEUR SAUCE

5 oz. mushrooms
½ oz. (1 tablespoonful) butter
1 tablespoonful (1¼ tablespoonfuls) olive oil
a little shallot
3 tablespoonfuls (3¾ tablespoonfuls) brandy
6 tablespoonfuls (9 tablespoonfuls) dry white wine
½ pint (1¼ cups) demi-glace sauce
2–3 tablespoonfuls (2½–3¾ tablespoonfuls) tomato sauce
a little meat jelly
parsley

In a mixture of butter and olive oil, brown the chopped mushrooms slightly. Add the chopped shallot and brandy. In another pan reduce the dry white wine by half and add this as well. Finally add the *demi-glace* sauce, tomato sauce and meat jelly. Boil for a minute or two and add a little chopped parsley. This sauce is admirable with tournedos or fillet of beef.

ROBERT SAUCE

1 medium-sized onion
butter
⅙ pint (⅓ cup) dry white wine
½ pint (1¼ cups) demi-glace sauce
1 dessertspoonful (½ tablespoonful) meat glaze
mustard
caster sugar

Mince a medium-sized onion finely and fry it with a little butter without letting it colour. Now dilute with the dry white wine, and reduce this by a third. Add ½ pint of demi-glace sauce (*see* p. 209), and simmer for 20 minutes. When the sauce is ready, finish it with a dessertspoonful of meat glaze, some mustard and a small pinch of caster sugar.

TOMATO SAUCE

Chop 1–1½ lb. tomatoes. Melt 1 tablespoonful (1¼ tablespoonfuls) of olive oil and 1 oz. (2 tablespoonfuls) butter in a shallow pan. Add the tomatoes and a clove of garlic. Fresh or dried basil, caster sugar and celery leaves may be added at this point, if desired. Simmer all for about 15 minutes with the lid on. Sieve or put through a vegetable mill. Test for seasoning, which will be a matter of personal preference. To my mind, the skins should be left on the tomatoes during the cooking. They will disappear when the sauce is sieved. This sauce will keep well if a little melted butter is poured over it.

EMULSIFIED SAUCES

BÉARNAISE SAUCE

½ **glass dry white wine**
4 fl. oz. (½ cup) tarragon vinegar
2 level teaspoonfuls (2½ teaspoonfuls) chopped shallot
pinch of chopped tarragon
pinch salt
small pinch coarse pepper
1 oz. (2 tablespoonfuls) butter
3 yolks of eggs
8 oz. (1 cup) softened butter
cayenne pepper
chopped chervil

Put the wine, vinegar, shallot, herbs, seasonings and the butter into a saucepan, and boil till reduced by two-thirds. Cool, off the heat, for a few minutes, then add the egg yolks and over a *very low heat indeed* add the softened butter in small pieces, beating each addition in till dissolved. Keep stirring with a wooden spoon till the sauce thickens. Serve *warm*. If it should curdle, take another egg yolk and start again.

CHORON SAUCE
This is a Béarnaise sauce with the addition of tomato purée. The amount of tomato purée to be added is a quarter of the Béarnaise sauce and it should be added at the last minute and the tarragon and chervil omitted.

SAUCE TARTARE
This can either be a mayonnaise to which has been added finely chopped gherkins, capers, olives, parsley and chives, or it can be a mayonnaise made with hard-boiled egg yolk, garnished with finely chopped onions and chives and highly seasoned.

MISCELLANEOUS SAUCES

MADEIRA SCALLION SAUCE

12 spring onions **2 oz. (¼ cup) butter** **1 oz. (¼ cup) flour** **6 fl. oz. (¾ cup) water** **salt, pepper** **ketchup** **parsley** **½ glass Madeira**	Chop up the onions finely and gently sauté in the butter for 5 minutes. Add the flour and brown slightly, then gradually stir in the hot water and cook for a further 5 minutes till it has thickened. Now chop or mince the parsley. Add the seasoning, ketchup, parsley and Madeira and bring to the boil just before serving.

MEAT GLAZE

This is nothing more than the reduction of good stock (brown or white). As it reduces, so it thickens and the preliminary process may be done fairly quickly, though the final stages are done very gently over a moderate heat, so that the glaze attains a syrupy consistency, which will coat the back of a spoon. It should be used carefully.

MELTED BUTTER SAUCE

This is not to be confused with melted butter (*beurre fondue*), as it is often called 'Melted Butter' (the word 'sauce' being understood) in some old cookery books.

1 oz. (2 tablespoonfuls) butter **1 oz. (¼ cup) flour** **½ pint (1¼ cups) water** **salt, pepper**	Make a roux with the butter and flour and mix with it the water, which should be hot but not quite boiling. Stir till it thickens, bring to the boil, simmer for a few minutes and season with salt and pepper.

MINT SAUCE

Wash and dry 2 tablespoonfuls (2½ tablespoonfuls) of fresh mint leaves, and chop very finely. Add 3–4 tablespoonfuls (3¾–5 tablespoonfuls) caster sugar and pour over ⅛ pint (¼ cup) boiling water to keep the mint green. Then add ¼ pint (⅓ pint) good vinegar and serve cold.

ONION SAUCE

Blanch ½ lb. onions, then put them into cold water with a little salt and cook about 1 hour till quite tender. Drain and chop finely and add to a pint of white sauce. Season with bay leaf or a little nutmeg if you prefer.

THE MATCHMAKING OF MEAT AND WINE

by André L. Simon

The best of all partnerships is that in which the partners understand each other perfectly and when they are willing and able to help one another.

Wine and cheese, for instance, are said to be good partners; so they are good partners, but not the best of partners. Why? Because the cheese does all, or most of the giving, whilst the wine gives nothing or very little in return. It is the wine merchant who will give you cheese when he is asking you to taste the wines which he wishes you to buy, but has any grocer ever been known to offer a glass of wine to any prospective cheese buyer? It may well be said that exactly the reverse is the case with fish and wine: it is the wine that does all the giving! It is all the more praiseworthy because the white wine which so graciously helps the fish, does not like fish, and red wine simply detests it! Nobody will deny that fish loses most of its fishiness when cooked in white wine, and that it tastes much better if served with a nice fresh white wine, but has any fish ever been known to return the compliment and help wine?

It is only when we come to meat and wine that we find the best or ideal partnership, when both partners really do help one another. There must be, of course, the very important proviso that they must be well matched! As it happens, however, there is a very great variety not so much of meat but of ways and means of preparing meat for the table, and there is also a very considerable number of different wines available for us to choose the right partner. This means that if we will give a little attention and care to the problem – it might be better to call it a game or a hobby than a problem – of wine and meat matchmaking, we have every chance to succeed.

It is generally accepted as a sound or basic rule to look for a red wine to partner any kind of red meat, and for a white wine to partner white meat, such as veal and pork, as well as most offals. Like all rules, of course, it has its exceptions.

Another rule, one which has very few, if any, exceptions, is that all meat and meat dishes are better partnered with dry wines, still or sparkling, but never sweet.

Yet another rule, maybe the last but certainly not the least, is that the best wine

THE MATCHMAKING OF MEAT AND WINE

is the wine which you happen to have or the one you are able to get: it is up to you to make the best of it, and there is no cause to worry if the name on its label is not that mentioned in your cookery book. Labels are not for drinking; the wine in the bottle is! So, if you are going to have a *Boeuf Bourguignon* or a *Boeuf à la Bordelaise*, and the book tells you to serve Burgundy with the one and Bordeaux with the other, do so by all means should you have both red wines in your cellar to choose from; however, if you have only one or the other, there is no need whatever to be unhappy about it. Red Bordeaux and Burgundy are not, like port and sherry, entirely different types of wine; they are both naturally fermented from the ripe juice of different black grapes, and a red Bordeaux will partner quite well a *Boeuf Bourguinon*, just as a red Burgundy will also partner happily a *Boeuf à la Bordelaise* if and when you do not happen to have what may be called the 'correct' wine to partner the dish.

Of course, when in doubt – and in funds – serve Champagne, dry Champagne. Happily there are but few people who suffer from an unbalanced or over-sensitive diaphragm that will not tolerate bubbles, and although Champagne is by no means an ideal partner for all kinds of meat, it is the most generally welcome wine at all times!

In the list of suggested wine and meat partnerships, the wines mentioned are merely suggestions based on the presumption that the finer and more costly wines are best with the more costly meat dishes, but one must bear in mind that nobody ever had the monopoly of good taste. The partnerships on our list are not necessarily better than other possible combinations on less extravagant levels, but there is no harm in aiming high for a special occasion. More modest wines than those on our list, particularly those from the same *communes*, would be very good partners for whichever dish you enjoy.

WINE AND MEAT MATCH IN EXCELSIS

Boeuf Bourguignon	Chambertin Clos de Bèze, Gevrey-Chambertin
Boeuf à la Mode	Château Cheval Blanc, Graves de St Emilion
Beef Stroganoff	Château Margaux, Margaux
Entrecôte Mirabeau	Château Lafite, Pauillac
Miroton of beef	Château Maucaillou, Moulis-Médoc
Silverside	Château Pontet-Canet, Pauillac
Roast Sirloin	Clos Fourtet, St Emilion
Grilled steak	Château Montrose, St Estèphe
Stewed steak	Château La Pointe, Pomerol
Tournedos Béarnaise	Château Ducru-Beaucaillou, St Julien
Tournedos sauté chasseur	Les Amoureuses, Chambolle-Musigny

Lamb chops	Château Mouton-Rothschild, Pauillac
Lamb cutlets	Château Gris, Nuits St Georges
Roast leg of lamb	Romanée St Vivant, Vosne-Romanée
Roast loin of lamb	Bonnes-Mares, Chambolle-Musigny
Crown roast of lamb	Clos de Vougeot, Vougeot
Noisettes of lamb	Château Léoville-Barton, St Julien
Saddle of mutton	Le Chambertin, Gevrey-Chambertin
Shoulder of lamb	Clos St Jean, Morey-St Denis
Blanquette of veal	Corton-Charlemagne, Aloxe-Corton
Veal Escalopes	Riesling d'Alsace
Roast loin of veal	Meursault Perrières, Meursault
Wiener Schnitzel	Bâtard-Montrachet, Puligny-Montrachet
Pork chops	Scharzberger, Saar
Roast loin of pork	Niersteiner, Rhinehesse
Baked ham	Bernkasteler, Moselle
Sucking pig	Johannisberger, Rhinegau

Acknowledgments

The publishers and producers of this book wish to express their thanks to the proprietors of Stone's Chophouse and À L'Écu de France restaurants, London, and to their staffs for their assistance and advice in the preparation of the drawings. The dishes for the photographs were prepared by Betty Coy.

They would also like to thank the following publishers for permission to quote from the sources given: Blackie and Sons Ltd, *The Scots Kitchen* by Marian McNeill; Faber and Faber Ltd, *Small Meat Dishes* by Ambrose Heath; William Heinemann Ltd, *A Guide to Modern Cookery* by Auguste Escoffier.

Comparative Cookery Terms and Measures

BRITISH MEASURES	AMERICAN MEASURES	AMERICAN CUP EQUIVALENTS
1 teaspoon	1¼ teaspoons	
1 tablespoon	1¼ tablespoons	
1 fluid ounce	1 fluid ounce or 2 tablespoons	
2 fluid ounces	2 fluid ounces or 4 tablespoons	¼ cup
2⅔ fluid ounces	5⅓ tablespoons	⅓ cup
4 fluid ounces	8 tablespoons	½ cup
5⅓ fluid ounces	10⅔ tablespoons	⅔ cup
8 fluid ounces	8 fluid ounces or ½ U.S. pint	1 cup
10 fluid ounces or ½ Imperial pint	10 fluid ounces	1¼ cups
16 fluid ounces	1 U.S. pint	2 cups
20 fluid ounces or 1 Imperial pint	1¼ U.S. pints	2½ cups
1⅗ Imperial pints	2 U.S. pints or 1 U.S. quart	4 cups
2 Imperial pints or 1 Imperial quart	2½ U.S. pints	5 cups
6⅖ Imperial pints	8 U.S. pints or 1 U.S. gallon	16 cups
8 Imperial pints or 1 Imperial gallon	10 U.S. pints	20 cups

COMPARATIVE COOKERY TERMS AND MEASURES

British and American Equivalent Ingredients

BRITISH	AMERICAN
Icing sugar	Confectioners sugar
Cornflour	Cornstarch
Sultanas	Raisins
Rusk	Zwieback
Single cream	Light cream
Double cream	Heavy cream
Bicarbonate of soda	Baking soda
Scone	Biscuit
Soft brown sugar	Brown sugar
100 per cent wholemeal flour	Graham flour
Digestive biscuits	Graham crackers
Trex or Spry	Soft shortening
Butter or margarine	Shortening
1 oz. cooking chocolate	1 square chocolate
$\frac{2}{3}$ oz. bakers yeast, or 3 level teaspoonfuls dried yeast	1 cake yeast
Okra	Gumbo
$\frac{1}{3}$ oz. powdered gelatine, or 1 level tablespoonful	1 envelope gelatine
Caster sugar	Granulated sugar
Biscuit	Cookie or Cracker
Minced meat	Ground meat
2 oz. egg (standard)	2 oz. egg (large)

Equivalent Gas and Electric Oven Temperatures

GAS	$\frac{1}{4}$	$\frac{1}{2}$	1	2	3	4	5	6	7	8	9
ELECTRICITY	240°	265°	290°	310°	335°	355°	380°	400°	425°	445°	470°

1 British fluid ounce is equal to 1 U.S. fluid ounce
British Standard Measuring Cup is equivalent to 10 fluid ounces
American Standard Measuring Cup is equivalent to 8 fluid ounces

In general British and American solid weights are equivalent

Throughout this book English measures are given first: the American equivalents for both solids and liquids follow in brackets

Vintage Chart

0 = No Good   7 = The Best

CHAMPAGNE	WHITE BURGUNDY	SAUTERNES	RHINE	RHÔNE	BURGUNDY	CLARET	PORT	YEAR
6	5	5	6	6	6	6	5	1966
5	4	3	3	3	5	4	4	1965
7	6	3	6	7	6	6	4	1964
4	5	5	2	4	5	4	6	1963
6	5	6	6	6	5	6	5	1962
6	6	5	5	5	5	7	4	1961
4	3	4	5	5	5	4	7	1960
7	7	7	7	7	6	6	3	1959
5	4	5	5	6	4	5	5	1958
2	5	3	3	5	4	5	5	1957
4	3	4	3	5	2	3	2	1956
7	6	6	5	7	6	6	7	1955
3	4	3	3	5	4	4	5	1954
7	7	6	7	7	6	6	5	1953
7	6	6	6	7	7	6	4	1952
2	3	3	2	4	3	3	3	1951
3	6	4	5	6	4	6	6	1950
6	6	5	7	6	6	7	4	1949
4	5	4	5	4	5	6	7	1948
7	7	7	6	7	7	7	7	1947

0 = No Good   7 = The Best

CHAMPAGNE	WHITE BURGUNDY	SAUTERNES	RHINE	RHÔNE	BURGUNDY	CLARET	PORT	YEAR
3	5	3	4	4	4	3	5	1946
6	6	7	6	6	7	6	7	1945
3	2	4	3	3	2	4	4	1944
5	6	6	5	6	5	5	6	1943
5	4	4	5	5	3	3	6	1942
4	1	0	2	3	1	1	4	1941
3	1	3	3	2	2	3	5	1940
2	2	2	3	3	2	2	3	1939
4	4	3	4	5	3	4	5	1938
5	7	7	6	6	5	5	4	1937
2	4	3	1	5	2	3	3	1936
3	5	2	5	3	4	2	7	1935
6	6	5	7	5	6	6	6	1934
5	5	2	6	6	6	4	4	1933
2	2	0	3	2	2	0	1	1932
2	1	2	2	0	0	2	6	1931
1	3	0	3	1	1	1	2	1930
7	7	7	5	7	6	7	3	1929
1	6	5	1	6	5	6	1	1928
1	2	2	4	6	1	1	7	1927

Fresh Food in its Best Season

	JANUARY	FEBRUARY	MARCH	APRIL	MAY	JUNE	JULY	AUGUST	SEPTEMBER	OCTOBER	NOVEMBER	DECEMBER
MEAT												
Beef							x	x	x			
Beef, stall-fed	x	x	x	x								
Grass lamb						x	x					
House lamb	x	x										x
Mutton	x	x	x	x	x	x	x	x	x	x	x	x
Pork	x	x								x	x	x
Sucking-pig	x	x	x									
Veal	x	x	x	x	x	x	x	x	x	x	x	x
POULTRY												
Chicken	x	x	x	x	x	x	x	x	x	x	x	x
Duck	x	x	x	x	x	x	x	x	x	x	x	x
Duckling					x	x						
Goose	x								x	x	x	x
Guinea-fowl		x	x	x	x	x	x	x				
Muscovy duck	x	x	x							x	x	x
Turkey	x			x	x	x	x	x	x	x	x	x
GAME												
Blackgame								x	x	x		
Capercailzie								x	x	x	x	
Golden Plover	x								x	x	x	x
Grouse								x	x	x	x	
Hare	x								x	x	x	x
Partridge	x								x	x	x	x
Pheasant	x									x	x	x
Snipe	x									x	x	x
Venison	x	x	x							x	x	x
Wild duck	x								x	x	x	x
Wild goose	x									x	x	x

	JANUARY	FEBRUARY	MARCH	APRIL	MAY	JUNE	JULY	AUGUST	SEPTEMBER	OCTOBER	NOVEMBER	DECEMBER
GAME (*continued*)												
Wild pigeons and doves	x	x						x	x	x	x	x
Wild rabbit	x	x						x	x	x	x	x
Woodcock	x								x	x	x	x
FISH												
Bass	x	x	x	x	x	x	x	x	x	x	x	x
Bream	x	x	x	x	x	x	x	x	x	x	x	x
Brill				x	x	x	x	x				
Carp		x	x									
Cod	x	x								x	x	x
Dab			x	x	x	x	x	x	x	x		
Eel	x	x				x	x	x	x	x	x	x
Flounder			x	x	x	x	x	x	x			
Grayling									x	x	x	
Grey mullet	x	x	x	x	x	x	x	x	x	x	x	x
Haddock	x	x	x	x	x	x	x	x	x	x	x	x
Hake			x	x	x	x	x	x	x			
Halibut	x	x	x	x	x	x	x	x	x	x	x	x
Herring				x	x	x	x	x	x	x		
John Dory	x	x	x	x	x	x	x	x	x	x	x	x
Lamprey	x	x										
Lemon sole			x	x	x	x	x	x	x			
Mackerel					x	x	x					
Pike	x	x	x					x	x	x	x	x
Pilchard				x	x	x	x	x	x	x		
Plaice			x	x	x	x	x	x	x			
Red mullet					x	x	x	x	x	x	x	x
Rock salmon	x	x	x	x	x	x	x					x
Salmon		x	x	x	x	x	x	x	x			
Salmon trout		x	x	x	x	x	x	x	x			
Sardine	x	x	x	x	x	x						
Skate	x	x	x	x	x	x	x	x	x	x	x	x
Smelt	x	x	x	x						x	x	x
Sole			x	x	x	x	x	x	x			
Sprat										x	x	
Sturgeon	x	x	x	x	x	x	x	x	x	x	x	x
Trout	x	x	x	x	x	x	x	x	x	x	x	x
Turbot	x	x	x	x	x	x	x	x	x	x	x	x
Whitebait	x	x	x	x	x	x	x	x	x	x	x	x
Whiting	x	x	x	x	x	x	x	x	x	x	x	x

FRESH FOOD IN ITS BEST SEASON

	JANUARY	FEBRUARY	MARCH	APRIL	MAY	JUNE	JULY	AUGUST	SEPTEMBER	OCTOBER	NOVEMBER	DECEMBER
CRUSTACEANS												
Crab	x	x	x	x	x	x	x	x	x	x	x	x
Crawfish	x	x	x	x	x	x	x	x	x	x	x	x
Crayfish	x	x	x	x	x	x	x	x	x	x	x	x
Lobster	x	x	x	x	x	x	x	x	x	x	x	x
Prawns	x	x	x	x	x	x	x	x	x	x	x	x
Shrimps	x	x	x	x	x	x	x	x	x	x	x	x
MOLLUSCS												
Mussel	x	x	x	x					x	x	x	x
Oyster	x	x	x	x					x	x	x	x
Scallop	x	x	x	x					x	x	x	x
FRESH VEGETABLES												
Artichoke, globe						x	x	x	x			
Artichoke, Jerusalem	x	x									x	x
Asparagus					x	x	x					
Bean, broad					x	x	x					
Bean, French						x	x					
Bean, haricot						x	x					
Bean, runner							x	x	x			
Beetroot	x	x	x							x	x	x
Broccoli										x	x	x
Brussels sprouts	x	x								x	x	x
Cabbage	x	x	x	x					x	x	x	x
Cabbage, red	x	x	x							x	x	x
Cabbage, savoy	x	x								x	x	x
Carrot					x	x	x	x	x			
Cauliflower						x	x	x	x			
Celery	x									x	x	x
Chestnut	x	x	x								x	x
Cucumber						x	x	x	x			
Curly kale								x	x	x	x	x
Endive	x	x	x	x					x	x	x	x
Leek	x	x	x	x							x	x
Lettuce					x	x	x	x	x			
Mushroom								x	x	x		
Onion	x	x	x	x	x	x	x	x	x	x	x	x
Onion, spring					x	x	x					
Parsnip										x	x	x

	JANUARY	FEBRUARY	MARCH	APRIL	MAY	JUNE	JULY	AUGUST	SEPTEMBER	OCTOBER	NOVEMBER	DECEMBER
FRESH VEGETABLES (*continued*)												
Pea						x	x					
Potato	x	x	x	x	x	x	x	x	x	x	x	x
Potato, new						·x	x					
Pumpkin							x	x	x		x	x	x
Radish						x	x	x				
Rhubarb				x	x	x						
Sea kale									x	x	x	
Shallot								x	x	x		
Spinach				x	x	x	x	x	x	x		
Swede	x									x	x	x
Sweet corn								x	x	x	x	
Tomato					x	x	x	x	x			
Turnip	x									x	x	x
Vegetable marrow							x	x	x	x		
Watercress	x	x	x	x	x	x	x	x	x	x	x	x
FRUITS												
Apple, cooking	x	x	x	x				x	x	x	x	x
Apple, eating	x	x	x						x	x	x	x
Apricot					x	x	x	x	x			
Biackberry								x	x	x		
Blueberry								x	x			
Cherry						x	x	x				
Crabapple								x	x			
Currant						x	x					
Damson								x	x	x		
Gooseberry						x	x	x	x			
Green fig										x	x	
Greengage								x	x			
Loganberry								x				
Medlar											x	
Melon					x	x	x	x	x			
Nectarine								x	x			
Peach						x	x	x				
Plum							x	x	x			
Quince										x		
Raspberry						x	x	x				
Sloe										x		
Strawberry					x	x	x	x				

General Index

Numbers in *italics* refer to illustrations

Alsace, special recipe:
    Bakenoff, 144
America, *see* United States of America
amourette, 194
Austria, special recipes:
    boiled pork Wienerwald, 150
    Wiener Schnitzel, 82

bacon:
    Canadian, 159
    colour, 159
    cuts (English):
        back, long, 160
        back and ribs, 160
        back, short, 160
        back, top, 160
        chops, 160
        collar, end, 160
        collar, prime, 160
        flank, 160
        fore hock, 159
        oyster, 160
        streaky, prime, 160
        streaky, thin, 160
        streaky, top, 160
    preparation, 159
    Scottish, 159
    storage, 159
    vacuum packed, 159
    see also gammon
baking, 13–15
barbecues, 15
beef:
    accompaniments, 27
    carving, *see separate heading,* carving
    categories, 23
    colour, 23
    cuts (English):
        aitchbone, 24
        bladebone, 24
        brisket, *22,* 24, *29*
        buttock, *22,* 24
        chuck, 24
        clod, *22,* 24
        fillet (undercut of sirloin), *22,* 24, *56*
        flank, thick, *22,* 24
        flank, thin, *22,* 24
        forequarter, *22,* 24
        head, *22*
        leg, *22,* 23
        leg of mutton cut, 24
        neck piece, *22,* 24
        ribs, *22, 29*
        ribs, back, 24
        ribs, flat, 24
        ribs, fore, 24
        ribs, top, 24
        rump steak, *22,* 24
        rump, top, *22,* 24
        shin, *22,* 24
        silverside, 24, *202*
        sirloin, *22,* 24, *26, 56*
        skirt, thick, 23
        skirt, thin, 23
        topside, 24
    cuts (French):
        for French equivalents of English cuts
        see p. 25
    cuts (U.S.A.):
        for U.S. equivalents of English cuts
        see p. 25
    nutriment, 23
    roasting times, 25
    sauces with, 27
    wine with, 215
Belgium, special recipes:

carbonnades flamandes, 46
paupiettes de boeuf flamandes, 50
boiling, 16, 18–19
Boulestin, Marcel, *on* roast pork
    Périgourdine, 136
Bradenham ham, 166
brains, preparation, 178
braising, 17–18
broiling, 16
butchers, 11

calf's head, carving, 21, 92
Calves' feet jelly, 180
carving:
  beef, boiled silverside, 20, 202
    brisket, 20, 29
    roast fillet, 20, 56
    roast rib, 20, 29
    roast sirloin, 19, 26
    rolled sirloin, 20, 56
  calf's head, 21, 92
  gammon, 21, 163
  ham, 21, 163
  lamb, crown roast, 20, 115
    neck, best end of, 21, 115
    roast leg, 20, 111
    stuffed loin, 20, 111
  mutton, roast leg, 20, 111
    roast saddle, 20–1, 115
    roast shoulder, 20, 112
    stuffed loin, 20, 111
  ox tongue, 21, 202
  pork, roast rib of, 21, 140
  sucking pig, 21, 142
  veal, stuffed breast, 20, 92
Cuts, *see* bacon; beef; gammon; lamb;
    mutton; pork; steak; veal

deep frying, *see* frying
Denmark, special recipe:
  pickled salt pork and cabbage, 149

England, special recipes:
  boiled Bradenham ham, 169
  Epping sausages, 153
  Oxford sausages, 153
  see also Old English
Escoffier:
  on brains, 179
  on palate, 195
  on sweetbreads, 196

Fanny Farmer's Boston Cook Book, 37
feet, 180
France, special recipes:
  baked Alsace ham, 170
  baked Auvergne ham, 170
  Basque pork fillet, 144
  beef à la mode, 45
  beef Arlésienne, 69
  boeuf Bourguignon, 46
  beef Lyonnaise, 69
  beef Provençale, 69
  blanquette of veal (blanquette de veau à
    l'ancienne), 93
  boiled ham, 169
  brains à la ravigote, 180
  brains with black butter (cervelles au
    beurre noir), 178
  braised beef, 43
  Carcassonne cassoulet, 145
  croûte au pot, 57
  daube Avignonnaise, 121
  daube Provençale, 47
  fillet de boeuf poêlé à l'Anglaise, 27
  filet de boeuf en croute, 64
  hâchis en portefeuille, 71
  paupiettes de boeuf, 50
  pepper steak, 40
  pork accompaniments, 132
  pot-au-feu, 55
  skinless sausages, 158
  steak garnishes, 35
  tourte Lorraine, 151
  tripe à la mode de Caen, 205
  veal kidney Liègeoise, 187
  veal matelot, 94
Frying, deep, 16
  shallow, 17

GENERAL INDEX

gammon, 160
   carving, 21, *163*
   cuts:
      corner, 161, *163*
      hock, 161
      middle, 161
      slipper, 161
      steaks, 161
Germany, special recipes:
   Bavarian veal chops, 79
   pork chop sandwiches, 143
   Würstelbraten, 49
Greece, special recipes:
   moussaka, 127
   shish kebab, 123
   souvlakia, 118
grilling, 15–16

Ham:
   accompaniments, 167
   Belgian, 167
   Bradenham, 166
   carving, 21, *163*
   cooking, 168–9
   French, 167–8
   German, 167
   Irish, 166
   Italian, 167
   jambon d'Ardennes, 167
   jambon de Bayonne, 167
   Kentucky, 166
   preparing, 167, 168–9
   prosciutto di Parma, 167
   Suffolk (Seager), 166
   Virginia, 166
   Westphalia, 167
   Wiltshire, 166
   wine with, 216
   York, 166
heads, 181
hearts, 182
Holland, special recipes:
   fricadelles, 49
   pig's trotters and peas, 181
Hungary, special recipe:

goulash of beef, 48

India, special recipes:
   lamb curry, 122
   mutton curry, 122
Irish ham, 167
Italy, special recipes:
   garofolato, 48
   pork chops with capers, 147
   pork chops stewed in wine, 148
   saltimbocca, 88
   stewed shin of veal (osso buco), 96
   veal with marsala (piccate alla marsala), 83

jambons de compagne, 167
jambon glacé (Jambon de Paris), 168

Kentucky ham, 167
Kettner (*Book of the Table*), *on* Pork, 131
kidneys, 184

lamb:
   best joints, 107
   Canterbury, 107
   carving, *see separate heading*, Carving
   colour, 107
   cuts (English):
      breast, 108
      chops, 108, *109*, *119*, *120*
      cutlets, 108
      leg, 72, 107, *111*
      loin, 72, 108, *111*
      neck, best end, 72, 108, *115*
      neck, middle, 72, 108
      noisettes, 108, *120*
      scrag, 108
      shin, 72
      shoulder, 72, 108
   cuts (French):
      for French equivalents of English cuts see p. 108
   cuts (U.S.A.):
      for U.S. equivalents of English cuts see p. 108

districts, 107
New Zealand, 107
pré-salé, 107
temperatures, 107
wine with, 216
liver, 188

McNeill, Marian (*The Scots Kitchen*):
  on beef-ham, 60
  on mutton ham, 124
Marrow, 194
meat:
  buying, 11–12
  carving, *see separate heading*, Carving
  choosing, 11–12
  cooking, seven main methods, 13
    two main sections, 10
  hanging, 12–13
  keeping, 12–13
  national differences, 9
  preparation, 11
  refrigeration, 12–13
  sources, five main, 9
Mexico, special recipes:
  chili con carne, 48
  pork chops, 146
Middle East, special recipe:
  shish kebab, 118
mutton:
  best joints, 107
  carving, *see separate heading*, Carving
  colour, 107
  cuts:
    breast, 108
    chops, 108, *109*, *119*, *120*
    cutlets, 108
    leg, 107, *111*
    loin, 108, *111*
    neck, best end, 108, *115*
    neck, middle, 108
    noisettes, 108, *120*
    scrag, 108
    shoulder, 108, *112*
  districts, 107
  prime age, 107
  temperatures, 107
  wine with, 216

Offal (U.K.), 178
Old English, special recipes:
  bacon froise, 164
  fidget pie, 165
  minced collops of beef, 64
Oliver, Raymond, *on* filet de boeuf en croûte, 65
Ox tongue, carving, 21, *202*

Palate, 195–6
Poêling, 15
Poland, special recipe:
  veal kromeskis, 105
Pork:
accompaniments, 131
  carving, *see separate heading*, Carving
  colour, 131
  crackling, 131, 133
  cuts (English):
    bladebone, 132
    chops, 132
    fillet, 132
    leg, 132
    loin, 132
    ribs, short, 132, *140*
    ribs, spare, 132, *140*
    shoulder (hand), 132
    tenderloin, 132
  cuts (French):
    for French equivalents of English cuts see p. 133
  cuts (U.S.A.):
    for U.S. equivalents of English cuts see p. 133
  preparation, 131, 133
  summertime superstition about, 131
  temperatures, 133
  wine with, 216
  see also Ham, sucking pig
Potroasting, 15
Prague ham, 168
Pressure cooking, 19

GENERAL INDEX

Refrigeration, 12-13
Roasting, 13-15
Rundell, Mrs, *on* marrow bones, 195
Russia, special recipes:
    beef Stroganoff, 41
    bifteck à la Russe, 62

Sauce, *see* Index of Recipes
Sautéing, 17
Scotland, special recipes:
    beef-ham, 60
    mutton ham, 124
    mutton pies, 125
Seager ham, 166
Soyer, Alexis:
    on black puddings, 152
    on cold salt beef, 58
Spain, special recipe:
    lamb Catalane, 122
Steak:
    butter for, 32, 35
    cuts:
        Chateaubriand, *31*, 32
        club, 32, *38*
        entrecôte, 30, *31*
        entrecôte, double, 30, *31*
        filet mignon, 30, *38*
        fillet, 30, *36*
        minute, 30, *31*
        point, 32
        porterhouse, 32, *36*
        portmanteau, 32
        rump, 32
        T-bone, 32, *38*
        tournedos, 30, *31*, 32
    garnishes for, 32, 35
    preparation, 35
    sauces, 32, 35
    temperatures, 35
    wine with, 215
stewing, 18
sucking pig:
    carving, 21, *142*
    wine with, 216
Suffolk ham, 166

sweetbreads, 196

tails, 200
thermometer, meat, 14
tongue, 201
tripe, 204
Turkey, special recipe:
    mutton hash, 127

United States of America, special recipes:
    baked ham, 171, 173, 174
    baked Missouri ham, 170
    beef Cecils, 70
    boiled fresh beef, 55
    boiled Virginia ham, 169
    Confederate veal (Missouri), 94
    corned beef, 59
    Creole ham grillades, 173
    Creole veal kidney, 184
    devilled pork fillet, 146
    Fort Lincoln, 158
    glazed corned beef, 60
    glazed ham, 172
    ham baked with apples, 173
    ham baked in milk, 174
    ham, country style, 175
    ham with noodles, 176
    lamb chop casseroles, 122
    minted lamb cutlets, 129
    New England boiled dinner, 59
    pork accompaniments, 132
    pork chops and cranberries, 135
    pork chops, stuffed, 136
    pressed beef, 58
    quenelles, 194
    steak garnishes, 35
    steak tartare, 63
    veal Holstein, 97
    veal knots, 83
    veal olives, 88
    veal sweetbreads, country style, 198
    veal sweetbreads with mushrooms, 199
    Virginia boiled tongue, 203
Variety meats (U.S.A.), 178
Veal:

accompaniments, 73
carving, *see separate heading*, Carving
colour, 73
cuts:
    breast, 74, *92*
    chops, 74, *75*
    escalopes, 74
    fillet, 74
    grenadins, 74
    knuckle, 74
    leg, *72*
    loin, *72*, 74
    medaillons, 74
    mignonettes, 74
    neck, best end, *72*, 74
    neck, middle and scrag, *72*, 74
    noisettes, 74
    shin, *72*
    shoulder, 74
cuts (French):
    for French equivalents of English cuts see p. 77
cuts (U.S.A.):
    for U.S. equivalents of English cuts see p. 77
wine with, 216
Virginia ham, 167

Wiltshire ham, 166
wine:
    with beef, 215
    with ham, 216
    with lamb, 216
    with mutton, 216
    with pork, 216
    with steak, 215
    with sucking pig, 216
    with veal, 216

York ham, 166

zampino, 168

Index of recipes

Apple sauce, 139
Apples, and baked ham, 173
Apples, with sausages, 154
Apricots, with pork chops, 141
Aspic, for cold tongue, 201

Bacon, baked, 161
Bacon, boiled, 162
Bacon, braised, 162
Bacon with braised veal and sour cream, 87
Bacon and calves' liver, 191
Bacon and egg pie, 164
Bacon, fidget pie, 165
Bacon, fried, 165
Bacon, froise, 164
Bacon, gammon steaks with wine and cream, 164
Bacon, grilled, 165
Bacon and mushrooms in pastry, 164
Bacon and onion tart, 164

Bacon with pork chop pie, 151
Bacon, roasted, 161
Bacon roly-poly pudding, 165
Bacon in veal kromeskis, 102
Bacon with veal sweetbreads, 197
Bacon, *see also* Gammon
Baked Alsace ham, 170
Baked Auvergne ham, 170
Baked bacon, 161
Baked ham, 171
Baked ham with apples, 173
Baked ham in milk, 174
Baked ham in pastry, 170
Baked ham with pineapple, 175
Baked Missouri ham, 170
Bakenoff, 144
Bananas with sausages, 153
Batter for fried brains, 179
Bavarian veal chops, 79
Béarnaise sauce, 212

INDEX OF RECIPES

Béchamel sauce, 206
Beef à la mode, 45
Beef Arlésienne, 69
Beef and beans, 58
Beef, bifteck à l'Americaine, 63
Beef, bifteck à la Russe, 62
Beef, boiled au gratin, 68
Beef, boiled fresh, 55
Beef, boiled silverside, 51, 52
Boeuf Bourguignon, 46
Beef, braised, 42
Beef, braised with anchovies, 41
Beef, braised (France), 43
Beef, cannelon of, 70
Beef, carbonnades flamandes, 46
Beef Cecils, 70
Beef, corned, 59
Beef, corned, hash, 69
Beef, Cornish pasty, 67
Beef, Croûte au pot, 57
Beef curry, 54
Beef, Daube Provençale, 47
Beef doves, 53
Beef, filet de boeuf en croûte, 64
Beef, filet de boeuf poêle à l'Anglaise, 27
Beef, fricadelles, 49
Beef, garofolato, 48
Beef, glazed corn, 60
Beef, goulash of, 48
Beef, hâchis en portefeuille, 71
Beef-ham, 60
Beef left-overs, 68
Beef Lyonnaise, 69
Beef, meat balls, 62
Beef, mince, 63
Beef, minced, 61
Beef, minced collops of, 64
Beef, miroton of, 70
Beef olives, 50
Beef paupiettes, 50
Beef, paupiettes à la crème, 53
Beef, paupiettes flamandes, 50
Beef with peas, 44
Beef, pot-au-feu, 55
Beef, potroasted, 28

Beef, pressed, 58
Beef provençale, 69
Beef, roast, 25, 26, 29, 33, 34, 56
Beef salad, 71
Beef, salt, boiled, 59
Beef, salt, cold, 58
Beef, salt, in New England boiled dinner, 59
Beef sausages, 67
Beef sausages in beer, 68
Beef, silverside, 51, 52
Beef, sirloin, 33, 34
Beef, spiced, 60
Beef, spicy stewed, 45
Beef, stewed, 44
Beef Stroganoff, 41
Beef, Würstelbraten, 49
Beef, *see also* Steak
Bifteck à l'Americaine, 63
Bifteck à la Russe, 62
Black puddings, 152
Blanquette de veau à l'ancienne, 93
Boiled bacon, 162
Boiled beef, 55
Boiled beef au gratin, 68
Boiled Bradenham ham, 169
Boiled calf's head, 182
Boiled fresh beef, 55
Boiled gammon, 162
Boiled ham, 169
Boiled lamb, 124
Boiled mutton, 124
Boiled ox tongue, 201
Boiled pork with pease pudding, 149
Boiled pork Wienerwald, 150
Boiled salt beef, 59
Boiled stuffed breast of mutton with caper sauce, 125
Boiled sweetbreads, 197
Boiled Virginia ham, 169
Boiled Virginia tongue, 203
Bordelaise sauce, 210
Brains à la ravigote, 180
Brains with black butter, 178
Brains in court-bouillon, 179

Brains, fried, 179
Braised bacon, 162
Braised beef, 42
Braised beef (France), 43
Braised beef with anchovies, 41
Braised calves' tongues, 203
Braised ham, 171
Braised lamb, 121
Braised loin of veal, 84
Braised mutton, 121
Braised ox tongue, 203
Braised topside of veal, 84
Braised veal sweetbreads, 197
Brown gravy, for potroast, 28

Calf's foot, with tripe à la mode de Caen, 205
Calf's head, boiled, 182
Calf's head, fried, 182
Calf's heart à l'Hongroise, 183
Calves' liver and bacon, 191
Calves' liver casserole, 188
Calves' liver, devilled, 193
Calves' liver dumplings, 188
Calves' liver en papillotes, 192
Calves' liver, grilled, 193
Calves' liver loaf, 191
Calves' liver Lyonnaise, 191
Calves' liver, mock terrapin, 193
Calves' liver with mushrooms, 192
Calves' liver, stuffed and baked, 192
Calves' liver, in veal and ham pie, 99
Calves' tongues, braised, 203
Cannelon of beef, 70
Caper sauce, 125
Carbonnades flamandes, 46
Carcassonne cassoulet, 145
Casserole, calves' liver, 188
Casserole, ox heart, 183
Casserole, ox kidneys, 185
Casserole, lamb chop, 122
Cervelles au beurre noir, 178
Chasseur sauce, 211
Cheese sauce, 206
Chili con carne, 48

Chops, lamb, with apricots, 117
  lamb, casserole, 122
  lamb, roasted, 114
  lamb, stuffed, 114
  pork, à la Maréchale, 143
  pork, à l'Auvergnate, 143
  pork, with apricots, 141
  pork, with capers, 147
  pork, and cranberries, 135
  pork, Mexico, 146
  pork, with mustard and cream, 135
  pork, with orange, 141
  pork, pan-fried, 141
  pork, with pineapple, 141
  pork, sandwiches, 143
  pork, stuffed, 136
  veal, Bavarian, 79
  veal, Bordelaise, 79
  veal, fried, 80
Choron sauce, 212
Cider sauce, 171
Confederate veal, 94
Corned beef, 59
Corned beef, glazed, 60
Corned beef hash, 69
Cornish pasty, 67
Court-bouillon, 179
Creole ham grillades, 173
Creole veal kidney, 184
Cranberries, with pork chops, 135
Croûte au pot, 57
Curry, beef, 54
  lamb, 122
  mutton, 122
  pork, 146
  quick, 128
  sauce, 128
Cutlets, lamb, jugged, 121
  lamb, Milanaise, 117
  lamb, minted, 129
  lamb Suédoise, 118
  mutton, Murillo, 117
pork, à l'étuvé, 147
  pork, au gratin, 136
  pork, with horseradish, 143

INDEX OF RECIPES 233

    pork, Marseillaise, 139
    pork, with turnips, 147
    pork, villageoise, 144
    veal, à la Créole, 97
    veal, with cucumber, 80
    veal, with sour cream, 91
    veal, Suédoise, 80

Daube Avignonnaise, 121
Daube Provençale, 147
Demi-glace sauce, 209
Devilled mutton, 126
Devilled pork fillet, 146
Devilled sauce, 209

Egg and bacon pie, 164
Egg and ham cocottes, 177
Egg and ham pie, 175
Eggs in bacon and onion tart, 164
Eggs in Scotch eggs, 158
Entrecôte Mirabeau, 41
Entrecôte sauté maître d'hôtel, 39
Epping sausages, 153
Espagnole sauce, 209

Feet, 180
Fidget pie, 165
Filet de boeuf en croûte, 64
Filet de boeuf poêlé à l'Anglaise, 27
Fladgeon of veal, 100
Fort Lincoln, 158
Fricadelles, 49
Fricandeau of veal, 87
Fried bacon, 165
Fried beef, 130
Fried brains, 179
Fried breast of lamb, 117
Fried lamb, 116
Fried ox palates, 196
Fried pork, 141
Fried steak, 39
Fried veal, 79
Fried veal chop, 80

Gammon bacon steaks with wine and
    cream, 164
Gammon, boiled, 162
Garofolato, 48
Goulash, beef, 48
Grilled bacon, 166
Grilled beef, 30
Grilled breast of mutton, 116
Grilled calves' liver, 193
Grilled lamb, 116
Grilled ox palates, 196
Grilled pork, 141
Grilled steak, 35

Hâchis en Portefeuille, 71
Ham, Alsace, baked, 170
Ham, Auvergne, baked, 170
Ham, baked, 170, 171
Ham, baked, with apples, 173
Ham, baked in milk, 174
Ham, baked, with pineapple, 175
Ham, baked in pastry, 170
Ham, boiled, 169
Ham, Bradenham, boiled, 169
Ham, braised, 171
Ham, country style, 175
Ham, Creole, grillades, 173
Ham, devilled, 174
Ham and egg cocottes, 177
Ham and egg pie, 175
Ham, glazed, 172, *207, 208*
Ham, glazed, U.S.A., 172
Ham in hors d'oeuvre, 168
Ham hotpot, 177
Ham, Missouri, baked, 170
Ham and mushroom pie, 176
Ham with noodles, 176
Ham with ox-tongue in sweet-sour sauce, 204
Ham pancakes, 176
Ham parsley, 172
Ham, in saltimbocca, with veal, 88
Ham, in veal and calves' liver pie, 99
Ham, in veal kromeskis, 102
Ham and veal pie, 99
Ham, Virginia, boiled, 169

Hamburger steak, 61
Hamburger steak, planked, 62
Haricot beans, with beef, 58
Hash, corned beef, 69
Hash, mutton, 128
Hash, mutton, Turkey, 127
Heads, 181
Hearts, 182
Horseradish sauce, 27
Hotpot, ham, 177
Hotpot, Lancashire, 123
Hotpot, sausage, 157

Irish stew, 123

Jugged lamb cutlets, 121

Kidney, ox, en casserole, 185
Kidney, ox, in mince, 63
Kidney and pork stew, 148
Kidney rolls, sheep's, 187
Kidney, sheep's devilled, 185
Kidney, sheeps', en brochette, 185
Kidney, sheeps', in potato, 185
Kidney and steak pie, 65
Kidney, veal, Ali-bab, 186
Kidney, veal, creole, 184
Kidney, veal, croquettes, 186
Kidney, veal, en cocotte, 186
Kidney, veal, flambé, 187
Kidney, veal, Liégeoise, 187
Kidney, veal, soufflé, 187

Lamb, breast of, à la Sainte-Ménéhoulde, 121
Lamb, breast of, fried, 117
Lamb Catalane, 122
Lamb chops with apricots, 117
Lamb chops casserole, 122
Lamb chops, roasted, 114
Lamb chops, stuffed, 114
Lamb, Cornish pasty, 67
Lamb, crown roast, 110, *156*
Lamb curry, 122
Lamb cutlets, jugged, 121

Lamb cutlets Milanaise, 117
Lamb cutlets, minted, 129
Lamb cutlets Murillo, 117
Lamb cutlets Suédoise, 118
Lamb, Devonshire squab pie, 126
Lamb, fried, 116
Lamb left-overs, 126
Lamb, leg of, boiled, 124
Lamb, leg of, roast, *103, 104*, 110
Lamb, loin of baby, roast, *111*, 113
Lamb, Moussaka, 127
Lamb, neck of, dressed, *154*
Lamb pie, 126
Lamb rissoles, 129
Lamb, roast, *103, 104*, 110, *111, 137, 138*
Lamb, saddle of, *137, 138*
Lamb, Shepherd's pie, 128
Lamb, shish kebab, Greece, 123
Lamb, shish kebab, Middle East, 118
Lamb, shoulder, roast stuffed, 114
Lamb, Souvlakia, 118
Lambs' tails stew, 200
Lancashire hotpot, 123
Liver, 188
Liver, calves', and bacon, 191
Liver, calves', casserole, 188
Liver, calves', devilled, 193
Liver, calves', dumplings, 188
Liver, calves', grilled, 193
Liver, calves', loaf, 191
Liver, calves', Lyonnaise, 191
Liver, calves', mock terrapin, 193
Liver, calves', with mushrooms, 192
Liver, calves', en papillotes, 192
Liver, calves', stuffed and baked, 192
Liver, pig's, and sausage pie, 194
Liver, pork, pâté, 193
Loose-vinken, *see* paupiettes
Lyonnaise potatoes, 71

Madeira sauce, 209
Madeira scallion sauce, 213
Madeira veal steak, 96
Marbled veal, 101
Marinade for boiled calf's head, 182

INDEX OF RECIPES

Marinade for lamb cutlets Suédoise, 118
Marrow bones, 195
Marrow patties, 195
Marrow toasts, 195
Matignon, 15
Meat balls, beef, 62
Meat glaze, 213
Melted butter sauce, 213
Mince, 63
Minced collops of beef, 64
Mint sauce, 213
Mint stuffing, 116
Miroton of beef, 70
Mock geese, 145
Mock goose, 135
Mock terrapin, 193
Moussaka, 127
Mushrooms and bacon in pastry, 164
Mushrooms and calves' liver, 192
Mushrooms with devilled calves' liver, 193
Mushrooms and ham pie, 176
Mushrooms with veal sweetbreads, 199
Mushrooms with veal sweetbread flan, 198
Mustard sauce, 206
Mutton, breast of, grilled, 116
Mutton, breast of, stuffed, boiled, with caper sauce, 125
Mutton, Cornish pasty, 67
Mutton curry, 122
Mutton cutlets Murillo, 117
Mutton, daube Avignonnaise, 121
Mutton, devilled, 126
Mutton, Devonshire squab pie, 126
Mutton, grilled, 116
Mutton ham, 124
Mutton hash, 128
Mutton hash, Turkey, 127
Mutton, in Irish stew, 123
Mutton, in Lancashire hotpot, 123
Mutton left-overs, 126
Mutton, leg of, boiled, 124
Mutton, leg of, roast, marinated with port, 110
Mutton, Moussaka, 127
Mutton pie, 125

Mutton, roast, 110, *112*
Mutton, roast saddle of, *137, 138*
Mutton, saddle of, 114, *137, 138*
Mutton, shepherd's pie, 128
Mutton, shish kebab, 118
Mutton, shoulder of, roast stuffed, *112*, 114
Mutton, Welsh venison, 122

New England boiled dinner, 59
Noodles, with ham, 176

Offal (England), 178
Oiseaux sans têtes, *see* paupiettes
Onions, with tripe, 204
Onion sauce, 213
Oranges, with pork chops, 141
Osso buco, 96
Ox-foot, with tripe à la mode de Caen, 205
Oxford sausages, 153
Ox heart casserole, 183
Ox kidneys en casserole, 185
Ox kidneys, in mince, 63
Ox palate, fried, 196
Ox palate, grilled, 196
Oxtail, stewed, 200
Ox tongue, boiled, 201
Ox tongue, braised, 203
Ox tongue in sweet-sour sauce, 204
Ox tongue, Virginia boiled, 203
Oysters, and steak pie, 65

Piccate alla marsala, 83
Pancakes, ham, 176
Pan-grilled steak, 37
Pastry, for mutton pies, 125
Pastry, shortcrust, 65
Pâté, pork liver, 193
Patty, marrow, 195
Paupiettes, 50, *76*
Paupiettes de boeuf, 50
Paupiettes de boeuf à la crème, 53
Paupiettes de boeuf flamandes, 50
Paupiettes, veal, 88
Paupiettes, veal, à la crème with anchovies, 89

Pease pudding, 149
Pepper steak, 40
Périgueux sauce, 64
Pies, bacon and egg, 164
    Cornish pasty, 67
    Devonshire squab, 126
    fidget, 165
    ham and egg, 175
    ham and mushroom, 176
    lamb, 126
    mutton, 125
    pig's liver and sausage, 194
    pork chop, 151
    raised pork, 151
    Shepherd's, 128
    steak, 65
    steak and kidney, 65
    steak and oyster, 65
    steak and potato, 66
    veal and ham, 99
    veal, ham and calves' liver, 99
    veal pot, 98
    veal sweetbread flan, 198
Pig's liver and sausage pie, 194
Pig's trotters and peas, 181
Pineapple, with baked ham, 175
Pineapple, with pork, 148
Pineapple, with pork chops, 141
Pineapple, with sausages, 154
Piquante sauce, 210
Planked hamburger steak, 62
Planked steak, 37
Poached veal, 98
Poivrade sauce, 210
Pork, Bakenoff, 144
Pork, boiled, with pease pudding, 149
Pork, boiled, Wienerwald, 150
Pork cake, 158
Pork, Carcassonne cassoulet, 145
Pork cheese, 156
Pork chops à l'Auvergnate, 143
Pork chops à la Maréchale, 143
Pork chops with apricots, 141
Pork chops with capers, 147
Pork chops and cranberries, 135
Pork chops with oranges, 141
Pork chops, pan-fried, 141
Pork chops with pineapple, 141
Pork chops Mexico, 146
Pork chops with mustard and cream, 135
Pork chops pie, 151
Pork chops sandwiches, 143
Pork chops, stuffed, 136
Pork curry, 146
Pork cutlets à l'étuvé, 147
Pork cutlets au gratin, 136
Pork cutlets with horseradish, 143
Pork cutlets Marseillaise, 139
Pork cutlets with turnips, 147
Pork cutlets villageoise, 144
Pork fillet, Basque, 144
Pork fillet with cream, 147
Pork fillet, devilled, 146
Pork fillet with red peppers, 144
Pork, Fort Lincoln, 158
Pork and kidney stew, 148
Pork liver pâté, 193
Pork, loin of, with prunes, 133
Pork, loin of, roast, 133, *189*, *190*
Pork, mock geese, 145
Pork, mock goose, 135
Pork and onion pudding, 150
Pork with pineapple, 148
Pork, pickled salt, and cabbage, 149
Pork, pickled salt, with veal, sweetbreads, country style, 198
Pork pie, raised, 151
Pork, roast, 133, *189*, *190*
Pork, roast, Périgourdine, 136
Pork, roast, with vegetables and apple sauce, 139
Pork, spare ribs with sauerkraut, 148
Pork stewed in red wine, 148
Pork, tourte Lorraine, 151
Pork, *see also* Sausages
Potatoes, Lyonnaise, 71
Pot-au-Feu, 55
Potroast, 28
Potroast with vegetables, 30
Pressed beef, 58

INDEX OF RECIPES

Prunes, with loin of pork, 133
Prune sauce, 141
Puddings, bacon roly-poly, 165
    black, 152
        pork and onion, 150
        steak, 66
        veal, 100

Ragoût of veal, 89
Ragoût of veal à la Creole, 90
Ragoût of veal with peas, 90
Ravigote sauce, 180
Rissoles, lamb, 129
Roast bacon, 161
Roast beef, 25
Roast, crown, of lamb, 110, *156*
Roast lamb, 110
Roast lamb chops, 114
Roast leg of lamb, 110
Roast leg of mutton, 110
Roast leg of mutton marinated with port, 110
Roast loin of baby lamb, 113
Roast loin of veal, 77
Roast loin of veal with kidney, 78
Roast mutton, 110
Roast pork, 133
Roast pork Périgourdine, 136
Roast pork with vegetables and apple sauce, 139
Roast stuffed shoulder of lamb, 114
Roast stuffed shoulder of mutton, 114
Roast sucking pig, 141
Roast veal, 77
Roast veal with vegetables, 78
Robert sauce, 211

Salad, beef, 71
    sheep's trotter, 181
    sweetbread, 197
    veal, 105
Salpicon of veal, 102
Saltimbocca, 88
Sauce, apple, 139
    Béarnaise, 212

Béchamel, 206
Bordelaise, 210
brown, 209
caper, 125
Chasseur, 211
cheese, 206
Choron, 212
cider, 171
curry, 128
demi-glace, 209
devilled, 209
Espagnole, 209
Fort Lincoln, 156
horseradish, 27
Madeira, 209
Madeira scallion, 213
meat glaze, 213
melted butter, 213
mint, 213
mustard, 206
onion, 213
Périgueux, 64
piquante, 210
Poivrade, 210
prune, 141
ravigote, 180
Robert, 211
steak platter, 35
sweet-sour, 204
tartare, 212
tomato, 150, 211
Sausagemeat, 152
Sausagemeat and pig's liver pie, 194
Sausagemeat, Scotch egg, 158
Sausages with apples, 154
Sausages with bananas, 153
Sausages, beef, 67, 68
Sausages in beer, 68, 157
Sausages, black pudding, 152
Sausages, boiled, 153
Sausages with cabbage, 154
Sausages, Epping, 153
Sausages, hotpot, 157
Sausages, Oxford, 153
Sausages with pineapple, 154

Sausage rolls, 157
Sausages, skinless, 158
Sausage Toad-in-the-hole, 157
Sausages, veal, 101
Sausages, veal and oyster, 101
Sausages with white wine, 154
Sauté de veau printanière, 95
Savoury grilled steak, 39
Scotch eggs, 156
Sheep's kidney, devilled, 185
Sheep's kidney en brochette, 185
Sheep's kidney in potato, 185
Sheep's kidney rolls, 187
Sheep's trotter salad, 181
Sheep's trotters, Lancashire, 180
Shepherd's pie, 128
Shish kebab, Greece, 123
Shish kebab, Middle East, 118
Shortcrust pastry, 65
Souvlakia, 118
Spiced beef, 60
Spicy stewed beef, 45
Steak, bifteck à l'Americaine, 63
Steak, butter for, 35
Steak, chili con carne, 48
Steak Diane, 40
Steak, entrecôte Mirabeau, 41
Steak, entrecôte sauté maître d'hôtel, 39
Steak, filet de boeuf en croûte, 64
Steak, fried, 39
Steak, garnishes for, English, 32
Steak, garnishes for, French, 33
Steak, garnishes for, U.S.A., 33
Steak, grilled, 35
Steak, grilled savoury, 39
Steak, hamburger, 61
Steak, hamburger, planked, 62
Steak and kidney pie, 65
Steak and oyster pie, 65
Steak, pan-grilled, 37
Steak, pepper, 40
Steak pie, 65
Steak, planked, 37
Steak platter sauce, 35
Steak and potato pie, 66

Steak pudding, 66
Steak, raw, 63
Steak, savoury grilled, 39
Steak, stewed, 44
Steak tartare, 63
Steak, tournedos sauté chasseur, 39
Steak, *see also* Beef
Stewed beef, 44
Stewed knuckle of veal, 90
Stewed lamb, 121
Stewed lamb's tails, 200
Stewed mutton, 121
Stewed oxtail, 200
Stewed shin of veal, 96
Stewed steak, 44
Stewed stuffed breast of veal, 93
Stew, Irish, 123
Stew, lambs' tails, 200
Stew, pork and kidney, 148
Stuffed veal sandwich, 89
Stuffing, mint, 116
Stuffings, for hearts, 182, 183
Sucking pig, roast, 141
Sweetbreads à la crème, 198
Sweetbreads à la Nantua, 199
Sweetbreads au jus, 199
Sweetbreads in bacon, 197
Sweetbreads, braised, 197
Sweetbreads, country style, 198
Sweetbread flan, 198
Sweetbreads, grilled, 197
Sweetbreads with mushrooms, 199
Sweetbread salad, 197
Sweet-sour sauce, 204

Tails, 200
Tartare sauce, 212
Toad-in-the-hole, sausage, 157
Tomato sauce, 211
Tomato sauce for boiled pork Weinerwald, 150
Tongue, 201
Tongue, aspic for, 201
Tongue, calves', braised, 203
Tongue, ox, boiled, 201

INDEX OF RECIPES

Tongue, ox, braised, 203
Tournedos sauté chasseur, 39
Tourte Lorraine, 151
Tripe à la mode de Caen, 205
Tripe and onions, 204

Variety meats (U.S.A.), 178
Veal, blanquette of, 93
Veal, braised, with bacon and sour cream, 87
Veal chops, Bavarian, 79
Veal chops, Bordelaise, 79
Veal chops, fried, 80
Veal, Confederate, 94
Veal cutlets à la Créole, 97
Veal cutlets with cucumber, 80
Veal cutlets with sour cream, 91
Veal cutlets Suédoise, 80
Veal en brochette, 83
Veal en coquilles, 102
Veal escalopes à la crème moutardée, 81
Veal escalopes Bolognese, 81
Veal escalopes Maréchale, 81
Veal escalopes Modenese, 80
Veal escalopes persillées, 82
Veal escalopes Savoyarde, 82
Veal, fillet of, en cocotte, 79
Veal, fladgeon of, 100
Veal, fricandeau of, 87
Veal fricassee, 85, 86, 91
Veal, fried, 79
Veal, ham and calves' liver pie, 99
Veal and ham pie, 99
Veal Holstein, 97
Veal kidney ali-bab, 186
Veal kidney, Creole, 184
Veal kidney croquettes, 186
Veal kidney en cocotte, 186
Veal kidney flambé, 187
Veal kidney Liégeoise, 187
Veal kidney soufflé, 187
Veal knots, 83
Veal knuckles, stewed, 90
Veal knuckle paysanne, 91
Veal kromeskis, 102

Veal left-overs, 101
Veal, leg of, bourgeoise, 95
Veal, loin of, braised, 84
Veal, loin of, roast, 77
Veal, loin of, roast, with kidney, 78
Veal, Madeira steak, 96
Veal, marbled, 101
Veal with Marsala, 83
Veal matelote, 94
Veal olives, 88
Veal and oyster sausages, 101
Veal paupiettes à la crème with anchovies, 89
Veal, poached, 98
Veal pot pie, 98
Veal pudding, 100
Veal quenelles, 98
Veal, ragoût of, 89
Veal ragoût à la Créole, 90
Veal ragoût with peas, 90
Veal, roast, with vegetables, 78
Veal, saddle of, 77
Veal salad, 105
Veal, salpicon of, 102
Veal, saltimbocca, 88
Veal sandwich, stuffed, 89
Veal and sausage loaf, 100
Veal sausages, 101
Veal, sauté de veau printanière, 95
Veal sauté marengo, 97
Veal sauté menagère, 96
Veal, shin of, stewed, 96
Veal, shoulder of, stuffed, 84
Veal, shoulder of, stuffed à la bourgeoise, 87
Veal, stewed knuckle of, 90
Veal, stewed shin of, 96
Veal, stewed stuffed breast of, 93
Veal stock, 73
Veal sweetbreads à la crème, 198
Veal sweetbreads à la Nantua, 199
Veal sweetbreads au jus, 199
Veal sweetbreads in bacon, 197
Veal sweetbreads, braised, 197
Veal sweetbreads, country style, 198

Veal sweetbread flan, 198
Veal sweetbreads with mushrooms, 199
Veal Tetrazzini, 105
Veal topside, braised, 84
Veal, tourte Lorraine, 151
Venison, Welsh, 122
Viennese steak, *see* Hamburger steak

Virginia boiled tongue, 203

Welsh venison, 122
Wiener Schnitzel, 82
Wienerwald, boiled pork, 150
Würstelbraten, 49

Yorkshire pudding, 27

The Wine and Food Society

The Wine and Food Society was founded in 1933 by André L. Simon, C.B.E., as a world-wide non-profit making society.

The first of its various aims has been to bring together and serve all who believe that a right understanding of wine and food is an essential part of personal contentment and health; and that an intelligent approach to the pleasures and problems of the table offers far greater rewards than the mere satisfaction of appetite.